Philosophy in the Twentieth Century

Philosophy in the Twentieth Century

AN ANTHOLOGY

Volume Four

Edited and with Introductions
by

WILLIAM BARRETT

New York University

and

HENRY D. AIKEN

Harvard University

Random House : *New York*

First Trade Edition

© Copyright, 1962, by William Barrett and Henry D. Aiken

Contents

Volume One

Volume Two

PART TWO

The Rise of Analytical Philosophy in England

F. H. BRADLEY

G. E. MOORE

Contents

Volume Three

PART THREE

Positivism

PART FOUR

Phenomenology and Existentialism

Volume Four

PART FIVE

Marxism and the Philosophy of History

PART FIVE

Marxism and the Philosophy of History

Introduction

The philosophy of history is a distinctly modern development within philosophy. Though the classical philosophers made observations from time to time on history, and though great and far-reaching schemes of human history were conceived before the modern epoch, the philosophical search to understand history as a distinct field within philosophy does not properly begin until Hegel in the nineteenth century. Though he had forebears in the eighteenth century—notably Vico, Herder, and Condillac—the achievements of these men took on the character of specific descriptions of what in their view the course of history had been rather than a philosophical analysis of what historical phenomena and historical knowledge essentially are. Indeed, the historical point of view may be Hegel's greatest contribution to philosophy.

Now, there is a very good reason why the philosophy of history should be such a late arrival on the philosophic scene. This reason, it so happens, is also historical in character: the fact is that the modern sense of history, without which no such distinct discipline as a philosophy of history would ever have been created, is itself an historical fact that emerges only in modern times—to be precise, with the outburst of the French Revolution at the end of the eighteenth century. Everything human is within history, including man's sense of history itself.

The history of the sense of history would alone be a volume, but here we shall merely indicate the main guide lines that can place in proper perspective the historical philosophy of the twentieth century.

The Greeks—and Plato and Aristotle would be prime philosophical examples—thought of history in terms of cycles. The eternal cycle of the heavens was imitated by the cycles of the seasons, and these in turn by the cycles of human history: the rise and fall of empires and men. Plato speaks of the cosmic Great Year (some 36,000 ordinary solar years) at the end of which all human things have decayed and go again through their old patterns. Aristotle remarks that the arts and the sciences have been discovered and have perished numberless times in the past. Through Homer the Greeks celebrated the fall of Troy in myth and archetype, but this race, so intellectually curious in all other ways, never went into the archaeology of Troy.

The eruption of Christianity into the classical world brought with it a changed consciousness of history. Since the world was created out of nothing, time had a beginning; and since the whole creation moved toward one end, which would be the Last Judgment, time also had an end; and having thus both beginning and end, time also had a direction, a unique irreversible arrow. The present did not merely repeat the past, like the cycles of the cosmos without beginning and end, but it was a step further from the beginning and a step closer to the end. History was a distinctly human, not a merely natural, affair, since it issued from the covenant of God with the children of Israel and reached its climax in the actual coming of a Savior who redeemed all of human history.

But though this Christian sense of history held for man's religious and moral destiny, medieval Christianity succeeded in imposing its historical picture upon a timeless view of man in his social and secular world. Since the pattern of God's providence was believed to be known, all of human history was held within this timeless providential framework. In Dante's *Divine Comedy* the whole of human history is presented as a timeless present in which all human souls, ancient and modern, are arranged according to the degrees of their damnation or merit in an eternal and contemporaneous present. Moreover, so far as the actual social life of man was concerned, the future was thought of as repeating the past, even though the future carried with it the possibility of the religious apocalypse. All of human history was spread out as a simultaneous whole before the gaze of an eternal, and therefore, nonhistorical eye.

With the Renaissance a different and more secular consciousness began, but it was a long time before this new consciousness penetrated into the field of history. Even in the Age of Enlightenment in the eighteenth century, which saw a great outburst of historical writing and inquiry, the historians still performed their job essentially as moralists and humanists in the style of the great classical historians. Thus Gibbon takes Tacitus as his model.

The event that changed all this was the French Revolution, for this was the first event in human history that revealed that a revolution did not mean merely the exchange of rulers, the beggar riding on horseback with the rider dashed to the ground, but that the whole fabric of human life could be completely transformed from top to bottom. The future thus took on a new dimension of contingency: it could mean that the life of man in that future might be radically different from what it had been in the past. The English had had their revolution against absolute monarchy a century earlier in 1688; but this revolution left the basic fabric of social life virtually untouched. It was a limited not a total revolt, settling once and for all for the English that henceforth no Papist would be king and that bourgeois liberties were safe against the aspirations of any despot. It was a *reasonable* revolution, where the French Revolution was a *rational* one. It would simply not have been in the British character to have enthroned an actress as the Goddess of Reason in Canterbury Cathedral as the French did in Notre Dame. And with these unlimited and revolutionary claims of "Reason" began the Terror that has haunted modern history since.

Kant was the first philosopher to remark on these possibilities latent in the French Revolution. Just a few years after it had occurred, he described it as the most significant event in history up to that point, since it revealed for the first time that the conditions of human life could become totally different from what they were. However, none of this penetrated into Kant's philosophy proper: with him the forms and categories of the mind are necessary and a priori, fixed and eternal, not the creatures of historical evolution and change. It was Hegel, writing in the next generation, who was to make the imaginative leap from Kant's isolated perception to a new truth for the whole of philosophy.

This new truth was that all forms of the human spirit—including "reason"—are the product of historical development. Hegel belonged to the generation after Kant, a generation that had been set aflame by the aspirations of the French Revolution and later by the Napoleonic conquests that rent the whole traditional fabric of European life. Amid the thunder and lightning of these historical happenings it is no wonder that the youthful Hegel at times could see the World-spirit riding as the French conqueror on horseback. In addition, Hegel had been an aspiring poet in his youth—a fact which is often forgotten but which explains his extraordinary powers of imagination when turned in another direction, as in his great interpretations of the art of the past. These imaginative powers he was able to turn also on the evocation of past philosophies, and see them as a dialectical progression toward an ever more complete and comprehensive grasp of Truth. In the end, even logic itself, for Hegel, is to be understood in quasi-historical terms, as the successive stages in the development of the Absolute Concept.

Yet, though here for the first time in philosophy we seem to find man plunged up to his ears in history, in the end Hegel remains faithful to the classical tradition in philosophy that goes back to Plato in its insistence that the philosopher must try to see all things in the universe with unhistorical eyes in the aspect of eternity. For the Absolute, which is Reality, is beyond time, change, and history, which belong only to Appearance. Thus Hegel's labor to expound the historical point of view in all fields is curiously at odds with itself because history itself has already been completed in the fullness of the Absolute. The ordeals, the fire and bloodshed, of history, about which Hegel writes so eloquently, turn out to be a curious kind of game that the Absolute plays with Itself ("Himself" would be the language of traditional Theism) since It is already, in the fullness of Absolute Reality, beyond such frivolities of Appearance. Real contingency disappears from history, for the end is already given. What Hegel ends by giving us is a highly elaborate secular version of Christian theodicy, to which he had also annexed the optimistic eighteenth-century conviction of the inevitability of progress. Indeed, it may be questioned whether this belief in inevitable progress has not been in most men who have held it an unconscious surrogate of the older theological belief in God's providential governing of the affairs of the world.

With Karl Marx (1818-1883), disciple of Hegelian historicism, the historical consciousness takes another immense stride forward: Marx abolishes the timeless Reality of the Absolute, and plunges all things human so deeply in history that ideas, institutions, and moral attitudes are interpreted as rooted in the social relations of economic production. Here at last we would seem to have come upon a grasp of history as real and all-engulfing, without any taint of the supra-historical and supra-temporal perspective that had shaped, secretly or openly, the visions of philosophers hitherto. But Marx is also the child of the Enlightenment of the eighteenth century, and he accepts without question the belief of the Enlightenment in the inevitability of progress. The forward march of history is just as inexorable here as with Hegel, though it is no longer the march of the Absolute Spirit through time, but the transformation of the economic structure until we arrive at communism and the classless society. The Marxist scheme remains outside of history, a providential pattern which historical events fulfill but will never alter in its main designs. And this has tended to be all the more true as Marxism, becoming a party doctrine, hardened into absolute dogma: all other ideas, ideologies, philosophies the Marxists see as the creatures of history, and therefore with the human limitations of their historical contexts, but somehow Marxism itself is exempt, it has attained absolute truth and is the chosen collaborator of inevitable historical destiny. No doubt, this faith has been an enormous asset to Marxism in the political struggles of this century, since nothing strengthens the will of the faithful more than the conviction that they are the chosen of God and on the winning side. But as a philosophy of history it is much oversimplified, reductive, and a priori rather than empirical in its approach. Because the future is already determined, real contingency has here too, as with Hegel, disappeared from history;

and lacking this, it does not have that note of anxiety before history which is so typical of the new historical consciousness of our century.

This note of anxiety before history is first introduced by Sören Kierkegaard (1813-1855) and Friedrich Nietzsche (1844-1900), now commonly taken as the founding fathers of existentialism. Both reject the eighteenth century's assumption of inevitable and limitless progress. In the midst of a smug and bourgeois nineteenth century, secure in the sense of its own enlightenment, both Kierkegaard and Nietzsche sound a very dissident and pessimistic note. Both see their age as one of decadence in certain respects, and both have very marked fear of the mass society of the future.

It is with these last that there emerges a sense of history that has become more familiar to us in this century after two world wars and now with the fearful contingency of nuclear destruction on the horizon. If, following Kant, we recognize that the French Revolution revealed to modern man that it was possible for him to transform the total conditions of human life and therefore to create a future, which far from merely repeating the past with minor variations would represent a wholly new way of life, then we have also to recognize that with this positive possibility there goes inescapably the negative possibility: the man of the future can decline, regress, even destroy himself. Every possibility to be is also a possibility not to be. The axe always cuts both ways. If history is no longer viewed as the working out of God's providential design for man, or the mechanical interplay of social forces and classes leading to the triumph of communism, then it returns to the strictly human level—an affair of men made by men, and therefore exposed to the risks, hazards, and uncertainties of every human enterprise.

Though the existentialists have probably made the most eloquent pleas on this point, the position is not confined to their school alone. It is equally the position of pragmatism. That John Dewey happened to be an incurable optimist and progressive, that he exhibits nowhere any radical anxiety or malaise at the contingencies of history—these are accidents of his own temperament and of the historical period of naïve progressivism in America in which he grew up; but these temperamental accidents should not obscure for us his central philosophical understanding that man is totally within history and that there are no supra-historical points of view from which he can step outside of his world in order to be the Platonic spectator of it. But this line of historical thinking is less the product of any single philosopher or school of philosophers than of the actual labors of the historians themselves —particularly the historians of culture, of art, literature, and religion. The more deeply we investigate human culture the more deeply we find man in each age immersed in his own time. And if he touches th' eternal anywhere within his history, man does it always within forms and limits of his finite and historically rooted consciousness. The vessel receives according to its own shape; and its shape is always the mode of being of historical man in an actual and definite situation. The modern philosophers of history have merely elicited the ideas that were implicit in the interpretations of historians that have been accumulating during the last two centuries since historiography, the writing of history, itself took on modern form.

The selections in this section represent the historical thinking of an idealist (Croce), a Marxist (Lenin), and an existentialist (Jaspers). While these three provide a fairly representative sample of contemporary thought, the reader should be advised that these are not the only places in this book where the subject of history is touched upon. Questions in the philosophy of history are dealt with, directly or indirectly, in the selections from Dewey, Whitehead, Sartre, and Buber. Philosophy, as a specifically human activity, cannot be completely and snugly compartmentalized.

Once again our section begins with an Idealist, Benedetto Croce (1866-1952). Hegelian idealism had been the reigning influence in historical thinking within the academy. To be sure, Marx had already dropped his bombs in the midst of the nineteenth century, but they had not yet exploded among the "professional" philosophers. Again, the pattern of our century, here in the philosophy of history, is a departure from idealism.

Croce is an Hegelian, but the degree of his departure from Hegel has not been generally understood or else has been played down. The fact is that Croce has departed from Hegel much more than thinkers like F. H. Bradley or Josiah Royce, to name two other Hegelians in this volume. In the first place, Croce discards the Absolute and refuses to interpret history as a theodicy in the manner of Hegel. There is more than a touch of pragmatism in Croce, however idealistic his turns of phrase. Croce, in fact, is a thoroughly secular mind, one of the shining examples of that militantly anti-clerical and liberal generation that grew up in Italy after the unification and founding of the Italian nation in 1870, and that has displayed its liberal and humanistic ardor in the statue to Giordano Bruno in the Campo del Marzo at Rome, where Bruno had been burned by the Inquisition. Moreover, Croce has more than a little of that peculiarly Italian genius of mind, visible in Machiavelli and Vico, which is more rooted and concrete than its European neighbors to the north. Croce is altogether incapable of those sweeping and soaring excesses of the Teutonic mind of which Hegel is a principal example.

Accordingly, when Croce speaks of history as essentially spiritual activity, he does not assert the grandiose and audacious claims for the spirit made by German idealism: the spiritual here is to be understood in a thoroughly humanistic sense without any explicit or implicit religious overtones. To be sure, Hegel had already produced a kind of secularized version of Christian theodicy, but the theological elements never were cast out from the metaphysical sweep of Hegel's view of history. If, then, Hegel's is indeed a secularized Christian theodicy, we may say that Croce has gone a step further by secularizing Hegel. Croce does this by rejecting metaphysics as a legitimate philosophical discipline altogether—which means, of course, that his is an Hegelianism of a very different stripe and color than that of Bradley and Bosanquet. In this rejection of metaphysics, indeeed, Croce would seem to be very strangely in the company of the positivists, whom on other grounds he criticized unceasingly throughout his whole life. But unlike the positivists he does not propose to replace metaphysics by syntax and semantics, and generally the logical analysis of language, but by the history of philosophy itself! But this history of philosophy is not to be mere doxological history, the stringing out of successive opinions of the philosophers like so many garments on a washline. No; the real history of philosophy is itself philosophy—a point which Croce derives from Hegel but without attaching any metaphysical or theological speculation about the ultimate framework of history that lies beyond any possible experience. Philosophy is man's effort to comprehend totally, in their variety and unity, all the diverse activities of the human spirit. But since man is a thoroughly historical being, this comprehension must also be historical. This is anti-metaphysics, but a very far cry from positivism, which in our century at least has approached the problems of philosophy in a thoroughly unhistorical, even anti-historical, manner and has usually relegated the history of philosophy to a position of triviality and unimportance.

For Croce, then, it is the spiritual activity of man—his activity, that is, as a strictly human rather than animal being—that provides meaning within history, and consequently by connecting present and past produces meaningful history. But the writing of history also is a spiritual act on the part of the historian, and therefore itself an act of history. The historian can interpret a past period only to the degree that his own spiritual activity re-creates within himself the meanings of the past. He, for example, can understand the historical necessity of the Protestant Reformation only to the degree that he has lived through something of its inner crises in the forging of his own individuality against the Catholic collective, a fact both social and psychological, in which he was raised. And this is not merely a matter of inner sympathy on the part of the historian that makes it possible for him to have historical insight; more than this, it is an act of history that perpetuates, renews, and furthers the inner meanings of the historical past. For this reason Croce is uncompromisingly opposed to all the positivistic historians and positivistic philosophers of history of the nineteenth century, who sought to reconstruct history out of isolated "facts" or else sought to reduce the human to the natural sciences by finding "laws" of history somewhat in the fashion of laws of physics. These "facts" usually turn out to be merely outward facts, and therefore give us only the external crust but never the inner meaning of any historical movement.

The inner meaning that connects the facts is discovered by the historian's active *intuition*. Historical understanding, according to Croce, is ultimately intuitive in nature because what it has to understand is always a concrete individual—whether it be an individual person, period, or institution—and never an abstract universal, which is grasped by *conceptual* intellect. Can we understand the New Deal, for example, as the pure interaction of impersonal social forces without that rather remarkable historical phenomenon, the individual personality of Franklin Delano Roosevelt? If individual men do make history, then history itself is not altogether comprehensible apart from the understanding of individual personalities and individual biographies; and biography, unlike the impersonal subject matter of the physical sciences, cannot be written without the active intuition of the biographer.

Since intuition is what is also required in the understanding of works of art, critics have often attacked the Crocean doctrine with the accusation that it turns history into poetry, making it a work of the imagination divorced from fact. This is a mistake, and a mistake all the more unpardonable since Croce has expressed himself with scorn on the subject of "poetic history." To be sure, the first of our selections here is from Croce's *Aesthetics,* but that is only because historical knowledge like aesthetic knowledge is ultimately of the individual. But the intuition that creates a work of art is different from the intuition that writes a work of history. If I create a character in a novel, my intuition of that character can be criticized by the critics (i.e., by the intuition of the critics) as lacking verisimilitude, profundity, or spiritual value. But it would be simply beside the point for the critic to say that the character in the novel was wrong because it did not resemble a certain historical personage. But the intuitions of the historian can be criticized for not corresponding with actual persons and events. A biography of Franklin Roosevelt presents us with a certain complex intuition of a given individual's character. The biographer's intuition can be criticized for colliding with facts—i.e., with all the varying and partial intuitions we have from different acts and words of Roosevelt's life. Intuition, too, is a self-corrective process, not the blind leap of the fortuneteller into the dark.

What is involved here is not merely a misinterpretation of a certain point in Croce but a misunderstanding and a dwindling of intuition that becomes more and more endemic to our epoch. As we remarked before, but perhaps all too briefly, apropos of Bergson, intuition itself has become the suspect thing in modern life. As life becomes more routinized, we need less and less intuition. The creative intuition is required only at the top of the social pyramid, among the men who invent new machines, new efficiency methods, or new processes of routinization; the rest of us are consigned to social functions where we have merely to check over accurately the items of an inventory like animated electric eyes. Soon we shall all dress in our functional uniforms, wear clothes of a prescribed cut or style, so that an observer will need only accurate external *sensation* to spot who and what we are. Naturally enough, with society going this way, there is bound also to be a steady production of academic robots who will teach that "intuition" is a meaningless word.

An interesting experiment to show how society conspires to crush the power of insight in its members was performed by the Gestalt psychologists in Berlin in the twenties. The Gestalt psychologists had become interested in the analysis of handwriting as an index of personality. One psychologist had the parallel idea of attempting to measure the natural ability of people to read character from handwriting. Among others, a group of children were selected and presented with a series of pairs of slides—the handwriting of a nun opposite that of an opera diva, a pillar of society against the handwriting of a criminal, etc. etc.—and told to guess whose handwriting was whose. The children scored conspicuously higher than the adults. Moreover, a follow-up on the experiment was taken: the same children were given a similar test in successive years. As the children got older, their scores got steadily lower. What had happened? Merely that the combined conspiracy of parents, nurses, governesses, social authorities had operated to crush or cause to atrophy the native power of intuition.

The reader may think at this point that this editor is going somewhat afield from the matters that concern this book. Such is not the case. The issue of intuition does not touch merely on the life of modern society, but also on the reconstruction within philosophy that has been going on in this century. It is the issue not only where the term "intuition" is explicitly used—as in Croce and Bergson—but even where for very definite philosophic strategies the term is eschewed. We meet the same issue when Heidegger extols a thinking that is rooted in Being over against the mere cerebration of reason. It is the issue behind Husserl's pronouncement that the task of philosophy in this century is a "reconstitution of reason" since classical rationalism is too schematic and no longer viable. It is also the issue in the difference between G. E. Moore's philosophy of Common Sense as against the Cartesian skepticism of Bertrand Russell, since some of the things Moore claims Common Sense knows without proof would have to be known by intuition, though Moore is entirely right to avoid the hornet's nest of problems that would be concealed in that word. Hence, our excuse for this little excursion on the subject of intuition—which we now proceed to continue.

A common attitude against intuition professed by a contemporary school of philosophy in America centers around a watered-down version of Charles Peirce's famous discussion of methods of fixing belief. Four such methods are enumerated:

1) the method of authority;
2) the method of faith;
3) the method of intuition;
4) the method of science.

This editor recalls that as a young student he had to spout these "methods" like the articles of a catechism together with the reason why the first three were to be knocked over like sitting ducks for the eventual triumph of scientific method. The gist of the argument was that the method of science is "self-corrective"—that is, scientific theories are constantly checked and changed by recourse to facts—while the other "methods" do not enjoy this advantage. Now, I do not know whether it makes any sense at all to speak of a "method of faith" or a "method of intuition," since neither faith nor intuition seem to enjoy the routines of a "method," but leaving this point aside, we can observe without any shadow of doubt that intuition is self-corrective. Anyone who has ever practiced literary criticism will know what it means to correct one's impressions of an author by diligent rereading, and indeed even by the experiences of one's own life. The whole effort of criticism, in fact, is a perpetual process of self-correction. The literary article the critic writes at one time will not stand up to his vision at a later time. And this is true not merely for the individual critic, but for the whole history of literary criticism itself, which as a perpetual correction of itself is also a perpetual recreation of the past. Authors who were dropped by the wayside are revived and re-evaluated. Today we read the history of English poetry differently from Matthew Arnold because the critical vision of T. S. Eliot has also changed our vision.

Indeed, Croce's view that historical knowledge is in the end intuitive is much more easily grasped when we realize how much of our essential knowledge of the past stems from its art and literature. If we had only the external "facts" about Greece and Rome, the dates of battles and conquests, without the classical literatures, the Greeks and Romans would be for us as meaningless as the Scythians or the Carthaginians. But literature can never be grasped by the purely "factual" or positivistic historian. Factual research is, of course, indispensable, and is sometimes of great value for the literary interpretation of a text; but the scholar who confines himself solely to digging into Shakespeare's laundry lists is likely to end cut off from Shakespeare as literature. The work of art is understood only to the degree that the critical interpreter enters in imagination into the world of the artist. This requires a positive act of intuition on the part of the historian of art or literature. But such intuition, when it genuinely illumines the work, is the farthest thing from mere "impressionism," or willful subjectivity. On the contrary, it stands open to perpetual correction by the critic's later intuitions or the intuitions of other critics. In the field of the humanities the activity of intuition is as "self-corrective" as scientific method in its own fields.

One reason for dwelling so insistently upon this issue is the urgency that the problem now takes on in the United States, where there has been a strong incursion of the quantitative and positivistic attitude into the humanities themselves. As a nation we Americans are hypnotized by "facts": nothing has quite the solidity for us as so-called solid facts, and we are so eager in our search for facts that it hardly seems to matter whether the facts are bound together by any insight or whether the facts in themselves are very worthwhile. This attitude has become all the more pronounced as the large foundations have begun to finance activities in the humanities, and the emphasis of the organizational mind—especially where money is being spent—is on what it fancies as "objective." Instances abound, but it would take us too far afield to go into them; what we have said should already be sufficient to indicate to the reader that Croce's position, like every genuine philosophical one, is not a merely technical or remote matter, but in fact touches on the vital attitudes of a whole society.

One final question on Croce, and then we move on to Marxism. Why, it may be asked, if Croce has eliminated the Hegelian Absolute and history is no longer for him theodicy but the activity of the human spirit—why is his position not essentially identical with that of the existentialists, who hold that a history is strictly an affair of men made by men? The difference, in one respect, is a matter of historical generations. Croce belongs much more to the nineteenth century and shares the vigorous optimism of an expanding bourgeoisie that had at last secured the national unification of Italy. His thought has not been hatched in the century of two world wars, and so does not bear the emotional coloration of existentialism. History, for Croce, is progress, and specifically a progress in human liberty as realized in continuing institutions. This is the position of Hegel, without the Hegelian Absolute; it is also the voice of pure nineteenth-century liberalism, and it is hard for younger philosophers to maintain this attitude against the harsh realities of this century with its global wars, concentration camps, and generally the appalling regimentation of individuals within modern mass society. Croce does not have any deep anxiety about the contingencies of history; historical disasters somehow will always be redeemed and reconciled in the harmonies of spirit. It is inconceivable that Croce could ever entertain the possibility that Jaspers throws out in one place: that it is not beyond the bounds of possibility that the whole human species could become psychotic! Nor could he share Heidegger's view that truth is essentially and inextricably involved with untruth, that with every great step forward into the light humanity may thrust part of itself back into darkness—as, particularly in Heidegger's case, the fear that the extraordinary technological advance of the present and near future may sever man from the primal source of Nature.

Croce remains an Hegelian in that he sees Enlightenment as a constantly expanding circle. For the existentialists this metaphor is incomplete: it may apply with some accuracy to the sciences, which become progressively broader and more accurate, but even if this circle of scientific light expands it would become possible for the human individuals, the finite bearers of truth, to shrivel up in other dimensions of their Being as compared with the past—in faith, art, the life of instinct, or in their wholeness and spontaneity of Being. For Croce, the idealist, human existence is ideal, the light and triumph of spirit, not at all the thoroughly and completely problematic thing it is to the existentialists.

Measured by the number of people whose life it has touched, by the upheaval among the nations it has brought about, and by the enormous shadow it now casts on the future, Marxism has to be reckoned as the greatest historical force of the nineteenth and twentieth centuries. As Marxism has solidified into orthodox communism, moreover, it has taken on the dogmatic features of a secular religion sweeping millions in its wake. Indeed, as an historical movement, it rather resembles a secularized Islam, pledged to win converts by fire and sword.

Yet with all its dimensions as an historical force, Marxism has had very few philosophers in this century. This is to be expected in view of the suppression of free thought in communist circles. Perhaps the gulf between East and West is such that we do not hear about the Soviet philosophers. In any case, communism seems to have captured only one first-rate European intellectual in recent years—we omit scientists and artists—the Hungarian scholar Georges Lukacs. But the bulk and the best of Lukacs' writing has been in literary interpretation, and thus not particularly usable in this volume. Hence we have been able to represent Marxism in this volume only by one selection, but fortunately from the one Marxist who has been also the most politically influential man of the century, Lenin. If there be irony in the fact that the movement most historically convulsive in this century should be represented by only one selection in a book concerned with philosophy in this century, the irony is not on the part of the editors: whatever other intellectual activities Marxism—at least Marxism in its orthodox Communist form—promotes, it does not seem to produce independent philosophers.

The irony is somewhat further compounded by the fact that Lenin's contribution to this volume is not directly upon the philosophy of history itself. No matter; for the Marxist version of history is visible between the lines throughout, and it is the basic point of view from which Lenin is attacking Ernst Mach and the positivists. The crucial thing for Lenin, after all, is not merely that Mach and the positivists are wrong, but that they are the spokesmen of a certain historical form of consciousness, the bourgeoisie in its decadence, and history has already moved beyond this.

Lenin's *Materialism and Empirio-Criticism* (from which our selection is taken) is not the work of a professional academic philosopher. No one knew this better than Lenin himself. He is writing as a man of action immersed in the world and with a grip upon History, for which he is the called and chosen spokesman. This involvment with action does not weaken the force of his argument or the sharpness of his insight. Academic philosophers have tended to slight Lenin's critique of positivism (and phenomenalism generally) as a mere party document. This is a mistake. Lenin had a powerful and acute mind, even if he did not always argue with the subtlety and politeness of an Oxford don.

For one thing, Lenin's objection against positivism in the name of the objective reality of material things maps out a road which British philosophy has traveled from the Humean position of Bertrand Russell to G. E. Moore's Common Sense. To be sure, the arguments that have brought contemporary British philosophers away from the belief in the supposed higher reality of sense-data to the everyday belief in chairs, tables, and other people, have been more refined and logical than Lenin's. But it may not always be the business of a philosopher to crawl forward so slowly through a net of tangled and halting reasons; sometimes his business is to know, and declare that he knows—the arguments can be found afterward. Whatever his philosophical manners, Lenin did know that the science of physics was about the material objects around us, not about sense-data. And he did get there before the British.

Of course, Lenin's materialism is a much more sweeping doctrine than the current trend among British analysts (and even, more recently, the positivists) to take for granted the reality of physical objects. Marxist materialism, in fact, is a much more sweeping metaphysical thesis than even the ordinary brand of "nineteenth-century materialism."

"Nineteenth-century materialism" has become today a stock epithet for a dominant attitude of the previous epoch. That it was such a dominant attitude in that period may come as a surprise to the reader since this volume has represented the development of twentieth-century philosophy as a breaking away on many fronts from the idealism that reigned at the end of the century. But this prevalence of idealism was mainly among academic philosophers. "Nineteenth-century materialism" was a much more widespread and endemic attitude. While it had its philosophic spokesmen, it really remained a kind of digest or compost of nineteenth-century physics. It seemed indeed to be the verdict of physical science itself about the world of nature and man. And so it had an uncontested validity for the popular mind, and so shaped the despair of poets and religious men. This physics was still Newtonian physics, dominated by the ideas of mechanics, and by the fundamental concepts of mass and inertia. Determinism was the iron law of nature everywhere, with no loophole anywhere for human freedom. Since mechanics was assumed to be basic and therefore all phenomena would be reducible to the factors of mass, space, and time, it seemed that human consciousness itself—together with its illusory feeling of freedom—was so reducible to the movements of matter. What happened, of course, was that physics itself blew wide open toward the end of the century. New discoveries and new concepts changed the general outlook of the science. Nineteenth-century materialism had been a footnote to the science of its day; if it is largely dead now, this has not been accomplished so much by philosophic refutation but by a change within science itself.

Marxist materialism is a much more complex, as also a more obscure, doctrine than this stock materialism of the previous century. Marxist materialism calls itself "Dialectical Materialism." The dialectic here referred to is derived from Hegel, who spoke of the processes of thought as well as of nature moving in the pattern of triads: first, thesis, then its opposing antithesis, and finally the synthesis that transcends and reconciles the two warring opposites. It is a pretty image; but the effort to force it as a universal law upon all phenomena, historical as well as natural, as Marxists have attempted, is rigid and indefensible. The real practical effect of this grand metaphor was the same for the Marxists as for Hegel: it allowed for the incorporation of the qualitative into the processes of the world, and so offered much richer possibilities for interpretation than did the stock materialism that was its contemporary.

Marxism also calls itself "Historical Materialism"—and here we come upon an aspect of its doctrine far more significant than its use of the mechanical ballet of the Hegelian dialectic. Historical materialism is the view that all events of human history are fundamentally conditioned or determined by the basic economic structure of the society. As the Marxist formula puts it, substructure determines superstructure —where by substructure is meant the economic basis, and by superstructure all the frosting on top of the social cake: the art, religion, culture, and even the thinking of mankind. As an all-embracing metaphysical thesis about history, this too becomes as questionable as the use of the dialectic. The material economic factor is a powerful one in history; yet there have been countless historical occasions when other factors have been as powerful, and sometimes more powerful, and where it is quite impossible to reduce their operation to that of hidden economic pressures. By taking a profound insight into one part of the whole truth as an all-embracing claim of truth, Marxism here becomes an *ideology* rather than a philosophy, as Karl Jaspers points out in a later piece in this section.

Nevertheless, historical materialism as a hermeneutic principle, as a guiding idea for interpretation, remains an extraordinarily important contribution to the philosophy of history. Its application to historical phenomena has yielded insight that would otherwise be denied us. And perhaps with some historians it is necessary to overstress the material aspect of events; for the historian all too often may be exclusively preoccupied with the ideal content of an historical epoch—its conscious expressions in ideas, art, and religious faith—so that he forgets the gritty and grubby conditions of economic life in which the men of that period sweated to feed, clothe, and house their bodies. The political dynamism of Marxism today is precisely among those peoples of the earth who feel the economic pinch the most so that every other historical factor—including personal and political liberty—seems relatively inconsequential and secondary.

With Karl Jaspers (1883-   ), the existentialist representative in this section, we arrive at a view of history that has more distinctly the stamp of the twentieth century upon it. Not that it can compete with Marxism as a view swaying the masses of mankind; but it does show the pressure of contemporary events and moods just as unmistakably as Marxism shows the traces of nineteenth-century ideology. Of course, this does not mean that it is necessarily a truer view; only later. The contingency of history extends also to the possibility of losing truth as well as gaining it.

(For another confrontation of existentialism with Marxism the reader is also referred to the critique by Sartre in the previous section.)

Jaspers is a good representative of existentialist views on history because for an academic thinker he has been unusually immersed in the world and has meditated deeply upon contemporary experience. As a disciple of the great German sociologist Max Weber, he has studied social problems intensively. Heidegger may have a bolder and more radical interpretation of Western history; but Heidegger's views on history are interspersed with his treatment of other problems. Jaspers also has the advantage of being unquestionably liberal on political matters; and since existentialism has been sometimes associated with less rational political feelings, it may set the balance right to have this particular note sounded.

Jaspers's view of history follows very closely from his own brand of existentialism. For Jaspers the goal of human life is the achievement of authentic existence through deeper and wider self-consciousness. Philosophy contributes to this task as the activity of illuminating existence. But the expansion of consciousness for Jaspers is not the Hegelian circle of knowledge ever widening and widening toward the Absolute. The raising of human consciousness toward authenticity is a much more complex matter than the simple expansion of a circle. Self-consciousness may come with the "shipwreck" of a sweeping intellectual system, for in the foundering of his theories man comes to know the finitude of his own mental powers and therefore of his own being, and he is returned to himself from the tyranny of those ideas. Man is always more than any of his ideas or even the sum of his ideas, says Jaspers; and if man forgets this, he becomes the fanatical partisan of an ideology. If Hegel had given up the System, he would have come face to face with the man Hegel. It is out of this kind of encounter with the Self that is more than all of our ideas, this encounter of reason with non-reason, that authentic existence springs. And authentic existence continues only as the perpetual tension between reason and non-reason. In practice Jaspers is an uncompromising rationalist, but his brand of rationalism is at opposite poles from Hegel's; for here, with Jaspers, reason has its meaning only through what perpetually lies beyond reason itself.

Given this emphasis, it is perfectly in order that Jaspers should see human history as pivoting around the drama of self-consciousness. The Axial Age in human history, according to Jaspers, the age in which humanity properly speaking begins, is the period between 800-200 B.C., when the first sages and prophets emerge to reflect upon human existence. It is the period that in China produces Lao-tse and Confucius, in India the sages of the Upanishads and Buddha, among the Hebrews the prophets, among the Persians Zoroaster, and in Greece Socrates and the philosophers. What unites all these movements for Jaspers is not an identity of metaphysical and cosmological speculation. Such speculation is only a byproduct of the deeper historical revolution that changed human consciousness in that period! The essential thing was that in their different ways and in their different cultures *men for the first time asked themselves about the meaning of their own existence.* And despite the varying answers, there is implicit in all of these sages the realization that meaning comes into human existence only through the struggle for a lucid consciousness and the moral courage for that struggle. At the moment when man asks "What is my meaning?" there dawns the possibility of freedom from the trammels of fate. For, whatever his answer, in his very asking of this question it has become clear that only he can establish or decide to accept the meaning of his own existence. In this act, humanity, as strictly human, emerges from the depths of the primeval.

If the emergence of self-consciousness as deliberate reflection is the axis around which the whole of human history turns, then the goal of history is not hard to descry: it is to raise and enrich the self-consciousness of man. History begins when man takes the first step toward authentic human existence; it continues as the struggle, with all its tensions and setbacks, toward ever greater authenticity. Modern civilization has brought great progress and enlightenment in many fields —Jaspers does not doubt this; he remains a staunch champion of science and the Enlightenment; what he does question is whether the actual organization of the world today does not threaten to swamp the possibilities of authenticity for the individual.

It is perhaps as a critic of modern mass society that Jaspers is most valuable. Such critics have abounded in recent years; but none seems to have spoken with quite the intellectual richness and flexibility of Jaspers or with the depth of his moral seriousness. To read Jaspers on history is to have one's anxieties on the present and future greatly heightened, but also one's hopes renewed. It is, in fact, the tension between these two that makes up the struggle for authenticity. Jaspers holds that philosophy is not a body of doctrine but essentially an activity—an activity intended to awaken in oneself and other human beings the possibilities for a genuinely meaningful life. There can be no doubt that his own philosophy succeeds in doing this, whatever eventual status as a thinker the future may accord him.

W.B.

Benedetto Croce

ART AND PHILOSOPHY [1]

The two forms of knowledge, æsthetic and intellectual or conceptual, are indeed different, but this does not altogether amount to separation and disjunction, as of two forces each pulling in its own direction. If we have shown that the æsthetic form is altogether independent of the intellectual and suffices to itself without external support, we have not said that the intellectual can stand without the æsthetic. To describe the independence as *reciprocal* would not be true.

What is knowledge by concepts? It is knowledge of the relations of things, and things are intuitions. Concepts are not possible without intuitions, just as intuition is itself impossible without the matter of impressions. Intuitions are: this river, this lake, this brook, this rain, this glass of water; the concept is: water, not this or that appearance and particular example of water, but water in general, in whatever time or place it be realized; the material of infinite intuitions, but of one single constant concept.

But the concept, the universal, if it be no longer intuition in one respect, is intuition in another respect, and cannot fail of being intuition. The man who thinks has impressions and emotions, in so far as he thinks. His impression and emotion will be not love or hate, not the passion of the man who is not a philosopher, not hate or love for certain objects and individuals, but *the effort of his thought itself,* with the pain and the joy, the love and the hate joined to it. This effort cannot but assume an intuitive form, in becoming objective to the spirit. To speak is not to think logically; but to *think logically* is also to *speak.*

[1] From: *Aesthetic,* Benedetto Croce, Ch. 5. Farrar, Straus & Cudahy, Inc., New York. Reprinted by permission.

That thought cannot exist without speech, is a truth generally admitted. The negations of this thesis are all founded on equivocations and errors.

The first of the equivocations is that of those who observe that one can likewise think with geometrical figures, algebraical numbers, ideographic signs, without any word, even pronounced silently and almost insensibly within one; that there are languages in which the word, the phonetic sign, expresses nothing, unless the written sign also be examined, and so on. But when we said "speak," we intended to employ a synecdoche, by which was to be understood "expression" in general, for we have already remarked that expression is not only so-called verbal expression. It may or may not be true that certain concepts may be thought without phonetic manifestations. But the very examples adduced to show this also prove that those concepts never exist without expressions.

Others point out that animals, or certain animals, think and reason without speaking. Now as to how, whether, and what animals think, whether they be rudimentary men, like savages who refuse to be civilized, rather than physiological machines, as the old spiritualists maintained, are questions that do not concern us here. When the philosopher talks of animal, brutal, impulsive, instinctive nature and the like, he does not base himself on such conjectures as to dogs or cats, lions or ants; but upon observations of what is called animal and brutal in man: of the animal side or basis of what we feel in ourselves. If individual animals, dogs or cats, lions or ants, possess something of the activity of man, so much the better, or so much the worse, for them. This means that in respect to them also we must talk, not of "nature" as a whole, but of its animal basis, as being perhaps larger and stronger in them than the animal basis of man. And if we suppose that animals think and form concepts, what kind of conjecture would justify the assertion that they do so without corresponding expressions? Analogy with man, knowledge of the spirit, human psychology, the instrument of all our conjectures as to animal psychology, would constrain us on the contrary to suppose that if they think in any way, they also somehow speak.

Another objection is derived from human psychology, and indeed literary psychology, to the effect that the concept can exist without the word, for it is certainly true that we all know books *well thought and ill written:* that is to say, a thought which remains *beyond* the expression, or *notwithstanding* faulty expression. But when we talk of books well thought and ill written, we cannot mean anything but that in such books are parts, pages, periods or propositions well thought and well written, and other parts (perhaps the least important) ill thought and ill written, not really thought and so not really expressed. Where Vico's *Scienza nuova* is really ill written, it is also ill thought. If we pass from the consideration of big books to a short sentence, the error or inaccuracy of such a contention will leap to the eyes. How could a single sentence be clearly thought and confusedly written?

All that can be admitted is that sometimes we possess thoughts (concepts) in an intuitive form, which is an abbreviated or rather peculiar expression, sufficient for us, but not sufficient to communicate it easily to any other given person or persons. Hence it is incorrect to say that we have the thought without the expression; whereas we should rather say that we have, indeed, the expression, but in such a form that it is not easy to communicate it to others. This, however, is a very variable, relative fact. There are always those who catch our thought on the wing, prefer it in this abbreviated form, and would be wearied by the greater development of it required by others. In other words, the thought considered abstractly and logically will be the same; but æsthetically we are dealing with two different intuition-expressions, into which different psychological elements enter. The same argument suffices to destroy, that is, to interpret correctly, the altogether empirical distinction between an *internal* and an *external* language.

The most lofty manifestations, the summits of intellectual and of intuitive knowledge shining from afar, are called, as we know, Art and Science. Art and Science, then, are different and yet linked together; they meet on one side, which is the æsthetic side. Every scientific work is also a work of art. The æsthetic side may remain little noticed when our mind is altogether taken up with the effort to understand the thought of the man of science and to examine its truth. But it is no longer unnoticed when we pass from the activity of understanding to that of contemplation and see that thought either develops itself before us, limpid, exact, well-shaped, without superfluous or insufficient words, with appropriate rhythm and intonation; or confused, broken, embarrassed, tentative. Great thinkers are sometimes called great writers, while other equally great thinkers remain more or less fragmentary writers even if their fragments have the scientific value of harmonious, coherent, and perfect works.

We pardon thinkers and men of science their literary mediocrity. The fragments, the flashes, console us for the whole, because it is far easier to recover the well-arranged composition from the fragmentary work of genius, to liberate the flame latent in the spark, than to achieve the discovery of genius. But how can we pardon mediocre expression in pure artists? *"Mediocribus esse poetis non di, non homines, non concessere columnae."* The poet or painter who lacks form, lacks everything, because he lacks *himself*. Poetical material permeates the souls of all: the expression alone, that is to say, the form, makes the poet. And here appears the truth of the view which denies all content to art, just the intellectual concept being understood as content. In this sense, when we take "content" as equal to "concept" it is most true, not only that art does not consist of content, but also that *it has no content*.

The distinction between *poetry and prose* also cannot be justified, save as that between art and science. It was seen in antiquity that such distinction could not be founded on external elements, such as rhythm and metre, or on rhymed or unrhymed form; that it was, on the contrary, altogether internal. Poetry is the language of feeling, prose of the intellect; but since the intellect is also feeling, in its concreteness and reality, all prose has its poetical side.

The relation between intuitive knowledge or expression and intellectual knowledge or concept, between art and science, poetry and prose, cannot be otherwise defined than by saying that it is one of *double degree.* The first degree is the expression, the second the concept: the first can stand without the second, but the second cannot stand without the first. There is poetry without prose, but not prose without poetry. Expression, indeed, is the first affirmation of human activity. Poetry is "the mother tongue of the human race"; the first men "were by nature sublime poets." We assert this in another way, when we observe that the passage from soul to spirit, from animal to human activity, is effected by means of language. And this should be said of intuition or expression in general. But to us it appears somewhat inaccurate to define language or expression as an *intermediate* link between nature and humanity, as though it were a mixture of both. Where humanity appears, the other has already disappeared; the man who expresses himself, certainly emerges from the state of nature, but he really does emerge: he does not stand half within and half without, as the use of the phrase "intermediate link" would imply.

The cognitive spirit has no form other than these two. Expression and concept exhaust it completely. The whole speculative life of man is spent in passing from one to the other and back again.

Historicity is incorrectly held to be a third theoretical form. Historicity is not form, but content: as form, it is nothing but intuition or æsthetic fact. History does not seek for laws nor form concepts; it employs neither induction nor deduction; it is directed *ad narrandum, non ad demonstrandum;* it does not construct universals and abstractions, but posits intuitions. The this and here, the *individuum omnimode determinatum,* is its domain, as it is the domain of art. History, therefore, is included in the universal concept of art.

As against this doctrine, in view of the impossibility of conceiving a third mode of knowledge, objections have been brought forward which would lead to the affiliation of history to intellectual or scientific knowledge. The greater portion of these objections is animated by the prejudice that in refusing to history the character of conceptual science something of its value and dignity has been taken from it. This really arises from a false idea of art, conceived not as an essential theoretic function, but as an amusement, a superfluity, a frivolity. Without reopening a long debate, which so far as we are concerned is finally closed, we will mention here one sophism which has been and still is widely repeated. Its purpose is to show the logical and scientific nature of history. The sophism consists in admitting that historical knowledge has for its object the individual; but not the representation, it is added, but rather the concept of the individual. From this it is argued that history is also a logical or scientific form of knowledge. History, in fact, is supposed to work out the concept of a personage such as Charlemagne or Napoleon; of an epoch, like the Renaissance or the Reformation; of an event, such as the French Revolution and the Unification of Italy. This it is held to do in the same way as Geometry works out the concepts of spatial forms, or Æsthetic that of expression. But all this is untrue. History cannot do otherwise than *represent* Napoleon and Charlemagne, the Renaissance and the Reformation, the French Revolution and the Unification of Italy as individual facts with their individual physiognomy: that is, in the sense in which logicians use the word "represent" when they say that one cannot have a concept of the individual, but only a representation. The so-called concept of the individual is always a universal or general concept, full of characteristics, supremely full, if you like, but however full it be, incapable of attaining to that individuality to which historical knowledge, as æsthetic knowledge, alone attains.

To show how the content of history comes to be distinguished from that of art in the narrow sense, we must recall what has already been observed as to the ideal character of the intuition or first perception, in which all is real and therefore nothing is real. Only at a later stage does the spirit form the concepts of external and internal, of what has happened and what is desired, of object and subject, and the like: only at this later stage, that is, does it distinguish historical from non-historical intuition, the *real* from the *unreal,* real imagination from pure imagination. Even internal facts, what is desired and imagined, castles in the air, and countries of Cockaigne, have their reality, and the soul, too, has its history. His illusions form part of the biography of every individual as real facts. But the history of an individual soul is history, because the distinction between the real and the unreal is always active in it, even when the illusions themselves are the real. But these distinctive concepts do not appear in history like the concepts of science, but rather like those that we have seen dissolved and melted in the æsthetic intuitions, although in history they stand out in a manner altogether special to themselves. History does not construct the concepts of the real and unreal, but makes use of them. History, in fact, is not the theory of history. Mere conceptual analysis is of no use in ascertaining whether an event in our lives was real or imaginary. We must mentally reproduce the intuitions in the most complete form, as they were at the moment of production. Historicity is distinguished in the concrete from pure imagination as any one intuition is distinguished from any other: in memory.

Where this is not possible, where the delicate and fleeting shades between the real and unreal intuitions are so slight as to mingle the one with the other, we must either renounce for the time being at least the knowledge of what really happened (and this we often do), or we must fall back upon conjecture, verisimilitude, probability. The principle of verisimilitude and of probability in fact dominates all historical criticism. Examination of sources and authorities is devoted to establishing the most credible evidence. And what is the most credible evidence, save that of the best observers, that is, of those who best remember and (be it understood) have not wished to falsify, nor had interest in falsifying the truth of things?

From this it follows that intellectualistic scepticism finds it easy to deny the certainty of any history, for the certainty of history differs from that of science. It is the certainty of memory and of authority, not that of analysis and demonstration. To speak of historical induction or demonstration is to make a metaphorical use of these expressions, which bear a quite different meaning in history to that which they bear in science. The conviction of the historian is the undemonstrable conviction of the juryman, who has heard the witnesses, listened attentively to the case, and prayed Heaven to inspire him. Sometimes, without doubt, he is mistaken, but the mistakes are in a negligible minority compared with the occasions when he grasps the truth. That is why good sense is right against the intellectualists in believing in history, which is not a "fable agreed upon," but what the individual and humanity remember of their past. We strive to enlarge and to render as precise as possible this record, which in some places is dim, in others very clear. We cannot do without it, such as it is, and taken as a whole it is rich in truth. Only in a spirit of paradox can one doubt that there ever was a Greece or a Rome, an Alexander or a Cæsar, a feudal Europe overthrown by a series of revolutions, that on the 1st of November 1517 the theses of Luther were fixed to the door of the church at Wittemberg, or that the Bastile was taken by the people of Paris on the 14th of July 1789.

"What proof hast thou of all this?" asks the sophist, ironically. Humanity replies: "I remember it."

The world of what has happened, of the concrete, of historical fact, is the world called real, natural, including in this definition both the reality called physical and that called spiritual and human. All this world is intuition; historical intuition, if it be shown as it realistically is; imaginary or artistic intuition in the narrow sense, if presented in the aspect of the possible, that is to say, of the imaginable.

Science, true science, which is not intuition but concept, not individuality but universality, cannot be anything but science of the spirit, that is, of what reality has of universal: Philosophy. If natural *sciences* be spoken of, apart from philosophy, we must observe that these are not perfect sciences: they are aggregates of cognitions, arbitrarily abstracted and fixed. The so-called natural sciences indeed themselves recognize that they are surrounded by limitations, and these limitations are nothing but historical and intuitive data. They calculate, measure, establish equalities and uniformities, create classes and types, formulate laws, show in their own way how one fact arises out of other facts; but while doing this they are constantly running into facts known intuitively and historically. Even geometry now states that it rests altogether on hypotheses, since three-dimensional or Euclidean space is but one of the possible spaces, selected for purposes of study because more convenient. What is true in the natural sciences is either philosophy or historical fact. What of properly naturalistic they contain, is abstraction and caprice. When the natural sciences wish to become perfect sciences, they must leave their circle and enter philosophy. They do this when they posit concepts which are anything but naturalistic, such as those of the unextended atom, of ether or vibration, of vital force, of non-intuitional space, and the like. These are true and proper attempts at philosophy, when they are not mere words void of meaning. The concepts of natural science are, without doubt, most useful; but one cannot obtain from them that *system* which belongs only to the spirit.

These historical and intuitive data which cannot be eliminated from the natural sciences furthermore explain not only how, with the advance of knowledge, what was once believed to be true sinks gradually to the level of mythological belief and fantastic illusion, but also how among natural scientists some are to be found who call everything in their sciences upon which reasoning is founded *mythical facts, verbal expedients,* or *conventions.* Natural scientists and mathematicians who approach the study of the energies of the spirit without preparation, are apt to carry thither such mental habits and to speak in philosophy of such and such conventions as "decreed by man." They make conventions of truth and morality, and a supreme convention of the Spirit itself! But if there are to be conventions, something must exist which is no convention, but is itself the author of conventions. This is the spiritual activity of man. The limitation of the natural sciences postulates the illimitability of philosophy.

These explications have firmly established that the pure or fundamental forms of knowledge are two: the intuition and the concept— Art, and Science or Philosophy. With these are to be included History, which is, as it were, the product of intuition placed in contact with the concept, that is, of art receiving in itself philosophic distinctions, while remaining concrete and individual. All other forms (natural sciences and mathematics) are impure, being mingled with extraneous elements of practical origin. Intuition gives us the world, the phenomenon; the concept gives us the noumenon, the Spirit.

IDEAL GENESIS AND DISSOLUTION OF
THE 'PHILOSOPHY OF HISTORY'[1]

1.

The conception of the so-called 'philosophy of history' is perpetually opposed to and resisted by the deterministic conception of history. Not only is this clearly to be seen from inspection, but it is also quite evident logically, because the 'philosophy of history' represents the transcendental conception of the real, determinism the immanent.

But on examining the facts it is not less certain that historical determinism perpetually generates the 'philosophy of history'; nor is this fact less evidently logical than the preceding, because determinism is naturalism, and therefore immanent, certainly, but insufficiently and falsely immanent. Hence it should rather be said that it wishes to be, but is not, immanent, and whatever its efforts may be in the contrary direction, it becomes converted into transcendency. All this does not present any difficulty to one who has clearly in mind the conceptions of the transcendent and of the immanent, of the philosophy of history as transcendency and of the deterministic or naturalistic conception of history as a false immanence. But it will be of use to see in more detail how this process of agreements and oppositions is developed and solved with reference to the problem of history.

"First collect the facts, then connect them causally"; this is the way that the work of the historian is represented in the deterministic conception. *Après la collection des faits, la recherche des causes,* to repeat the very common formula in the very words of one of the most eloquent and picturesque theorists of that school, Taine. Facts are brute, dense, real indeed, but not illumined with the light of science, not intellectualized. This intelligible character must be conferred upon them

[1] From: *History, Its Theory and Practice,* Benedetto Croce, Ch. 4. George G. Harrap & Co., Ltd., London. Reprinted by permission. Russell and Russell, Inc., New York, 1961.

by means of the search of causes. But it is very well known what happens when one fact is linked to another as its cause, forming a chain of causes and effects: we thus inaugurate an infinite regression, and we never succeed in finding the cause or causes to which we can finally attach the chain that we have been so industriously putting together.

Some, maybe many, of the theorists of history get out of the difficulty in a truly simple manner: they break or let fall at a certain point their chain, which is already broken at another point at the other end (the effect which they have undertaken to consider). They operate with their fragment of chain as though it were something perfect and closed in itself, as though a straight line divided at two points should include space and be a figure. Hence, too, the doctrine that we find among the methodologists of history: that it is only necessary for history to seek out 'proximate' causes. This doctrine is intended to supply a logical foundation to the above process. But who can ever say what are the 'proximate causes'? Thought, since it is admitted that it is unfortunately obliged to think according to the chain of causes, will never wish to know anything but 'true' causes, be they near or distant in space and time (space, like time, *ne fait rien à l'affaire*). In reality, this theory is a fig-leaf, placed there to cover a proceeding of which the historian, who is a thinker and a critic, is ashamed, an act of will which is useful, but which for that very reason is wilful. The fig-leaf, however, is a sign of modesty, and as such has its value, because, if shame be lost, there is a risk that it will finally be declared that the 'causes' at which an arbitrary halt has been made are the 'ultimate' causes, the 'true' causes, thus raising the caprice of the individual to the rank of an act creative of the world, treating it as though it were God, the God of certain theologians whose caprice is truth. I should not wish again to quote Taine just after having said this, for he is a most estimable author, not on account of his mental constitution, but of his enthusiastic faith in science; yet it suits me to quote him nevertheless. Taine, in his search for causes, having reached a cause which he sometimes calls the 'race' and sometimes the 'age,' as for instance in his history of English literature, when he reaches the concept of the 'man of the North' or 'German,' with the character and intellect that would be suitable to such a person—coldness of the senses, love of abstract ideas, grossness of taste, and contempt for order and regularity—gravely affirms: *Là s'arrête la recherche: on est tombé sur quelque disposition primitive, sur quelque trait propre à toutes les sensations, à toutes les conceptions d'un siècle ou d'une race, sur quelque particularité inséparable de toutes les démarches de son esprit et de son cœur. Ce sont là les grandes causes, les causes universelles et permanentes.* What that primitive and insurmountable thing contained was known to Taine's imagination, but criticism is ignorant of it; for criticism demands that the genesis of the facts or groups of facts designated as 'age' and 'race' should be given, and in demanding their genesis declares that they are neither 'universal' nor 'permanent,' because no universal and permanent 'facts' are known, as far as I am aware, certainly not *le Germain* and *l'homme du Nord;* nor are mummies facts, though they last some thousands of years, but not for ever—they change gradually, but they do change.

Thus whoever adopts the deterministic conception of history, provided that he decides to abstain from cutting short the inquiry that he has undertaken in an arbitrary and fanciful manner, is of necessity obliged to recognize that the method adopted does not attain the desired end. And since he has begun to think history, although by means of an insufficient method, no course remains to him save that of beginning all over again and following a different path, or that of going forward but changing his direction. The naturalistic presupposition, which still holds its ground ("first collect the facts, then seek the causes": what is more evident and more unavoidable than that?), necessarily leads to the second alternative. But to adopt the second alternative is to supersede determinism, it is to transcend nature and its causes, it is to propose a method opposite to that hitherto followed—that is to say, to renounce the category of cause for another, which cannot be anything but that of end, an extrinsic and transcendental end, which is the analogous opposite, corresponding to the cause. Now the search for the transcendental end is the 'philosophy of history.'

The consequent naturalist (I mean by this he who 'continues to think,' or, as is generally said, to draw the consequences) cannot avoid this inquiry, nor does he ever avoid it, in whatever manner he conceive his new inquiry. This he cannot even do, when he tries, by declaring that the end or 'ultimate cause' is unknowable, because (as elsewhere remarked) an unknowable affirmed is an unknowable in some way known. Naturalism is always crowned with a philosophy of history, whatever its mode of formulation: whether it explain the universe as composed of atoms that strike one another and produce history by means of their various shocks and gyrations, to which they can also put an end by returning to their primitive state of dispersion, whether the hidden God be termed Matter or the Unconscious or something else, or whether, finally, He be conceived as an Intelligence which avails itself of the chain of causes in order to actualize His counsels. And every philosopher of history is on the other hand a naturalist, because he is a dualist and conceives a God and a world, an idea and a fact in addition to or beneath the Idea, a kingdom of ends and a kingdom or sub-kingdom of causes, a celestial city and one that is more or less diabolical or terrene. Take any deterministic historical work and you will find or discover in it, explicit or understood, transcendency (in Taine, for example, it goes by the name of 'race' or of *'siècle,'* which are true and proper deities); take any work of 'philosophy of history' and dualism and naturalism will be found there (in Hegel, for example, when he admits rebellious and impotent facts which resist or are unworthy of the dominion of the idea). And we shall see more and more clearly how from the entrails of naturalism comes inevitably forth the 'philosophy of history.'

2.

But the 'philosophy of history' is just as contradictory as the deterministic conception from which it arises and to which it is opposed. Having both accepted and superseded the method of linking brute facts together, it no longer finds facts to link (for these have already been linked together, as well as might be, by means of the category of cause), but brute facts, on which it must confer rather a 'meaning' than a linking, representing them as aspects of a transcendental process, a theophany. Now those facts, in so far as they are brute facts, are mute, and the transcendency of the process requires an organ, not that of thought that thinks or produces facts, but an extra-logical organ, in order to be conceived and represented (such, for example, as thought which proceeds abstractly *a priori,* in the manner of Fichte), and this is not to be found in the spirit, save as a negative moment, as the void of effective logical thought. The void of logical thought is immediately filled with *praxis,* or what is called sentiment, which then appears as poetry, by theoretical refraction. There is an evident poetical character running through all 'philosophies of history.' Those of antiquity represented historical events as strife between the gods of certain peoples or of certain races or protectors of certain individuals, or between the god of light and truth and the powers of darkness and lies. They thus expressed the aspirations of peoples, groups, or individuals toward hegemony, or of man toward goodness and truth. The most modern of modern forms is that inspired by various national and ethical feelings (the Italian, the Germanic, the Slav, etc.), or which represents the course of history as leading to the kingdom of liberty, or as the passage from the Eden of primitive communism, through the Middle Ages of slavery, servitude, and wages, toward the restoration of communism, which shall no longer be unconscious but conscious, no longer Edenic but human. In poetry, facts are no longer facts but words, not reality but images, and so there would be no occasion to censure them, if it remained pure poetry. But it does not so remain, because those images and words are placed there as ideas and facts—that is to say, as myths: progress, liberty, economy, technique, science are myths, in so far as they are looked upon as agents external to the facts. They are myths no less than God and the Devil, Mars and Venus, Jove and Baal, or any other cruder forms of divinity. And this is the reason why the deterministic conception, after it has produced the 'philosophy of history,' which opposes it, is obliged to oppose its own daughter in its turn, and to appeal from the realm of ends to that of causal connexions, from imagination to observation, from myths to facts.

The reciprocal confutation of historical determinism and the philosophy of history, which makes of each a void or a nothing—that is to say, a single void or nothing—seems to the eclectics as usual to be the reciprocal fulfilment of two entities, which effect or should effect an alliance for mutual support. And since eclecticism flourishes in contemporary philosophy, *mutato nomine,* it is not surprising that besides the duty of investigating the causes to history also is assigned that of ascertaining the 'meaning' or the 'general plan' of the course of history (see the works on the philosophy of history of Labriola, Simmel, and Rickert). Since, too, writers on method are wont to be empirical and therefore eclectic, we find that with them also history is divided into the history which unites and criticizes documents and reconstructs events, and 'philosophy of history' (see Bernheim's manual, typical of all of them). Finally, since ordinary thought is eclectic, nothing is more easy than to find agreement as to the thesis that simple history, which presents the series of facts, does not suffice, but that it is necessary that thought should return to the already constituted chain of events, in order to discover there the hidden design and to answer the questions as to whence we come and whither we go. This amounts to saying that a 'philosophy of history' must be posited side by side with history. This eclecticism, which gives substance to two opposite voids and makes them join hands, sometimes attempts to surpass itself and to mingle those two fallacious sciences or parts of science. Then we hear 'philosophy of history' defended, but with the caution that it must be conducted with 'scientific' and 'positive' method, by means of the search for the cause, thus revealing the action of divine reason or providence.[2] Ordinary thought quickly consents to this programme, but afterward fails to carry it out.[3]

There is nothing new here either for those who know: 'philosophy of history' to be constructed by means of 'positive methods,' transcen-

---

[2] See, for example, the work of Flint; but since, less radical than Flint, Hegel and the Hegelians themselves also ended in admitting the concourse of the two opposed methods, traces of this perversion are also to be found in their 'philosophies of history.' Here, too, is to be noted the false analogy by which Hegel was led to discover the same relation between *a priori* and historical facts as between mathematics and natural facts: *Man muss mit dem Kreise dessen, worin die Prinzipien fallen, wenn man es so nennen will,* a priori *vertraut sein, so gut als Kepler mit den Ellipsen, mit Kuben und Quadraten und mit den Gedanken von Verhältnissen derselben* a priori *schon vorher bekannt sein musste, ehe er aus den empirischen Daten seine unsterblichen Gesetze, welche aus Bestimmungen jener Kreise von Vorstellungen bestehen, erfinden konnte.* (Cf. *Vorles. üb. d. Philos. d. Gesch.,* ed. Brunstäd, pp. 107-108.)

[3] Not even the above-mentioned Flint carried it out, for he lost himself in preliminaries of historical documentation and never proceeded to the promised construction.

dency to be demonstrated by means of the methods of false immanence, is the exact equivalent in the field of historical studies to that
"metaphysic to be constructed by means of the experimental method"
which was recommended by the neocritics (Zeller and others), for it
claimed, not indeed to supersede two voids that reciprocally confute
one another, but to make them agree together, and, after having given
substance to them, to combine them in a single substance. I should not
like to describe the impossibilities contained in the above as the prodi-
gies of an alchemist (the metaphor seems to be too lofty), but rather
as the medleys of bad cooks.

3.

The true remedy for the contradictions of historical determinism and
of the 'philosophy of history' is quite other than this. To obtain it, we
must accept the result of the preceding confutation, which shows that
both are futile, and reject, as lacking thought, both the 'designs' of the
philosophy of history and the causal chains of determinism. When these
two shadows have been dispersed we shall find ourselves at the starting-
place: we are again face to face with disconnected brute facts, with
facts that are connected, but not understood, for which determinism
had tried to employ the cement of causality, the 'philosophy of history,'
the magic wand of finality. What shall we do with these facts? How
shall we make them clear rather than dense as they were, organic
rather than inorganic, intelligible rather than unintelligible? Truly, it
seems difficult to do anything with them, especially to effect their desired transformation. The spirit is helpless before that which is, or is
supposed to be, external to it. And when facts are understood in that
way we are apt to assume again that attitude of contempt of the philosophers for history which has been well-nigh constant since antiquity almost to the end of the eighteenth century (for Aristotle history was
"less philosophical" and less serious than poetry, for Sextus Empiricus
it was "unmethodical material"; Kant did not feel or understand history).
The attitude amounts to this: leave ideas to the philosophers and brute
facts to the historians—let us be satisfied with serious things and leave
their toys to the children.

But before having recourse to such a temptation, it will be prudent
to ask counsel of methodical doubt (which is always most useful),
and to direct the attention precisely upon those brute and disconnected
facts from which the causal method claims to start and before which
we, who are now abandoned by it and by its complement, the philosophy of history, appear to find ourselves again. Methodical doubt will
suggest above all things the thought that those facts are a *presupposition* that has *not been proved,* and it will lead to the inquiry as to
whether the proof can be obtained. Having attempted the proof, we

shall finally arrive at the conclusion that *those facts really do not exist.*

For who, as a matter of fact, affirms their existence? Precisely the spirit, at the moment when it is about to undertake the search for causes. But when accomplishing that act the spirit does not already possess the brute facts (*d'abord la collection des faits*) and then seek the causes (*après, la recherche des causes*); but it makes the *facts brute* by that very act—that is to say, it posits them itself in that way, because it is of use to it so to posit them. The search for causes, undertaken by history, is not in any way different from the procedure of naturalism, already several times illustrated, which abstractly analyses and classifies reality. And to illustrate abstractly and to classify implies at the same time to judge in classifying—that is to say, to treat facts, not as acts of the spirit, conscious in the spirit that thinks them, but as external brute facts. The *Divine Comedy* is that poem which we create again in our imagination in all its particulars as we read it and which we understand critically as a particular determination of the spirit, and to which we therefore assign its place in history, with all its surroundings and all its relations. But when this actuality of our thought and imagination has come to an end—that is to say, when that mental process is completed—we are able, by means of a new act of the spirit, separately to analyse its elements. Thus, for instance, we shall classify the concepts relating to 'Florentine civilization,' or to 'political poetry,' and say that the *Divine Comedy* was an effect of Florentine civilization, and this in its turn an effect of the strife of the communes, and the like. We shall also thus have prepared the way for those absurd problems which used to annoy de Sanctis so much in relation to the work of Dante, and which he admirably described when he said that they arise only when lively aesthetic expression has grown cold and poetical work has fallen into the hands of dullards addicted to trifles. But if we stop in time and do not enter the path of those absurdities, if we restrict ourselves purely and simply to the naturalistic moment, to classification, and to the classificatory judgment (which is also causal connexion), in an altogether practical manner, without drawing any deductions from it, we shall have done nothing that is not perfectly legitimate; indeed, we shall be exercising our right and bowing to a rational necessity, which is that of naturalizing, when naturalization is of use, but not beyond those limits. Thus the materialization of the facts and the external or causal binding of them together are altogether justified as pure naturalism. And even the maxim which bids us to stop at 'proximate' causes—that is to say, not to force classification so far that it loses all practical utility—will find its justification. To place the concept of the *Divine Comedy* in relation to that of 'Florentine civilization' may be of use, but it will be of no use whatever, or infinitely less use, to place it in relation to the class of 'Indo-European civilization' or to the 'civilization of the white man.'

4.

Let us then return with greater confidence to the point of departure, the true point of departure—that is to say, not to that of facts already disorganized and naturalized, but to that of the mind that thinks and constructs the fact. Let us raise up the debased countenances of the calumniated 'brute facts,' and we shall see the light of thought resplendent upon their foreheads. And that true point of departure will reveal itself not merely as a point of departure, but both as a point of arrival and of departure, not as the first step in historical construction, but the whole of history in its construction, which is also its self-construction. Historical determinism, and all the more 'philosophy of history,' leave the *reality of history* behind them, though they directed their journey thither, a journey which became so erratic and so full of useless repetitions.

We shall make the ingenuous Taine confess that what we are saying is the truth when we ask him what he means by the *collection des faits* and learn from him in reply that the collection in question consists of two stages or moments, in the first of which documents are revived in order to attain, *à travers la distance des temps, l'homme vivant, agissant, doué de passions, muni d'habitudes, avec sa voix et sa physionomie, avec ses gestes et ses habits, distinct et complet comme celui que tout à l'heure nous avons quitté dans la rue;* and in the second is sought and found *sous l'homme extérieur l'homme intérieur, "l'homme invisible," "le centre," "le groupe des facultés et des sentiments qui produit le reste," "le drame intérieur," "la psychologie."* Something very different, then, from *collections de faits!* If the things mentioned by our author really do come to pass, if we really do make live again in imagination individuals and events, and if we think what is within them —that is to say, if we think the synthesis of intuition and concept, which is thought in its concreteness—history is already achieved: what more is wanted? There is nothing more to seek. Taine replies: "We must seek causes." That is to say, we must slay the living 'fact' thought by thought, separate its abstract elements—a useful thing, no doubt, but useful for memory and practice. Or, as is the custom of Taine, we must misunderstand and exaggerate the value of the function of this abstract analysis, to lose ourselves in the mythology of races and ages, or in other different but none the less similar things. Let us beware how we slay poor facts, if we wish to think as historians, and in so far as we are such and really think in that way we shall not feel the necessity for having recourse either to the extrinsic bond of causes, historical determinism, or to that which is equally extrinsic of transcendental ends, philosophy of history. The fact historically thought has no cause and no end outside itself, but only in itself, coincident with its real qualities and with its qualitative reality. Because (it is well to note in passing) the determination of facts as *real* facts indeed, but of *unknown nature,* asserted but not understood, is itself also an illusion of naturalism (which thus heralds its other illusion, that of the 'philosophy of history'). In thought, reality and quality, existence and essence, are all one, and it is not possible to affirm a fact as real without at the same time knowing what fact it is—that is, without qualifying it.

Returning to and remaining in or moving in the concrete fact, or, rather, making of oneself thought that thinks the fact concretely, we experience the continual formation and the continual progress of our historical thought and also make clear to ourselves the history of historiography, which proceeds in the same manner. And we see how (I limit myself to this, in order not to allow the eye to wander too far) from the days of the Greeks to our own historical understanding has always been enriching and deepening itself, not because abstract causes and transcendental ends of human things have ever been recovered, but only because an ever increasing consciousness of them has been acquired. Politics and morality, religion and philosophy and art, science and culture and economy, have become more complex concepts and at the same time better determined and unified both in themselves and with respect to the whole. Correlatively with this, the histories of these forms of activity have become ever more complex and more firmly united. We know 'the causes' of civilization as little as did the Greeks; and we know as little as they of the god or gods who control the fortunes of humanity. But we know the theory of civilization better than did the Greeks, and, for instance, we know (as they did not know, or did not know with equal clearness and security) that poetry is an eternal form of the theoretic spirit, that regression or decadence is a relative concept, that the world is not divided into ideas and shadows of ideas, or into potencies and acts, that slavery is not a category of the real, but a historical form of economic, and so forth. Thus it no longer occurs to anyone (save to the survivals or fossils, still to be found among us) to write the history of poetry on the principle of the pedagogic ends that the poets are supposed to have had in view: on the contrary, we strive to determine the forms expressive of their sentiments. We are not at all bewildered when we find ourselves before what are called 'decadences,' but we seek out what new and greater thing was being developed by means of their dialectic. We do not consider the work of man to be miserable and illusory, and aspiration and admiration for the skies and for the ascesis joined thereunto and averse to earth as alone worthy of admiration and imitation. We recognize the reality of power in the act, and in the shadows the solidity of the ideas, and on earth heaven. Finally, we do not find that the possibility of social life is lost owing to the disappearance of the system of slavery. Such a disappearance would have been the catastrophe of reality, if slaves were natural to reality—and so forth.

This conception of history and the consideration of historiographical work in itself make it possible for us to be just toward historical determinism and to the 'philosophy of history,' which, by their continual reappearance, have continually pointed to the gaps in our knowledge, both historical and philosophical, and with their false provisional solutions have heralded the correct solutions of the new problems which we have been propounding. Nor has it been said that they will henceforth cease to exercise such a function (which is the beneficial function of Utopias of every sort). And although historical determinism and the 'philosophy of history' have no history, because they do not develop, they yet receive a content from the relation in which they stand to history, which does develop—that is to say, history develops in them, notwithstanding their covering, extrinsic to their content, which compels to think even him who proposes to schematize and to imagine without thinking. For there is a great difference between the determinism that can now appear, after Descartes and Vico and Kant and Hegel, and that which appeared after Aristotle; between the philosophy of history of Hegel and Marx and that of gnosticism and Christianity. Transcendency and false immanency are at work in both these conceptions respectively; but the abstract forms and mythologies that have appeared in more mature epochs of thought contain this new maturity in themselves. In proof of this, let us pause but a moment (passing by the various forms of naturalism) at the case of the 'philosophy of history.' We observe already a great difference between the philosophy of history, as it appears in the Homeric world, and that of Herodotus, with whom the conception of the anger of the gods is a simulacrum of the moral law, which spares the humble and treads the proud underfoot; from Herodotus to the Fate of the Stoics, a law to which the gods themselves are subjected, and from this to the conception of Providence, which appears in late antiquity as wisdom that rules the world; from this pagan providence again to Christianity, which is divine justice, evangelical preparation, and educative care of the human race, and so on, to the refined providence of the theologians, which as a rule excludes divine intervention and operates by means of secondary causes, to that of Vico, which operates as dialectic of the spirit, to the Idea of Hegel, which is the gradual conquest of the consciousness of self, which liberty achieves during the course of history, till we finally reach the mythology of progress and of civilization, which still persists and is supposed to tend toward the final abolition of prejudices and superstitions, to be carried out by means of the increasing power and divulgation of positive science.

In this way the 'philosophy of history' and historical determinism sometimes attain to the thinness and transparency of a veil, which covers and at the same time reveals the concreteness of the real in thought. Mechanical causes thus appear idealized, transcendent deities humanized, and facts are in great part divested of their brutal aspect. But however thin the veil may be, it remains a veil, and however clear the truth may be, it is not altogether clear, for at bottom the false persuasion still persists that history is constructed with the 'material' of brute facts, with the 'cement' of causes, and with the 'magic' of ends, as with three successive or concurrent methods. The same thing occurs with religion, which in lofty minds liberates itself almost altogether from vulgar beliefs, as do its ethics from the heteronomy of the divine command and from the utilitarianism of rewards and punishments. Almost altogether, but not altogether, and for this reason religion will never be philosophy, save by negating itself, and thus the 'philosophy of history' and historical determinism will become history only by negating themselves. The reason is that as long as they proceed in a positive manner dualism will also persist, and with it the torment of scepticism and agnosticism as a consequence.

The negation of the philosophy of history, in history understood concretely, is its ideal dissolution, and since that so-called philosophy is nothing but an abstract and negative moment, our reason for affirming that *the philosophy of history is dead* is clear. It is dead in its positivity, dead as a body of doctrine, dead in this way, with all the other conceptions and forms of the transcendental. I do not wish to attach to my brief (but in my opinion sufficient) treatment of the argument the addition of an explanation which to some will appear to be (as it appears to me) but little philosophical and even somewhat trivial. Notwithstanding, since I prefer the accusation of semi-triviality to that of equivocation, I shall add that since the criticism of the 'concepts' of cause and transcendental finality does not forbid the use of these 'words,' when they are simple words (to talk, for example, in an imaginative way of liberty as of a goddess, or to say, when about to undertake a study of Dante, that our intention is to 'seek the cause' or 'causes' of this or that work or act of his), so nothing forbids our continuing to talk of 'philosophy of history' and of philosophizing history, meaning the necessity of treating or of a better treatment of this or that historical problem. Neither does anything forbid our calling the researches of historical gnoseology 'philosophy of history,' although in this case we are treating the history, not properly of *history,* but of *historiography,* two things which are wont to be designated with the same word in Italian as in other languages. Neither do we wish to prevent the statement (as did a German professor years ago) that the 'philosophy of history' must be treated as 'sociology'—that is to say, the adornment with that ancient title of so-called sociology, the empirical science of the state, of society and of culture.

These denominations are all permissible in virtue of the same right as that invoked by the adventurer Casanova when he went before the magistrates in order to justify himself for having changed his name— "the right of every man to the letters of the alphabet." But the question treated above is not one of the letters of the alphabet. The 'philosophy of history,' of which we have briefly shown the genesis and the dissolution, is not one that is used in various senses, but a most definite mode of conceiving history—the transcendental mode.

THE POSITIVITY OF HISTORY [1]

We therefore meet the well-known saying of Fustel de Coulanges that there are certainly "history and philosophy, but not the philosophy of history," with the following: there is neither philosophy nor history, nor philosophy of history, but history which is philosophy and philosophy which is history and is intrinsic to history. For this reason, all the controversies—and foremost of all those concerned with *progress*—which philosophers, methodologists of history, and sociologists believe to belong to their especial province, and flaunt at the beginning and the end of their treatises, are reduced for us to simple problems of philosophy, with historical motivation, all of them connected with the problems of which philosophy treats.

In controversies relating to progress it is asked whether the work of man be fertile or sterile, whether it be lost or preserved, whether history have an end, and if so of what sort, whether this end be attainable in time or only in the infinite, whether history be progress or regress, or an interchange between progress and regress, greatness and decadence, whether good or evil prevail in it, and the like. When these questions have been considered with a little attention we shall see that they resolve themselves substantially into three points: the conception of *development,* that of *end,* and that of *value.* That is to say, they are concerned with the whole of reality, and with history only when it is precisely the whole of reality. For this reason they do not belong to supposed particular sciences, to the philosophy of history, or to sociology, but to philosophy and to history in so far as it is philosophy.

When the ordinary current terminology has been translated into philosophical terms it calls forth immediately the thesis, antithesis, and

[1] From: *History, Its Theory and Practice,* Benedetto Croce, Ch. 5. George G. Harrap & Co., Ltd., London. Reprinted by permission. Russell and Russell, Inc., New York, 1961.

synthesis by means of which those problems have been thought and solved during the course of philosophy, to which the reader desirous of instruction must be referred. We can only mention here that the conception of reality as development is nothing but the synthesis of the two one-sided opposites, consisting of permanency without change and of change without permanency, of an identity without diversity and of a diversity without identity, for development is a perpetual surpassing, which is at the same time a perpetual conservation. From this point of view one of the conceptions that has had the greatest vogue in historical books, that of *historical circles,* is revealed as an equivocal attempt to issue forth from a double one-sidedness and a falling back into it, owing to an equivocation. Because either the series of circles is conceived as composed of identicals and we have only permanency, or it is conceived as of things diverse and we have only change. But if, on the contrary, we conceive it as circularity that is perpetually identical and at the same time perpetually diverse, in this sense it coincides with the conception of development itself.

In like manner, the opposite theses, as to the attainment or the impossibility of attainment of the end of history, reveal their common defect of position the end as *extrinsic* to history, conceiving of it either as that which can be reached in time (*progressus ad finitum*), or as that which can never be attained, but only infinitely approximated (*progressus ad infinitum*). But where the end has been correctly conceived as *internal*—that is to say, all one with development itself—we must conclude that it is attained at every instant, and at the same time not attained, because every attainment is the formation of a new prospect, whence we have at every moment the satisfaction of possession, and arising from this the dissatisfaction which drives us to seek a new possession.[2]

Finally, the conceptions of history as a passage from evil to good (progress), or from good to evil (decadence, regression), take their origin from the same error of entifying and making extrinsic good and evil, joy and sorrow (which are the dialectical construction of reality itself). To unite them in the eclectic conception of an alternation of good and evil, of progress and regress, is incorrect. The true solution is that of progress understood not as a passage from evil to good, as though from one state to another, but as the passage from the good to the better, in which the evil is the good itself seen in the light of the better.

These are all philosophical solutions which are at variance with the superficial theses of controversialists (dictated to them by sentimental motives or imaginative combinations, really mythological or resulting

---

[2] For the complete development of these conceptions, see my study of *The Conception of Becoming,* in the *Saggio sullo Hegel seguito da altriscritti di storia della filosofia,* pp. 149-175 (Bari, 1913). (English translation of the work on Hegel by Douglas Ainslie. Macmillan, London.)

in mythologies), to the same extent that they are in accordance with profound human convictions and with the tireless toil, the trust, the courage, which constitute their ethical manifestations.

By drawing the consequences of the dialectical conception of progress something more immediately effective can be achieved in respect to the practice and history of historiography. For we find in that conception the origin of a historical maxim, in the mouth of every one, yet frequently misunderstood and frequently violated—that is to say, that to history pertains not to *judge,* but to *explain,* and that it should be not *subjective* but *objective.*

Misunderstood, because the judging in question is often taken in the sense of logical judgment, of that judgment which is thinking itself, and the subjectivity, which would thus be excluded, would be neither more nor less than the subjectivity of thought. In consequence of this misunderstanding we hear historians being advised to purge themselves of theories, to refrain from the disputes arising from them, to restrict themselves to facts, collecting, arranging, and squeezing out the sap (even by the statistical method). It is impossible to follow such advice as this, as may easily be seen, for such 'abstention from thought' reveals itself as really abstention from 'seriousness of thought,' as a surreptitious attaching of value to the most vulgar and contradictory thoughts, transmitted by tradition, wandering about idly in the mind, or flashing out as the result of momentary caprice. The maxim is altogether false, understood or misunderstood in this way, and it must be taken by its opposite—namely, that history must always judge strictly, and that it must always be energetically subjective without allowing itself to be confused by the conflicts in which thought engages or by the risks that it runs. For it is thought itself, and thought alone, which gets over its own difficulties and dangers, without falling even here into that frivolous eclecticism which tries to find a middle term between our judgment and that of others, and suggests various *neutral* and insipid forms of judgment.

But the true and legitimate meaning, the original motive for that 'judging,' that 'subjectivity,' which it condemns, is that history should not apply to the deeds and the personages that are its material the qualifications of good and evil, as though there really were good and evil facts in the world, people who are good and people who are evil. And it is certainly not to be denied that innumerable historiographers, or those who claim to be historiographers, have really striven and still strive along those lines, in the vain and presumptuous attempt to reward the good and punish the evil, to qualify historical epochs as representing progress or decadence—in a word, to settle what is good and what is evil, as though it were a question of separating one element from another in a compound, hydrogen from oxygen.

Whoever desires to observe intrinsically the above maxim, and by doing so to set himself in accordance with the dialectic conception of progress, must in truth look upon every trace or vestige of propositions affirming evil, regression, or decadence as real facts, as a sign of imperfection—in a word, he must condemn every trace or vestige of *negative* judgments. If the course of history is not the passage from evil to good, or alternative good and evil, but the passage from the good to the better, if history should explain and not condemn, it will pronounce only *positive* judgments, and will forge chains of good, so solid and so closely linked that it will not be possible to introduce into them even a little link of evil or to interpose empty spaces, which in so far as they are empty would not represent good but evil. A fact that seems to be only evil, an epoch that appears to be one of complete decadence, can be nothing but a *non-historical* fact—that is to say, one which has not been historically treated, not penetrated by thought, and which has remained the prey of sentiment and imagination.

Whence comes the phenomenology of good and evil, of sin and repentance, of decadence and resurrection, save from the consciousness of the agent, from the act which is in labour to produce a new form of life? [3] And in that act the adversary who opposed us is in the wrong; the state from which we wish to escape, and from which we are escaping, is unhappy; the new one toward which we are tending becomes symbolized as a dreamed-of felicity to be attained, or as a past condition to restore, which is therefore most beautiful in recollection (which here is not recollection, but imagination). Every one knows how these things present themselves to us in the course of history, manifesting themselves in poetry, in Utopias, in stories with a moral, in detractions, in apologies, in myths of love, of hate, and the like. To the heretics of the Middle Ages and to the Protestant reformers the condition of the primitive Christians seemed to be most lovely and most holy, that of papal Christians most evil and debased. The Sparta of Lycurgus and the Rome of Cincinnatus seemed to the Jacobins to be as admirable as France under the Carlovingians and the Capetians was detestable. The humanists looked upon the lives of the ancient poets and sages as luminous and the life of the Middle Ages as dense darkness. Even in times near our own has been witnessed the glorification of the Lombard communes and the depreciation of the Holy Roman Empire, and the very opposite of this, according as the facts relating to these historical events were reflected in the consciousness of an Italian longing for the independence of Italy or of a German upholding the holy German empire of Prussian hegemony. And this will always happen, because such is the phenomenology of the practical consciousness, and these practical valuations will always be present to some extent in the works of historians. As works, these are not and cannot ever be pure history, quintessential history; if in no other way, then in their phrasing and use of metaphors they will reflect the repercussion of practical needs

[3] For what relates to this section, see my treatment of *Judgments of Value,* in the work before cited.

and efforts directed toward the future. But the historical consciousness, as such, is logical and not practical consciousness, and indeed makes the other its object; history once lived has become in it thought, and the antitheses of will and feeling that formerly offered resistance have no longer a place in thought.

For if there are no good and evil facts, but facts that are always good when understood in their intimate being and concreteness, there are not opposite sides, but that wider side that embraces both the adversaries and which happens just to be historical consideration. Historical consideration, therefore, recognizes as of equal right the Church of the catacombs and that of Gregory VII, the tribunes of the Roman people and the feudal barons, the Lombard League and the Emperor Barbarossa. History never metes out justice, but always *justifies;* she could not carry out the former act without making herself unjust— that is to say, confounding thought with life, taking the attractions and repulsions of sentiment for the judgments of thought.

Poetry is satisfied with the expression of sentiment, and it is worthy of note that a considerable historian, Schlosser, wishing to reserve for himself the right and duty of judging historical facts with Kantian austerity and abstraction, kept his eyes fixed on the *Divine Comedy*— that is to say, a poetical work—as his model of treatment. And since there are poetical elements in all myths, we understand why the conception of history known as *dualistic*—that is to say, of history as composed of two currents, which mix but never resolve in one another their waters of good and evil, truth and error, rationality and irrationality— should have formed a conspicuous part, not only of the Christian religion, but also of the mythologies (for they really are such) of humanism and of illuminism. But the detection of this problem of the duality of values and its solution in the superior unity of the conception of development is the work of the nineteenth century, which on this account and on account of other solutions of the same kind (certainly not on account of its philological and archæological richness, which was relatively common to the four preceding centuries) has been well called 'the century of history.'

Not only, therefore, is history unable to discriminate between facts that are good and facts that are evil, and between epochs that are progressive and those that are regressive, but it does not begin until the psychological conditions which rendered possible such antitheses have been superseded and substituted by an act of the spirit, which seeks to ascertain what function the fact or the epoch previously condemned has fulfilled—that is to say, what it has produced of its own in the course of development, and therefore what it has produced. And since all facts and epochs are productive in their own way, not only is not one of them to be condemned in the light of history, but all are to be praised and venerated. A condemned fact, a fact that is repugnant, is not yet a historical proposition, it is hardly even the premiss of a historical problem to be formulated. A negative history is a non-history so long as its negative process substitutes itself for thought, which is affirmative, and does not maintain itself within its practical and moral bounds and limit itself to poetical expressions and empirical modes of representation, in respect of all of which we can certainly speak (speak and not think), as we do speak at every moment, of bad men and periods of decadence and regression.

If the vice of negative history arises from the separation, the solidification, and the opposition of the dialectical antitheses of good and evil and the transformation of the ideal moments of development into entities, that other deviation of history which may be known as *elegiac* history arises from the misunderstanding of another necessity of that conception—that is to say, the perpetual constancy, the perpetual conservation of what has been acquired. But this is also false by definition. What is preserved and enriched in the course of history is history itself, spirituality. The past does not live otherwise than in the present, as the force of the present, resolved and transformed in the present. Every particular form, individual, action, institution, work, thought, is destined to perish: even art, which is called eternal (and is so in a certain sense), perishes, for it does not live, save to the extent that it is reproduced, and therefore transfigured and surrounded with new light, in the spirit of posterity. Finally, truth itself perishes, particular and determined truth, because it is not rethinkable, save when included in the system of a vaster truth, and therefore at the same time transformed. But those who do not rise to the conception of pure historical consideration, those who attach themselves with their whole soul to an individual, a work, a belief, an institution, and attach themselves so strongly that they cannot separate themselves from it in order to objectify it before themselves and think it, are prone to attribute the immortality which belongs to the spirit in universal to the spirit in one of its particular and determined forms; and since that form, notwithstanding their efforts, dies, and dies in their arms, the universe darkens before their gaze, and the only history that they can relate is the sad one of the agony and death of beautiful things. This too is poetry, and very lofty poetry. Who can do otherwise than weep at the loss of a beloved one, at separation from something dear to him, cannot see the sun extinguished and the earth tremble and the birds cease their flight and fall to earth, like Dante, on the loss of his beloved "who was so beautiful"? But history is never *history of death,* but *history of life,* and all know that the proper commemoration of the dead is the knowledge of what they did in life, of what they produced that is working in us, the history of their life and not of their death, which it behoves a gentle soul to veil, a soul barbarous and perverse to exhibit in its miserable nakedness and to contemplate with unhealthy persistence. For this reason all histories which narrate the death and not the life of peoples, of states, of institutions, of customs, of literary and artistic ideals, of religious conceptions, are to be considered false, or, we repeat, simply poetry, where they attain to the level of poetry. People grow sad and suffer and lament because that which was is no longer. This would resolve itself into a mere tautology (because if it was, it is evident that it is no longer), were it not conjoined to the neglect of recognizing what of that past has not perished—that is to say, that past in so far as it is not past but present, the eternal life of the past. It is in this neglect, in the incorrect view arising out of it, that the falsity of such histories resides.

It sometimes happens that historians, intent upon narrating those scenes of anguish in a lugubrious manner and upon celebrating the funerals which it pleases them to call histories, remain partly astounded and partly scandalized when they hear a peal of laughter, a cry of joy, a sigh of satisfaction, or find an enthusiastic impulse springing up from the documents that they are searching. How, they ask, could men live, make love, reproduce their species, sing, paint, discuss, when the trumps were sounding east and west to announce the end of the world? But they do not see that such an end of the world exists only in their own imaginations, rich in elegiac motives, but poor in understanding. They do not perceive that such importunate trumpet-calls have never in reality existed. These are very useful, on the other hand, for reminding those who may have forgotten it that history always pursues her indefatigable work, and that her apparent agonies are the travail of a new birth, and that what are believed to be her expiring sighs are moans that announce the birth of a new world. History differs from the individual who dies because, in the words of Alcmæon of Crete, he is not able τὴν ἀρχὴν τῷ τέλει προσάψαι, to join his beginning to his end: history never dies, because she always joins her beginning to her end.

PHILOSOPHY AND METHODOLOGY[1]

Having established the unity of philosophy and historiography, and shown that the division between the two has but a literary and didactic value, because it is founded upon the possibility of placing in the foreground of verbal exposition now one and now the other of the two dialectical elements of that unity, it is well to make quite clear what is the true object of the treatises bearing the traditional title of philosophic 'theory' or 'system': to what (in a word) *philosophy can be reduced.*

Philosophy, in consequence of the new relation in which it has been placed, cannot of necessity be anything but the *methodological moment of historiography:* a dilucidation of the categories constitutive of historical judgments, or of the concepts that direct historical interpretation. And since historiography has for content the concrete life of the spirit, and this life is life of imagination and of thought, of action and of morality (or of something else, if anything else can be thought of), and in this variety of its forms remains always one, the dilucidation moves in distinguishing between æsthetic and logic, between economic and ethic, uniting and dissolving them all in the philosophy of the spirit. If a philosophical problem shows itself to be altogether sterile for the historical judgment, we have there the proof that such problem is otiose, badly stated, and in reality does not exist. If the solution of a problem—that is to say, of a philosophical proposition—instead of making history more intelligible, leaves it obscure or confounds it with others, or leaps over it and lightly condemns or negates it, we have there the proof that such proposition and the philosophy with which it is connected are arbitrary, though it may preserve interest in other respects, as a manifestation of sentiment or of imagination.

[1] From: *History, Its Theory and Practice,* Benedetto Croce, Appendix 3. George G. Harrap & Co., Ltd., London. Reprinted by permission. Russell and Russell, Inc., New York, 1961.

The definition of philosophy as 'methodology' is not at first exempt from doubts, even on the part of one ready to accept in general the tendency that it represents; because philosophy and methodology are terms often contrasted, and a philosophy that leads to a methodology is apt to be tainted with empiricism. But certainly the methodology of which we are here speaking is not at all empirical; indeed, it appears just for the purpose of correcting and taking the place of the empirical methodology of professional historians and of other such specialists in all that greater part of it where it is a true and proper, though defective, attempt toward the philosophical solution of the theoretical problems raised by the study of history, or toward philosophical methodology and philosophy as methodology.

If, however, the above-mentioned dispute is settled as soon as stated, this cannot be said of another, where our position finds itself opposed to a widely diffused and ancient conception of philosophy as the solver of the mystery of the universe, knowledge of ultimate reality, revelation of the world of noumena, which is held to be beyond the world of phenomena, in which we move in ordinary life and in which history also moves. This is not the place to give the history of that idea; but we must at least say this, that its origin is religious or mythological, and that it persisted even among those philosophers who were most successful in directing thought toward our earth as the sole reality, and initiated the new philosophy as methodology of the judgment or of historical knowledge. It persisted in Kant, who admitted it as the limit of his criticism; it persisted in Hegel, who framed his subtle researches in logic and philosophy of the spirit in a sort of mythology of the Idea.

Nevertheless, the diversity of the two conceptions manifested itself in an ever-increasing ratio, finding expression in various formulas of the nineteenth century, such as *psychology against metaphysic,* a philosophy of *experience and immanence, aprioristic* against *transcendental* philosophy, *positivism* against *idealism;* and although the polemic was as a rule ill conducted, going beyond the mark and ending by unconsciously embracing that very metaphysic, transcendency, and apriority, that very abstract idealism, which it had set out to combat, the sentiment that inspired it was legitimate. And the philosophy of methodology has made it its own, has combated the same adversary with better arms, has certainly insisted upon a psychological view, but a speculative psychological view, immanent in history, but dialectically immanent, differing in this from positivism, that while the latter made necessary the contingent, it made the contingent necessary, thus affirming the right of thought to the hegemony. Such a philosophy is just philosophy as history (and so history as philosophy), and the determination of the philosophical moment in the purely categorical and methodological moment.

The greater vigour of this conception in respect to the opposite, the superiority of philosophy as *methodology* over philosophy as *meta-*

physic, is shown by the capacity of the former to solve the problems of the latter by criticizing them and pointing out their origin. Metaphysic, on the other hand, is incapable of solving not only the problems of methodology, but even its own problems, without having recourse to the fantastic and arbitrary. Thus questions as to the reality of the external world, of soul-substance, of the unknowable, of dualisms and of antitheses, and so forth, have disappeared in gnoseological doctrines, which have substituted better conceptions for those which we formerly possessed concerning the logic of the sciences, explaining those questions as eternally renascent aspects of the dialectic or phenomenology of knowledge.

The view of philosophy as metaphysic is, however, so inveterate and so tenacious that it is not surprising that it should still give some sign of life in the minds of those who have set themselves free of it in general, but have not applied themselves to eradicating it in all its particulars, nor closed all the doors by which it may return in a more or less unexpected manner. And if we rarely find it openly and directly displayed now, we may yet discern or suspect it in one or other of its aspects or attitudes, persisting like kinks of the mind, or unconscious preconceptions, which threaten to drive philosophy as methodology back into the wrong path, and to prepare the return, though but for a brief period, of the metaphysic that has been superseded.

It seems to me opportune to provide here a clear statement of some of these preconceptions, tendencies, and habits, pointing out the errors which they contain and entail.

First of all the survivals of the past that are still common comes the view of philosophy as having a fundamental problem to solve. Now the conception of a fundamental problem is intrinsically at variance with that of philosophy as history, and with the treatment of philosophy as methodology of history, which posits, and cannot do otherwise than posit, the *infinity* of philosophical problems, all certainly connected with one another, but not one of which can be considered fundamental, for just the same reason that no single part of an organism is the foundation of all the others, but each one is in its turn foundation and founded. If, indeed, methodology take the substance of its problems from history, history in its most modest but concrete form of history of ourselves, of each one of us as an individual, this shows us that we pass on from one to another particular philosophical problem at the promptings of our life as it is lived, and that one or the other group of class of problems holds the field or has especial interest for us, according to the epochs of our life. And we find the same to be the case if we look at the wider but less definite spectacle afforded by the already mentioned general history of philosophy—that is to say, that according to times and peoples, philosophical problems relating sometimes to morality, sometimes to politics, to religion, or to the natural sciences and mathematics, have in turn the upper hand. Every particular philosophical problem has been a problem of the whole of philosophy, either openly or by inference, but we never meet with a *general problem of philosophy,* owing to the contradiction thereby implied. And if there does seem to be one (and it certainly does seem so), it is really a question of appearances, due to the fact that modern philosophy, which comes to us from the Middle Ages and was elaborated during the religious struggles of the Renaissance, has preserved a strong imprint of *theology* in its didactic form, not less than in the psychological disposition of the greater part of those addicted to it. Hence arises the fundamental and almost unique importance usurped by the problem of thought and being, which after all was nothing more than the old problem of this world and the next, of earth and heaven, in a critical and gnoseological form. But those who destroyed or who initiated the destruction of heaven and of the other world and of transcendental philosophy by immanent philosophy began at the same moment to corrode the conception of a fundamental problem, although they were not fully aware of this (for we have said above that they remained trammelled in the philosophy of the Thing in Itself or in the Mythology of the Idea). That problem was rightly fundamental for religious spirits, who held that the whole intellectual and practical dominion of the world was nothing, unless they had saved their own souls or their own thought in another world, in the knowledge of a world of noumena and reality. But such it was not destined to remain for the philosophers, henceforth restricted to the world alone or to nature, which has no skin and no kernel and is all of a piece. What would happen were we to resume belief in a fundamental problem, dominating all others? The other problems would either have to be considered as all dependent upon it and therefore solved with it, or as problems no longer philosophical but empirical. That is to say, all the problems appearing every day anew in science and life would lose their value, either becoming a tautology of the fundamental solution or being committed to empirical treatment. Thus the distinction between philosophy and methodology, between metaphysic and philosophy of the spirit, would reappear, the first transcendental as regards the second, the second aphilosophical as regards the first.

Another view, arising from the old metaphysical conception of the function of philosophy, leads to the rejection of distinction in favour of *unity,* thus conforming to the theological conception that all distinctions are unified by absorption in God, and to the religious point of view, which forgets the world and its necessities in the vision of God. From this ensues a disposition which may be described as something between indifferent, accommodating, or weak, in respect of particular problems, and the pernicious doctrine of the double faculty is almost tacitly renewed, that is, of intellectual intuition or other superior cognoscitive faculty, peculiar to the philosopher and leading to the vision of true reality, and of criticism or thought prone to interest itself in the contingent and thus greatly inferior in degree and free to proceed with a lack of speculative rigour not permissible in the other. Such a disposition led to the worst possible consequences in the philosophical treatises of the Hegelian school, where the disciples (differing from the master) generally gave evidence of having meditated but little or not at all upon the problems of the various spiritual forms, freely accepting vulgar opinions concerning them, or engaging in them with the indifference of men sure of the essential, and therefore cutting and mutilating them without pity, in order to force them into their pre-established schemes with all haste, thus getting rid of difficulties by means of this illusory arrangement. Hence the emptiness and tiresomeness of their philosophies, from which the historian, or the man whose attention is directed to the understanding of the particular and the concrete, failed to learn anything that could be of use to him in the direction of his own studies and in the clearer formulation of his own judgments. And since the mythology of the idea reappeared in positivism as mythology of evolution, here too particular problems (which are indeed the only philosophical problems) received merely schematic and empty treatment and did not progress at all. Philosophy as history and methodology of history restores honour to the virtue of acuteness or discernment, which the theological unitarianism of metaphysic tended to depreciate: discernment, which is prosaic but severe, hard and laborious but prolific, which sometimes assumes the unsympathetic aspect of scholasticism and pedantry, but is also of use in this aspect, like every discipline, and holds that the neglect of distinction for unity is also intimately opposed to the conception of philosophy as history.

A third tendency (I beg to be allowed to proceed by enumeration of the various sides of the same mental attitude for reasons of convenience), a third tendency also seeks the *definitive* philosophy, untaught by the historical fact that no philosophy has ever been definitive or has set a limit to thought, or has ever been thoroughly convinced that the perpetual changing of philosophy with the world which perpetually changes is not by any means a defect, but is the nature itself of thought and reality. Or, rather, such teaching, and the proposition that follows it, do not fail altogether of acceptance, and they are led to believe that the spirit, ever growing upon itself, produces thoughts and systems that are ever new. But since they have retained the presupposition of a fundamental problem which (as we have said) substantially consists of the ancient problem of religion alone, and each problem well determined implies a single solution, the solution given of the 'fundamental problem' naturally claims to be the definitive solution of the problem of philosophy itself. A new solution could not appear without a new problem (owing to the logical unity of problem and solution); but that problem, which is superior to all the others, is on the contrary the only one. Thus a definitive philosophy, assumed in the conception of the fundamental problem, is at variance with historical experience, and more irreconcilably, because in a more evidently logical manner, with philosophy as history, which, admitting infinite problems, denies the claim for and the expectation of a definitive philosophy. Every philosophy is definitive for the problem which it solves, but not for the one that appears immediately afterward, at the foot of the first, nor for the other problems which will arise from the solution of this. To close the series would be to turn from philosophy to religion and to rest in God.

Indeed, the fourth preconception, which we now proceed to state, and which links itself with the preceding, and, together with all the preceding, to the theological nature of the old metaphysic, concerns the *figure of the philosopher,* as Buddha or the Awakened One, who posits himself as superior to others (and to himself in the moments when he is not a philosopher), because he holds himself to be free from human passions, illusions, and agitations by means of philosophy. This is the case with the believer, who fixes his mind upon God and shakes off earthly cares, like the lover, who feels himself blessed in the possession of the beloved and defies the whole world. But the world soon takes its revenge both upon the believer and the lover, and does not fail to insist upon its rights. Such an illusion is impossible for the philosophical historian, who differs from the other in feeling himself irresistibly involved in the course of history, as at once both subject and object, and who is therefore led to negate felicity or beatitude, as he negates every other abstraction (because, as has been well said, *le bonheur est le contraire de la sensation de vivre*), and to accept life as it is, as joy that overcome sorrow and perpetually produces new sorrows and new unstable joys. And history, which he thinks as the only truth, is the work of tireless thought, which conditions practical work, as practical work conditions the new work of thought. Thus the primacy formerly attributed to the contemplative life is now transferred not to active life, but to life in its integrity, which is at once thought and action. And every man is a philosopher (in his circle, however wide or narrow it may appear), and every philosopher is a man, indissolubly linked to the conditions of human life, which it is not given to anyone to transcend. The mystical or apocalyptic philosopher of the Græco-Roman decadence was well able to separate himself from the world: the great thinkers, like Hegel, who inaugurated the epoch of modern philosophy, although they denied the primacy of the abstract contemplative life, were liable to fall back into the error of belief in this supremacy and to conceive a sphere of absolute spirit, a process of liberation through art, religion, and philosophy, as a means of reaching it; but the once sublime figure of the philosopher blessed in the absolute, when we try to revive it in this modern world of ours, becomes tinged with the comic. It is true that satire has now but little material upon which to exercise itself, and is reduced to aiming its shafts at the 'professors of philosophy' (according to the type of philosopher that has been created by modern universities, which is partly the heir of the 'master of theology' of the Middle Ages: against the professors, that is to say, to the extent that they continue to repeat mechanically abstract general propositions, and seem to be unmoved by the passions and the problems that press upon them from all sides and vainly ask for more concrete and actual treatment. But the function and the social figure of the philosopher have profoundly changed, and we have not said that the manner of being of the 'professors of philosophy' will not also change in its turn—that is to say, that the way of teaching philosophy in the universities and schools is not on the verge of experiencing a crisis, which will eliminate the last remains of the medieval fashion of formalistic philosophizing. A strong advance in philosophical culture should lead to this result: that all students of human affairs, jurists, economists, moralists, men of letters—in other words, all students of historical matters—should become conscious and disciplined philosophers, and that thus the philosopher in general, the *purus philosophus,* should find no place left for him among the professional specifications of knowledge. With the disappearance of the philosopher 'in general' would also disappear the last social vestige of the teleologist or metaphysician, and of the Buddha or Awakened One.

There is also a prejudice which to some extent inquinates the manner of *culture* of students of philosophy. They are accustomed to have recourse almost exclusively to the books of philosophers, indeed of philosophers 'in general,' of the metaphysical system-makers, in the same way as the student of theology formed himself upon the sacred texts. This method of culture, which is perfectly consequent when a start is made from the presupposition of a fundamental or single problem, of which it is necessary to know the different diverging and progressive solutions which have been attempted, is altogether inconsequent and inadequate in the case of a historical and immanent philosophy, which draws its material from all the most varied impressions of life and from all intuitions and reflections upon life. That form of culture is the reason for the aridity of the treatment of certain particular problems, for which is necessary a continued contact with daily experience (art and art criticism for æsthetic, politics, economy, judicial trials for the philosophy of rights, positive and mathematical sciences for the gnoseology of the sciences, and so on). To it is also due the aridity of treatment of those parts of philosophy themselves which are traditionally considered to constitute 'general philosophy,' for they too had their origin in life, and we must refer them back to life if we are to give a satisfactory interpretation of their propositions; we must plunge them into life again to develop them and to find in them new aspects. The *whole of history* is the foundation of philosophy as history, and to limit its foundation to the *history of philosophy* alone, and of 'general' or 'metaphysical' philosophy, is impossible, save by unconsciously ad hering to the old idea of philosophy, not as methodology but as meta-physic, which is the fifth of the prejudices that we are enumerating.

This enumeration can be both lengthened and ended with the mention of a sixth preconception, relating to *philosophical exposition.* Owing to this, philosophy is expected to have either an architectural form, as though it were a temple consecrated to the Eternal, or a warm poetical form, as though it were a hymn to the Eternal. But these forms were part of the old content, and that form is now changed. Philosophy shows itself to be a dilucidation of the categories of historical interpretation rather than the grandiose architecture of a temple or a sacred hymn running on conventional lines. Philosophy is discussion, polemic, rigorous didactic exposition, which is certainly coloured with the sentiments of the writer, like every other literary form, able also at times to raise its voice (or on the other hand to become slight and playful, according to circumstances), but not constrained to observe rules which appear to be proper to a theological or religious content. Philosophy treated as methodology has, so to speak, caused philosophical exposition to descend from poetry to prose.

All the preconceptions, habits, and tendencies which I have briefly described should in my opinion be carefully sought out and eliminated, for it is they that impede philosophy from taking the form and proceeding in the mode suitable and adequate to the consciousness of the unity with history which it has reached. If we look merely at the enormous amount of psychological observations and moral doubts accumulated in the course of the nineteenth century by poetry, fiction, and drama, those voices of our society, and consider that in great part it remains without critical treatment, some idea can be formed of the immense amount of work that falls to philosophy to accomplish. And if on the other hand we observe the multitude of anxious questions that the great European War has everywhere raised—as to the state, as to history, as to rights, as to the functions of the different peoples, as to civilization, culture, and barbarism, as to science, art, religion, as to the end and ideal of life, and so on—we realize the duty of philosophers to issue forth from the theologico-metaphysical circle in which they remain confined even when they refuse to hear of theology and meta-physic. For notwithstanding their protests, and notwithstanding the new conception accepted and professed by them, they really remain intellectually and spiritually attached to the old ideas.

Even the *history itself of philosophy* has hitherto been renewed only to a small extent, in conformity with the new conception of philosophy. This new conception invites us to direct our attention to thoughts and thinkers, long neglected or placed in the second rank and not considered to be truly philosophers because they did not treat directly the 'fundamental problem' of philosophy or the great *peut-être,* but were occupied with 'particular problems.' These particular problems, however, were destined to produce eventually a change of view as regards the 'general problem,' which emerged itself reduced to the rank of a 'particular' problem. It is simply the result of prejudice to look upon a Machiavelli, who posited the conception of the modern state, a Baltasar Gracian, who examined the question of acuteness in practical matters, a Pascal, who criticized the spirit of Jesuitry, a Vico, who renewed all the sciences of the spirit, or a Hamann, with his keen sense of the value of tradition, as minor philosophers, I do not say in comparison with some metaphysician of little originality, but even when compared with a Descartes or a Spinoza, who dealt with *other* but not *superior* problems. A schematic and bloodless history of philosophy corresponded, in fact, with the philosophy of the 'fundamental problem.' A far richer, more varied and pliant philosophy should correspond with philosophy as methodology, which holds to be philosophy not only what appertains to the problems of immanency, of transcendency, of this world and the next, but everything that has been of avail in increasing the patrimony of guiding conceptions, the understanding of actual history, and the formation of the reality of thought in which we live.

V. I. Lenin

HOW CERTAIN "MARXISTS" IN 1908
AND CERTAIN IDEALISTS IN 1710
REFUTED MATERIALISM[1]

Anyone in the least acquainted with philosophical literature must know that scarcely a single contemporary professor of philosophy (or of theology) can be found who is not directly or indirectly engaged in refuting materialism. They have declared materialism refuted a thousand times, yet are continuing to refute it for the thousand and first time. All our revisionists are engaged in refuting materialism, pretending, however, that actually they are only refuting the materialist Plekhanov, and not the materialist Engels, nor the materialist Feuerbach, nor the materialist views of J. Dietzgen—and, moreover, that they are refuting materialism from the standpoint of "recent" and "modern" positivism, natural science, and so forth. Without citing quotations, which anyone desiring to do so could cull by the hundred from the books above mentioned, I shall refer to those arguments by which materialism is being combated by Bazarov, Bogdanov, Yushkevich, Valentinov, Chernov[2] and other Machians. I shall use this latter term throughout as a synonym for "empirio-criticist" because it is shorter and simpler and has already acquired rights of citizenship in Russian literature. That Ernst Mach is

[1] From: *Materialism and Empirio-Criticism*, V. I. Lenin, pp. 13-31. International Publishers, New York, 1927.
[2] V. Chernov, *Philosophical and Sociological Studies*, Moscow, 1907. The author is as ardent an adherent of Avenarius and an enemy of dialectical materialism as Bazarov and Co.

the most popular representative in philosophical literature,[3] while Bogdanov's and Yushkevich's departures from "pure" Machism are of absolutely secondary importance, as will be shown later.

The materialists, we are told, recognise something unthinkable and unknowable—"things-in-themselves"—matter "outside of experience" and outside of our knowledge. They lapse into genuine mysticism by admitting the existence of something beyond, something transcending the bounds of "experience" and knowledge. When they say that matter, by acting upon our sense-organs, produces sensations, the materialists take as their basis the "unknown," nothingness; for do they not themselves declare our sensations to be the only source of knowledge? The materialists lapse into "Kantianism" (Plekhanov, by recognising the existence of "things-in-themselves," *i.e.,* things outside of our consciousness); they "duplicate" the world and preach "dualism," for the materialists hold that beyond the appearance there is the thing-in-itself; beyond the immediate sense data there is something else, some fetish, an "idol," an absolute, a source of "metaphysics," a double of religion ("hot matter," as Bazarov says).

Such are the arguments levelled by the Machians against materialism, as repeated and retold in varying keys by the afore-mentioned writers.

In order to test whether these arguments are new, and whether they are really directed against only one Russian materialist who "lapsed into Kantianism," we shall give some detailed quotations from the works of an old idealist, George Berkeley. This historical inquiry is all the more necessary in the introduction to our comments since we shall have frequent occasion to refer to Berkeley and his trend in philosophy, for the Machians misrepresent both the relation of Mach to Berkeley and the essence of Berkeley's philosophical line.

The work of Bishop George Berkeley, published in 1710 under the title *Treatise Concerning the Principles of Human Knowledge*[4] begins with the following argument: "It is evident to anyone who takes a survey of the *objects* of human knowledge, that they are either ideas actually imprinted on the senses; or else such as are perceived by attending to the passions and operations of the mind; or lastly, ideas formed by help of memory and imagination. . . . By sight I have the ideas of light and colours, with their several degrees and variations. By touch I perceive hard and soft, heat and cold, motion and resistance. . . . Smelling furnishes me with odours; the palate with tastes; and hearing conveys sounds. . . . And as several of these are observed to accompany each other, they come to be marked by one name, and so to be reputed as one thing. Thus, for example, a certain colour, taste, smell, figure and consistence having been observed to go together, are accounted one distinct thing, signified by the name apple; other collec-

[3] See, for instance, Dr. Richard Hönigswald, *Ueber die Lehre Humes von der Realität der Au Bendinge,* Berlin, 1904, S. 26.
[4] *Works of George Berkeley,* edited by A. C. Fraser, Oxford, 1871, Vol. I, p. 155.

tions of ideas constitute a stone, a tree, a book, and the like sensible things . . ." (§ 1).

Such is the content of the first section of Berkeley's work. We must remember that Berkeley takes as the basis of his philosophy "hard, soft, heat, cold, colours, taste, odours," etc. For Berkeley, things are "collections of ideas," this expression designating the aforesaid, let us say, qualities or sensations, and not abstract thoughts.

Berkeley goes on to say that besides these "ideas or objects of knowledge" there exists something that perceives them—"mind, spirit, soul or *myself*" (§ 2). It is self-evident, the philosopher concludes, that "ideas" cannot exist outside of the mind that perceives them. In order to convince ourselves of this it is enough to consider the meaning of the word "exist." "The table I write on I say exists, that is, I see and feel it; and if I were out of my study I should say it existed; meaning thereby that if I was in my study I might perceive it. . . ." That is what Berkeley says in § 3 of his work and thereupon he begins a polemic against the people whom he calls materialists (§§ 18, 19, etc.). "I cannot conceive," he says, "how it is possible to speak of the absolute existence of things without their relation to the fact that somebody perceives them. To exist means to be perceived" (their *esse* is *percipi*, § 3—a dictum of Berkeley's frequently quoted in textbooks on the history of philosophy). "It is indeed an opinion strangely prevailing amongst men, that houses, mountains, rivers, and in a word all sensible objects have an existence, natural or real, distinct from their being perceived by the understanding" (§ 4). This opinion is a "manifest contradiction," says Berkeley. "For, what are the afore-mentioned objects but the things we perceive by sense? and what do we perceive besides our own ideas or sensations? and is it not plainly repugnant that any one of these, or any combination of them, should exist unperceived?" (§ 4.)

The expression "collection of ideas" Berkeley now replaces by what to him is an equivalent expression, *combination of sensations,* and accuses the materialists of a "repugnant" tendency to go still further, of seeking some source of this complex—that is, of this combination of sensations. In § 5 the materialists are accused of trifling with an abstraction, for to divorce the sensation from the object, according to Berkeley, is an empty abstraction. "In truth," he says at the end of § 5, omitted in the second edition, "the object and the sensation are the same thing, and cannot therefore be abstracted from each other." Berkeley goes on: "But, say you, though the ideas themselves do not exist without the mind, yet there may be things like them, whereof they are copies or resemblances; which things exist without the mind, in an unthinking substance. I answer, an idea can be like nothing but an idea; a colour or figure can be like nothing but another colour or figure. . . . I ask whether those supposed originals, or external things, of which our ideas are the pictures or representations, be themselves perceivable or no? If they are, then they are ideas and we have gained our point; but if you say they are not, I appeal to anyone whether it be sense to assert a colour is like something which is invisible; hard or soft, like something which is intangible; and so of the rest" (§ 8).

As the reader sees, Bazarov's "arguments" against Plekhanov concerning the problem of whether things can exist apart from their action on us do not differ in the least from Berkeley's arguments against the materialists whom he does not mention by name. Berkeley considers the notion of the existence of "matter or corporeal substance" (§ 9) such a "contradiction," such a "repugnant" thing that it is really not worth wasting time exposing it. He says: "But because the tenet of the existence of Matter seems to have taken so deep a root in the minds of philosophers, and draws after it so many ill consequences, I choose rather to be thought prolix and tedious than omit anything that might conduce to the full discovery and extirpation of that prejudice" (§ 9).

We shall presently see to what ill consequences Berkeley is referring. Let us first finish with his theoretical arguments against the materialists. Denying the "absolute" existence of objects, that is, the existence of things outside human knowledge, Berkeley deliberately represents the views of his opponents as though they recognised the "thing-in-itself." In § 24 Berkeley writes in italics that the opinion which he is refuting recognises *the absolute existence of sensible objects in themselves, or without the mind*" (pp. 167-68, *op. cit.*). The two fundamental lines of philosophical outlook are here depicted with the straightforwardness, clarity and precision that distinguish the classical philosophers from the inventors of "new" systems in our day. Materialism is the recognition of "objects in themselves," or outside the mind; ideas and sensations are copies or images of those objects. The opposite doctrine (idealism) claims that objects do not exist "without the mind"; objects are "combinations of sensations."

This was written in 1710, fourteen years before the birth of Immanuel Kant, yet our Machians, supposedly on the basis of "recent" philosophy, made the discovery that the recognition of "objects in themselves" is a result of the infection or distortion of materialism by Kantianism! The "new" discoveries of the Machians are the product of an astounding ignorance of the history of the basic philosophical trends.

Their next "new" thought consists in this: that the concepts "matter" or "substance" are remnants of old uncritical views. Mach and Avenarius, you see, advanced philosophical thought, deepened analysis and eliminated these "absolutes," "unchangeable entities," etc. If you wish to check such assertions with the original sources, go to Berkeley and you will see that they are pretentious fictions. Berkeley says quite definitely that matter is "nonentity" (§ 68), that matter is *nothing* (§ 80). "You may," thus Berkeley ridicules the materialists, "if so it shall seem good, use the word *matter* in the same sense as other men use *nothing*" (pp. 196-97). At the beginning, says Berkeley, it was believed that colours, odours, etc., "really exist," but subsequently such views were renounced, and it was seen that they only exist in dependence on our sensations. But this elimination of old erroneous concepts was not completed; a remnant is the concept "substance" (§ 73), which is also a "prejudice" (p. 195), and which was finally exposed by Bishop Berkeley in 1710! In 1908 there are still wags who seriously believe Avenarius, Petzoldt, Mach and the rest, when they maintain that it was only "recent positivism" and "recent natural science" which at last succeeded in eliminating these "metaphysical" conceptions.

These same wags (among them Bogdanov) assure their readers that it was the new philosophy that explained the error of the "duplication of the world" in the doctrine of the eternally refuted materialists, who speak of some sort of a "reflection" by the human consciousness of things existing outside the consciousness. A mass of sentimental verbiage has been written by the above-named authors about this "duplication." Owing to forgetfulness or ignorance, they failed to add that these new discoveries had already been discovered in 1710. Berkeley says:

"Our knowledge of these [*i.e.,* ideas or things] has been very much obscured and confounded, and we have been led into very dangerous errors by supposing a twofold existence of the objects of sense—the one *intelligible* or in the mind, the other *real* and without the mind" (*i.e.,* outside consciousness). And Berkeley ridicules this "repugnant" notion, which admits the possibility of thinking the unthinkable! The source of the "repugnancy," of course, follows from our supposing a difference between *things* and *ideas* . . . the supposition of external objects" (§ 87). This same source—as discovered by Berkeley in 1710 and rediscovered by Bogdanov in 1908—engenders a faith in fetishes and idols. "The existence of Matter," says Berkeley, "or bodies unperceived, has not only been the main support of Atheists and Fatalists, but on the same principle doth Idolatry likewise in all its various forms depend" (§ 94).

Here we arrive at those "ill consequences" derived from the "repugnant" doctrine of the existence of an external world which compelled Bishop Berkeley not only to refute this doctrine theoretically, but passionately to persecute its adherents as enemies. "For as we have shown the doctrine of Matter or corporeal Substance to have been the main pillar and support of Scepticism, so likewise upon the same foundation have been raised all the impious schemes of Atheism and Irreligion. . . . How great a friend material substance has been to Atheists in all ages were needless to relate. All their monstrous systems have so visible and necessary a dependence on it, that when this cornerstone is once removed, the whole fabric cannot choose but fall to the ground, insomuch that it is no longer worth while to bestow a particular consideration on the absurdities of every wretched sect of Atheists (§ 92, p. 203).

"Matter being once expelled out of nature drags with it so many sceptical and impious notions, such an incredible number of disputes and puzzling questions ["the principle of economy of thought," discovered by Mach in the 'seventies, "philosophy as a conception of the world according to the principle of minimum expenditure of effort" —Avenarius in 1876!] which have been thorns in the sides of divines as well as philosophers, and made so much fruitless work for mankind, that if the arguments we have produced against it are not found equal to demonstration (as to me they evidently seem), yet I am sure all friends to knowledge, peace, and religion have reason to wish they were" (§ 96).

Frankly and bluntly did Bishop Berkeley argue! In our time these very same thoughts on the "economical" elimination of "matter" from philosophy are enveloped in a much more artful form, and confused by the use of a "new" terminology, so that these thoughts may be taken by naïve people for "recent" philosophy!

But Berkeley was not only candid as to the tendencies of his philosophy, he also endeavoured to cover its idealistic nakedness, to represent it as being free from absurdities and acceptable to "common sense." Instinctively defending himself against the accusation of what would nowadays be called subjective idealism and solipsism, he says that by our philosophy "we are not deprived of any one thing in nature" (§ 34). Nature remains, and the distinction between realities and chimeras remains, only "they both equally exist in the mind." "I do not argue against the existence of any one thing that we can apprehend, either by sense or reflection. That the things I see with my eyes and touch with my hands do exist, really exist, I make not the least question. The only thing whose existence we deny is that which *philosophers* [Berkeley's italics] call Matter or corporeal substance. And in doing this there is no damage done to the rest of mankind, who, I dare say, will never miss it. . . . The Atheist indeed will want the colour of an empty name to support his impiety. . . ."

This thought is made still clearer in § 37, where Berkeley replies to the charge that his philosophy destroys corporeal substance: " . . . if the word *substance* be taken in the vulgar sense, for a *combination* of sensible qualities, such as extension, solidity, weight, and the like —this we cannot be accused of taking away; but if it be taken in a philosophic sense, for the support of accidents or qualities without the mind—then indeed I acknowledge that we take it away, if one may be said to take away that which never had any existence, not even in the imagination."

Not without good cause did the English philosopher, Fraser, an idealist and adherent of Berkeleianism, who edited Berkeley's works and supplied them with his own annotations, designate Berkeley's doctrine by the term "natural realism" (*op. cit.,* p. x). This amusing terminology must by all means be noted, for it in fact expresses Berkeley's intention to counterfeit realism. In our further exposition we shall frequently find the "recent" "positivists" repeating the same stratagem or counterfeit in a different form and in a different verbal wrapping. Berkeley does not deny the existence of real things! Berkeley does not go counter to the opinion of all humanity! Berkeley denies "only" the teaching of the philosophers, *viz.*, the theory of knowledge, which seriously and resolutely takes as the foundation of all its reasoning the recognition of the external world and the reflection thereof in the minds of men. Berkeley does not deny natural science, which has always adhered (mostly unconsciously) to this, *i.e.*, the materialist, theory of knowledge. We read in § 59: "We may, from the experience[5] [Berkeley—a philosophy of "pure experience"] we have had of the train and succession of ideas in our minds . . . make . . . well-grounded predictions concerning the ideas we shall be affected with pursuant to a great train of actions, and be enabled to pass a right judgment of what would have appeared to us, in case we were placed in circumstances very different from those we are in at present. Herein consists the knowledge of nature, which [listen to this!] may preserve its use and certainty very consistently with what hath been said."

Let us regard the external world, nature, as "a combination of sensations" evoked in our mind by a deity. Acknowledge this and give up searching for the "ground" of these sensations outside the mind, outside men, and I will acknowledge within the framework of my idealist theory of knowledge *all* natural science and all the importance and authenticity of its deductions. It is precisely this framework, and only this framework, that I need for my deductions in favour of "peace and religion." Such is Berkeley's train of thought. It correctly expresses the essence of idealist philosophy and its social significance, and we shall encounter it later when we come to speak of the relation of Machism to natural science.

Let us now consider another recent discovery that was borrowed from Bishop Berkeley in the twentieth century by the recent positivist and critical realist, P. Yushkevich. This discovery is "empirio-symbolism." "Berkeley," says Fraser, "thus reverts to his favourite theory of a Universal Natural Symbolism" (*op. cit.*, p. 190). Did these words not occur in an edition of 1871, one might have suspected the English fideist philosopher Fraser of plagiarising both the modern mathematician and physicist Poincaré and the Russian "Marxist" Yushkevich!

This theory of Berkeley's which threw Fraser into raptures, is set forth by the Bishop as follows:

"The connexion of ideas [do not forget that for Berkeley ideas and things are identical] does not imply the relation of *cause* and *effect*, but only of a mark or *sign* with the thing *signified*" (§ 65). "Hence, it is evident that those things, which under the notion of a cause co-

[5] In his preface Fraser insists that both Berkeley and Locke "appeal exclusively to experience" (p. 117).

operating or concurring to the production of effects, are altogether in-explicable, and run us into great absurdities, may be very naturally ex-plained . . . when they are considered only as marks or signs for our information" (§ 66). Of course, in the opinion of Berkeley and Fraser, it is no other than the deity who informs us by means of these "empirio-symbols." The epistemological significance of *symbolism* in Berkeley's theory, however, consists in this, that it is to replace "the doctrine" which "pretends to explain things by corporeal causes" (§ 66).

We have before us two philosophical trends in the question of causality. One "pretends to explain things by corporeal causes." It is clear that it is connected with the "doctrine of matter" refuted as "repugnant" by Bishop Berkeley. The other reduces the "notion of causality" to the notion of a "mark or sign" which serves for "our in-formation" (supplied by God). We shall meet these two trends in a twentieth-century garb when we analyse the attitudes of Machism and dialectical materialism to this question.

Further, as regards the question of reality, it ought also to be re-marked that Berkeley, refusing as he does to recognise the existence of things outside the mind, tries to find a criterion for distinguishing be-tween the real and the fictitious. In § 36 he says that those "ideas" which the minds of men evoke at pleasure "are faint, weak, and un-steady in respect to others they perceive by sense; which, being im-pressed upon them according to certain rules or laws of nature, speak themselves about the effects of a Mind more powerful and wise than human spirits. These latter are said to have *more reality* in them than the former; by which is meant that they are more affecting, orderly and distinct, and that they are not fictions of the mind perceiv-ing them. . . ." Elsewhere (§ 84) Berkeley tries to connect the no-tion of reality with the simultaneous perception of the same sensa-tions by many people. For instance, how shall we resolve the question as to whether the transformation of water into wine, of which we are being told, is real? "If at table all who were present should see, and smell, and taste, and drink wine, and find the effects of it, with me there could be no doubt of its reality." And Fraser explains: "The simultaneous consciousness of . . . the 'same' *sense*-ideas by dif-ferent persons, as distinguished from the purely individual or personal consciousness of *imaginary* objects and emotions, is here referred to as a test of the *reality* of the former."

From this it is evident that Berkeley's subjective idealism is not to be interpreted as though it ignored the distinction between individual and collective perception. On the contrary, he attempts on the basis of this distinction to construct a criterion of reality. Deriving "ideas" from the action of the deity upon the human mind, Berkeley thus approaches objective idealism: the world proves to be not my idea but the product of a single supreme spiritual cause that creates both the "laws of nature" and the laws distinguishing "more real" ideas from those less real, and so forth.

In another work, *The Three Dialogues Between Hylas and Philonous* (1713), where he endeavours to present his views in an especially popular form, Berkeley sets forth the opposition between his doctrine and the materialist doctrine in the following way:

"I assert as well as you [materialists] that, since we are affected from without, we must allow Powers to be without, in a Being distinct from ourselves. . . . But then we differ as to the kind of this powerful being. I will have it to be Spirit, you Matter, or I know not what (I may add too, you know not what) third nature . . ." (p. 335).

Fraser comments: "This is the gist of the whole question. According to the Materialists, sensible phenomena are due to *material substance,* or to some unknown 'third nature'; according to Berkeley, to Rational Will; according to Hume and the Positivists, their origin is absolutely unknown, and we can only generalise them inductively, through custom, as facts."

Here the English Berkeleian, Fraser, approaches from his consistent idealist standpoint the same fundamental "lines" in philosophy which were so clearly characterised by the materialist Engels. In his work *Ludwig Feuerbach* Engels divides philosophers into "two great camps" —materialists and idealists. Engels—dealing with theories of the two trends much more developed, varied and rich in content than Fraser dealt with—sees the fundamental distinction between them in the fact that while for the materialists nature is primary and spirit secondary, for the idealists the reverse is the case. In between these two camps Engels places the adherents of Hume and Kant, who deny the possibility of knowing the world, or at least of knowing it fully, and calls them *agnostics.* In his *Ludwig Feuerbach* Engels applies this term only to the adherents of Hume (those people whom Fraser calls, and who like to call themselves, "positivists"). But in his article "On Historical Materialism," Engels explicitly speaks of the standpoint of *"the Neo-Kantian agnostic,"* regarding Neo-Kantianism as a variety of agnosticism.[6]

We cannot dwell here on this remarkably correct and profound judgment of Engels' (a judgment which is shamelessly ignored by the Machians). We shall discuss it in detail later on. For the present we shall confine ourselves to pointing to this Marxian terminology and to this meeting of extremes: the views of a consistent materialist and of a consistent idealist on the fundamental philosophical trends. In order to illustrate these trends (with which we shall constantly have to deal in our further exposition) let us briefly note the views of outstanding

[6] Friedrich Engels, *"Ueber historischen Materialismus," Neue Zeite,* XI. Jg., Bd. I (1892-93), Nr. 1, S. 18. Translated from the English by Engels himself. (This article was published as an introduction to the English translation of Engels' *Socialism: Utopian and Scientific.—Trans.*)

philosophers of the eighteenth century who pursued a different path from Berkeley.

Here are Hume's arguments. In his *An Enquiry Concerning Human Understanding,* in the chapter (XII) on sceptical philosophy, he says: "It seems evident, that men are carried, by a natural instinct or prepossession, to repose faith in their senses; and that, without any reasoning, or even almost before the use of reason, we always suppose an external universe, which depends not on our perception, but would exist though we and every sensible creature were absent or annihilated. Even the animal creations are governed by a like opinion, and preserve this belief of external objects, in all their thoughts, designs, and actions. . . .

"But this universal and primary opinion of all men is soon destroyed by the slightest philosophy, which teaches us, that nothing can ever be present to the mind but an image or perception, and that the senses are only the inlets, through which these images are conveyed, without being able to produce any immediate intercourse between the mind and the object. The table, which we see, seems to diminish, as we remove farther from it: But the real table, which exists independent of us, suffers no alteration: It was, therefore, nothing but its image, which was present to the mind. These are the obvious dictates of reason; and no man, who reflects, ever doubted, that the existences, which we consider, when we say, 'this house,' and 'that tree' are nothing but perceptions in the mind. . . .

"By what argument can it be proved, that the perceptions of the mind must be caused by external objects, entirely different from them, though resembling them (if that be possible), and could not arise either from the energy of the mind itself, or from the suggestion of some invisible and unknown spirit, or from some other cause still more unknown to us?

"How shall the question be determined? By experience surely; as all other questions of a like nature. But here experience is, and must be entirely silent. The mind has never anything present to it but the perceptions, and cannot possibly reach any experience of their connection with objects. This supposition of such a connection is, therefore, without any foundation in reasoning.

"To have recourse to the veracity of the Supreme Being, in order to prove the veracity of our senses, is surely making a very unexpected circuit . . . if the external world be once called in question, we shall be at a loss to find arguments, by which we may prove the existence of that Being, or any of his attributes." [7]

He says the same thing in his *Treatise of Human Nature* (Part IV, Sec. II, "On Scepticism Towards Sensations"): "Our perceptions are our only objects." By scepticism Hume means the refusal to explain

[7] David Hume, *An Enquiry Concerning Human Understanding. Essays and Treatises,* London, 1882. Vol. II, pp. 124-26.

sensations as the effects of objects, spirit, etc., a refusal to reduce perceptions to the external world, on the one hand, and to a deity or to an unknown spirit, on the other. And the author of the introduction to the French translation of Hume, F. Pillon—a philosopher of a trend akin to Mach (as we shall see below)—justly remarks that for Hume the subject and the object are reduced to "groups of various perceptions," to "elements of consciousness, to impressions, ideas, etc."; that the only concern should be with the "groupings and combinations of these elements." [8] The English Humean, Huxley, who coined the apt and correct term "agnosticism," in his *Hume* also emphasises the fact that Hume, regarding "sensations" as the "primary and irreducible states of consciousness," is not entirely consistent on the question how the origin of sensations is to be explained, whether by the effect of objects on man or by the creative power of the mind. "Realism and idealism are equally probable hypotheses" (*i.e.,* for Hume).[9] Hume does not go beyond sensations. "Thus the colours red and blue, and the odour of a rose, are simple impressions. . . . A red rose gives us a complex impression, capable of resolution into the simple impressions of red colour, rose-scent, and numerous others" (pp. 64-65, *op. cit.*). Hume admits both the "materialist position" and the "idealist position" (p. 82); the "collection of perceptions" may be generated by the Fichtean "ego" or may be a "signification" and even a "symbol" of a "real something." This is how Huxley interprets Hume.

As for the materialists, here is an opinion of Berkeley given by Diderot, the leader of the Encyclopædists: "Those philosophers are called *idealists* who, being conscious only of their existence and of the sensations which succeed each other within themselves, do not admit anything else. An extravagant system which, to my thinking, only the blind could have originated; a system which, to the shame of human intelligence and philosophy, is the most difficult to combat, although the most absurd of all." [10] And Diderot, who came very close to the standpoint of contemporary materialism (that arguments and syllogisms alone do not suffice to refute idealism, and that here it is not a question for theoretical argument), notes the similarity of the premises both of the idealist Berkeley, and the sensationalist Condillac. In his opinion, Condillac should have undertaken a refutation of Berkeley in order to avoid such absurd conclusions being drawn from the treatment of sensations as the only source of our knowledge.

In the "Conversation Between d'Alembert and Diderot," Diderot states his philosophical position thus: " . . . Suppose a piano to be endowed with the faculty of sensation and memory, tell me, would it not of its own accord repeat those airs which you have played on its

---

[8] *Psychologie de Hume. Traité de la nature humaine, etc.* Trad. par Ch. Renouvier et F. Pillon, Paris, 1878. Introduction, p. x.

[9] Thomas Huxley, *Hume,* London, 1879, p. 74.

[10] *Œuvres complètes de Diderot,* ed. par J. Assézat, Paris, 1875, Vol. I, p. 304.

keys? We are instruments endowed with sensation and memory. Our senses are so many keys upon which surrounding nature strikes and which often strike upon themselves. And this is all, in my opinion, that occurs in a piano organised like you and me." D'Alembert retorts that such an instrument would have to possess the faculty of finding food for itself and of reproducing little pianos. Undoubtedly, contends Diderot.—But take an egg. "This is what refutes all the schools of theology and all the temples on earth. What is this egg? A mass that is insensible until the embryo is introduced thither, and when this embryo is introduced, what is it then? An insensible mass, for in its turn, this embryo is only an inert and crude liquid. How does this mass arrive at a different organisation, arrive at sensibility and life? By means of heat. And what produces heat? Motion. . . . The animal that is hatched from the egg is endowed with all your sensations: it performs all your actions. Would you maintain with Descartes that this is a simple imitating machine? Little children will laugh at you, and the philosophers will reply that if this be a machine then you too are a machine. If you admit that the difference between these animals and you consists only in their organisation, you will prove your common sense and sagacity, you will be right. But from this will follow the conclusion that refutes you; namely, that from inert matter organised in a certain way, impregnated with another bit of inert matter, by heat and motion—sensibility, life, memory, consciousness, emotion, and thought are generated." One of the two, continues Diderot, either admit some "hidden element" in the egg, that penetrates to it in an unknown way at a certain stage of development, an element about which it is unknown whether it occupies space, whether it is material or whether it is created for the purpose—which is contradictory to common sense, and leads to inconsistencies and absurdities; or we must make "a simple supposition which explains everything, namely, that the faculty of sensation is a general property of matter, or a product of its organisation." To d'Alembert's objection that such a supposition implies a quality which in its essence is incompatible with matter, Diderot retorts:

"And how do you know that the faculty of sensation is essentially incompatible with matter, since you do not know the essence of any thing at all, either of matter, or of sensation? Do you understand the nature of motion any better, its existence in a body, its communication from one body to another?" D'Alembert: "Without knowing the nature of sensation, or that of matter, I see, however, that the faculty of sensation is a simple quality, single, indivisible, and incompatible with a divisible subject or substratum." Diderot: "Metaphysico-theological nonsense! What, do you not see that all qualities of matter, that all its forms accessible to our senses are in their essence indivisible? There cannot be a larger or a smaller degree of impenetrability. There may be half of a round body, but there is no half of roundness. . . . Be a physicist and admit the derivative character of the given effect when you see how it is derived, though you may be unable to explain the relation between the cause and the effect. Be logical and do not replace a cause that exists and explains everything by some cause which it is impossible to conceive, and the connection of which with the effect is even more difficult to conceive, and which engenders an infinite number of difficulties without solving a single one of them." D'Alembert: "And if I do proceed from this cause?" Diderot: "There is only one substance in the universe in men and in animals. A handorgan is of wood, man of flesh. A finch is of flesh, and a musician is of flesh, but differently organised; but both are of the same origin, of the same formation, have the same functions and the same purpose." D'Alembert: "And what establishes the similarity of sounds between your two pianos?" Diderot: " . . . The instrument endowed with the faculty of sensation, or the animal, has learned by experience that after a certain sound certain consequences follow outside of it; that other sentient instruments, like itself, or similar animals, approach, recede, demand, offer, wound, caress;—and all these consequences are associated in its memory and in the memory of other animals with the formation of sounds. Mark, in intercourse between people there is nothing beside sounds and actions. And to appreciate the power of my system, mark again that it is faced with that same insurmountable difficulty which Berkeley adduced against the existence of bodies. There was a moment of insanity when the sentient piano imagined that it was the only piano in the world, and that the whole harmony of the universe resided within it." [11]

This was written in 1769. And with this we shall conclude our brief historical inquiry. We shall have more than one occasion to meet "the insane piano" and the harmony of the universe residing within man when we come to analyse "recent positivism."

For the present we shall confine ourselves to one conclusion: the "recent" Machians have not adduced a single argument against the materialists that had not been adduced by Bishop Berkeley.

Let us mention as a curiosity that one of these Machians, Valentinov, vaguely sensing the falsity of his position, has tried to "cover up the traces" of his kinship with Berkeley and has done so in a rather amusing manner. On page 150 of his book we read: " . . . When those who, speaking of Mach, point to Berkeley, we ask, which Berkeley do they mean? Do they mean the Berkeley who traditionally regards himself [Valentinov wishes to say who is regarded] as a solipsist; or the Berkeley who defends 'the immediate presence and providence of the deity'? Generally, when speaking [?], do they mean Berkeley, the philosophising bishop, the destroyer of atheism, or Berkeley, the thoughtful analyser? With Berkeley the solipsist and preacher of religious metaphysics Mach indeed has nothing in com-

[11] *Ibid.*, Vol. II, pp. 114-18.

mon." Valentinov is muddled; he was unable to make clear to himself why he was obliged to defend the "thoughtful analyser" and idealist, Berkeley, against the materialist Diderot. Diderot drew a clear distinction between the fundamental philosophical trends. Valentinov confuses them, and while doing so very amusingly tries to console us: "We would not consider the 'kinship' of Mach to the idealist views of Berkeley as a philosophical crime," he says, "even if this actually were the case" (p. 149). To confound two irreconcilable fundamental trends in philosophy—really, what "crime" is that? But that is what the whole wisdom of Mach and Avenarius amounts to. We shall now proceed to an examination of this wisdom.

THE THEORY OF KNOWLEDGE OF
EMPIRIO-CRITICISM AND OF
DIALECTICAL MATERIALISM[1]

1.   *Sensations and complexes of sensations*

The fundamental premises of the theory of knowledge of Mach and Avenarius are frankly, simply and clearly expounded by them in their early philosophical works. To these works we shall now turn, postponing for later treatment an examination of the corrections and emendations subsequently made by these writers.

"The task of science," Mach wrote in 1872, "can only be: 1. To determine the laws of connection of ideas (Psychology). 2. To discover the laws of connection of sensations (Physics). 3. To explain the laws of connection between sensations and ideas (Psycho-physics)." [2] This is quite clear.

The subject matter of physics is the connection between sensations and not between things or bodies, of which our sensations are the image.

[1] From: *Materialism and Empirio-Criticism,* V. I. Lenin, pp. 32-93. International Publishers, New York, 1927.
[2] E. Mach, *Die Geschichte und die Wurzel des Satzes von der Erhaltung der Arbeit.* Vortrag, gehalten in der k. Böhm. Gesellschaft der Wissenchaften am 15. Nov. 1871. Prag 1872, S. 57-58.

And in 1883, in his *Mechanik,* Mach repeats the same thought: "Sensations are not 'symbols of things.' The 'thing' is rather a mental symbol for a complex of sensations of relative stability. Not the things (bodies) but colours, sounds, pressures, spaces, times (what we usually call sensations) are the real *elements* of the world." [3]

About this word "elements," the fruit of twelve years of "reflection," we shall speak later. At present let us note that Mach explicitly states here that things or bodies are complexes of sensations, and that he quite clearly sets up his own philosophical point of view against the opposite theory which holds that sensations are "symbols" of things (it would be more correct to say images or reflections of things). The latter theory is *philosophical materialism.* For instance, the materialist Frederick Engels—the not unknown collaborator of Marx and a founder of Marxism—constantly and without exception speaks in his works of things and their mental pictures or images (*Gedankenabbilder*), and it is obvious that these mental images arise exclusively from sensations. It would seem that this fundamental standpoint of the "philosophy of Marxism" ought to be known to everyone who speaks of it, and especially to anyone who comes out in print *in the name of* this philosophy. But because of the extraordinary confusion which our Machians have introduced, it becomes necessary to repeat what is generally known. We turn to the first section of *Anti-Dühring* and read: ". . . things and their mental images . . .";[4] or to the first paragraph of the philosophical part, which reads: "But whence does thought obtain these principles [*i.e.,* the fundamental principles of all knowledge]? From itself? No . . . these forms can never be created and derived by thought out of itself, but only from the external world . . . the principles are not the starting point of the investigation [as Dühring who would be a materialist, but cannot consistently adhere to materialism, holds], but its final result; they are not applied to nature and human history, but abstracted from them; it is not nature and the realm of humanity which conform to these principles, but the principles are only valid in so far as they are in conformity with nature and history. That is the only materialistic conception of the matter, and Herr Dühring's contrary conception is idealistic, makes things stand completely on their heads, and fashions the real world out of ideas" (pp. 43-44). Engels, we repeat, applies this "only materialistic conception" everywhere and without exception, relentlessly attacking Dühring for the least deviation from materialism to idealism. Anybody who reads *Anti-Dühring* and *Ludwig Feuerbach* with the slightest care will find scores of instances when Engels speaks of things and their reflections in the human brain, in our consciousness, thought, etc. En-

[3] E. Mach, *Die Mechanik in ihrer Entwicklung historisch-kritisch dargestellt,* 3. Auflage, Leipzig, 1897, S. 173.
[4] Frederick Engels, *Herr Eugen Dühring's Revolution in Science* (*Anti-Dühring*), English ed., 1935, p. 27.—*Trans.*

gels does not say that sensations or ideas are "symbols" of things, for consistent materialism must here use "image," picture, or reflection instead of "symbol," as we shall show in detail in the proper place. But the question here is not of this or that formulation of materialism, but of the opposition of materialism to idealism, of the difference between the two fundamental *lines* in philosophy. Are we to proceed from things to sensation and thought? Or are we to proceed from thought and sensation to things? The first line, *i.e.,* the materialist line, is adopted by Engels. The second line, *i.e.,* the idealist line, is adopted by Mach. No evasions, no sophisms (a multitude of which we shall yet encounter) can remove the clear and indisputable fact that Ernst Mach's doctrine of things as complexes of sensations is subjective idealism and a simple rehash of Berkeleianism. If bodies are "complexes of sensations," as Mach says, or "combinations of sensations," as Berkeley said, it inevitably follows that the whole world is but my idea. Starting from such a premise it is impossible to arrive at the existence of other people besides oneself: it is the purest solipsism. Much as Mach, Avenarius, Petzoldt and the others may abjure solipsism, they cannot in fact escape solipsism without falling into howling logical absurdities. To make this fundamental element of the philosophy of Machism still clearer, we shall give a few additional quotations from Mach's works. Here is a sample from the *Analyse der Empfindungen:*

"We see a body with a point S. If we touch S, that is, bring it into contact with our body, we receive a prick. We can see S without feeling the prick. But as soon as we feel the prick we find S on the skin. Thus, the visible point is a permanent nucleus, to which, according to circumstances, the prick is attached as something accidental. By frequent repetitions of analogous occurrences we finally accustom ourselves to regard *all* properties of bodies as 'effects' which proceed from permanent nuclei and are conveyed to the self through the medium of the body; which effects we call *sensations.* . . ." [5]

In other words, people "accustom" themselves to adopt the standpoint of materialism, to regard sensations as the result of the action of bodies, things, nature on our sense-organs. This "habit," so noxious to the philosophical idealists (a habit acquired by all mankind and all natural science!), is not at all to the liking of Mach, and he proceeds to destroy it:

". . . Thereby, however, these nuclei are deprived of their entire sensible content and are converted into naked abstract symbols. . . ."

An old song, most worthy Professor! This is a literal repetition of Berkeley who said that matter is a naked abstract symbol. But it is Ernst Mach, in fact, who goes naked, for if he does not admit that the "sensible content" is an objective reality, existing independently of us,

[5] E. Mach, *Analyse der Empfindungen,* Jena, 1900. S. 9 u. 10.—*Trans.*

there remains only a "naked abstract" *I*, an *I* infallibly written with a capital letter and italicised, equal to "the insane piano, which imagined that it was the sole existing thing in this world." If the "sensible content" of our sensations is not the external world then nothing exists save this naked *I* engaged in empty "philosophical" acrobatics. A stupid and fruitless occupation!

". . . It is then correct that the world consists only of our sensations. In which case we have knowledge *only* of sensations, and the assumption of those nuclei, and of their interaction, from which alone sensations proceed, turns out to be quite idle and superfluous. Such a view can only appeal to *half-hearted* realism or *half-hearted* criticism."

We have quoted the sixth paragraph of Mach's "antimetaphysical observations" in full. It is a sheer plagiarism on Berkeley. Not a single idea, not a glimmer of thought, except that "we sense only our sensations." From which there is only one possible inference, namely, that the "world consists only of *my* sensations." The word "our" employed by Mach instead of "my" is employed illegitimately. By this word alone Mach betrays that "half-heartedness" of which he accuses others. For if the "assumption" of the existence of the external world is "idle," if the assumption that the needle exists independently of me and that an interaction takes place between my body and the point of the needle is really "idle and superfluous," then primarily the "assumption" of the existence of other people is idle and superfluous. Only *I* exist, and all other people, as well as the external world, come under the category of idle "nuclei." Holding this point of view one cannot speak of *"our"* sensations; and when Mach does speak of them, it is only a betrayal of his own amazing half-heartedness. It only proves that his philosophy is a jumble of idle and empty words in which their author himself does not believe.

Here is a particularly graphic example of Mach's half-heartedness and confusion. In §6 of Chapter XI of the *Analyse der Empfindungen* we read: "If I imagine that while I am experiencing sensations, I or someone else could observe my brain with all possible physical and chemical appliances, it would be possible to ascertain with what processes of the organism particular sensations are connected . . ." (p. 198).

Very well! This means, then, that our sensations are connected with definite processes, which take place in the organism in general, and in our brain in particular? Yes, Mach very definitely makes this "assumption"—it would be quite a task not to make it from the standpoint of natural science! But is not this the very "assumption" of those very same "nuclei and their interaction" which our philosopher declared to be idle and superfluous? We are told that bodies are complexes of sensations; to go beyond that, Mach assures us, to regard sensations as a product of the action of bodies upon our sense-organs, is metaphysics, an idle and superfluous assumption, etc., à la Berkeley. But the brain is a body. Consequently, the brain also is no more than a complex of sensations. It follows, then, that with the help of a complex of sensations I (and *I* also am nothing but a complex of sensations) sense complexes of sensations. A delightful philosophy! First sensations are declared to be "the real elements of the world"; on this an "original" Berkeleianism is erected—and then the very opposite views are smuggled in, *viz.,* that sensations are connected with definite processes in the organism. Are not these "processes" connected with an exchange of matter between the "organism" and the external world? Could this exchange of matter take place if the sensations of the particular organism did not give it an objectively correct idea of this external world?

Mach does not ask himself such embarrassing questions when he mechanically jumbles fragments of Berkeleianism with the views of natural science, which instinctively adheres to the materialist theory of knowledge. . . . In the same paragraph Mach writes: "It is sometimes also asked whether (inorganic) 'matter' experiences sensation. . . ." Does this mean that there is no doubt that *organic* matter experiences sensation? Does this mean that sensation is not something primary but that it is one of the properties of matter? Mach skips over all the absurdities of Berkeleianism! . . . "The question," he avers, "is natural enough, if we proceed from the current widespread physical notions, according to which matter is the *immediate* and indisputably given *reality,* out of which everything, inorganic and organic, is constructed. . . ." Let us bear in mind this truly valuable admission of Mach's that the current widespread *physical* notions regard matter as the immediate reality, and that only one variety of this reality (organic matter) possesses the well-defined property of sensation. . . . Mach continues: "Then, indeed, sensation must suddenly arise somewhere in this structure [consisting of matter], or else have previously been present in the foundation. From *our* standpoint the question is a false one. For us matter is not what is primarily given. Rather, what is primarily given are the *elements* (which in a certain familiar relation are designated as sensations). . . ."

What is primarily given, then, are sensations, although they are "connected" only with definite processes in organic matter! And while uttering such absurdities Mach wants to blame materialism ("the current widespread physical notion") for leaving unanswered the question whence sensation "arises." This is a sample of the "refutation" of materialism by the fideists and their hangers-on. Does any other philosophical standpoint "solve" a problem before enough data for its solution has been collected? Does not Mach himself say in the very same paragraph: "As long as this problem (how far sensation extends in the organic world) has not been solved even in a single special case, no answer to the question is possible."

The difference between materialism and "Machism" in this particular question is thus reduced to the following. Materialism, in full agreement with natural science, takes matter as primary and regards consciousness, thought and sensation as secondary, because in its well-defined form sensation is associated only with the higher forms of matter (organic matter), while "in the foundation of the structure of matter" one can only surmise the existence of a faculty akin to sensation. Such, for example, is the supposition of the well-known German scientist Ernst Haeckel, the English biologist Lloyd Morgan and others, not to speak of Diderot's conjecture mentioned above. Machism holds to the opposite, the idealist point of view, and at once lands into an absurdity: since, in the first place, sensation is taken as primary, in spite of the fact that it is associated only with definite processes in matter organised in a definite way; and, since, in the second place, the basic premise that bodies are complexes of sensations is violated by the assumption of the existence of other living beings in general, of other "complexes" beside the given great *I*.

The word "element," which many naïve people (as we shall see) take to be some sort of a new discovery, in reality only obscures the question, for it is a meaningless term which creates the false impression that a solution or a step forward has been achieved. This impression is a false one, because there still remains to be investigated and reinvestigated how matter, apparently entirely devoid of sensation, is related to matter which, though composed of the same atoms (or electrons), is yet endowed with a well-defined faculty of sensation. Materialism clearly formulates the as yet unsolved problem and thereby stimulates the attempt to solve it, to undertake further experimental investigation. Machism, *i.e.,* a species of muddled idealism, befogs the issue and sidetracks it by means of the futile verbal trick, "element."

Here is a passage from Mach's latest, comprehensive and conclusive philosophical work that clearly betrays the falsity of this idealist trick. In his *Erkenntnis und Irrtum* we read: "While there is no difficulty in constructing (*aufzubauen*) *every physical* experience out of sensations, *i.e., psychical* elements, it is impossible to imagine (*ist keine Möglichkeit abzusehen*) how any *psychical* experience can be composed (*darstellen*) of the elements employed in modern physics, *i.e.,* mass and motion (in their rigidity—*Starrheit*—which is serviceable only for this special science)." [6]

Of the rigidity of the conceptions of many modern scientists and of their metaphysical (in the Marxian sense of the term, *i.e.,* anti-dialectical) views, Engels speaks repeatedly and very precisely. We shall see later that it was just on this point that Mach went astray, because he did not understand or did not know the relation between relativism and dialectics. But this is not what concerns us here. It is important for us here to note how glaringly Mach's *idealism emerges,*

[6] E. Mach. *Erkenntnis und Irrtum*, 2. Auflage, 1906, S. 12. Anmerkung.

in spite of the confused—ostensibly new—terminology. There is no difficulty, you see, in constructing any physical element out of sensations, *i.e.*, psychical elements! Oh yes, such constructions, of course, are not difficult, for they are purely verbal constructions, shallow scholasticism, serving as a loophole for fideism. It is not surprising after this that Mach dedicates his works to the immanentists; it is not surprising that the immanentists, who profess the most reactionary kind of philosophical idealism, welcome Mach with open arms. The "recent positivism" of Ernst Mach was only about two hundred years too late. Berkeley had already sufficiently shown that "out of sensations, *i.e.*, psychical elements," nothing can be "built" except *solipsism*. As regards materialism, against which Mach here, too, sets up his own views, without frankly and explicitly naming the "enemy," we have already seen in the case of Diderot what the real views of the materialists are. These views do not consist in deriving sensation from the movement of matter or in reducing sensation to the movement of matter, but in recognising sensation as one of the properties of matter in motion. On this question Engels shared the standpoint of Diderot. Engels dissociated himself from the "vulgar" materialists, Vogt, Büchner and Moleschott, for the very reason, among others, that they erred in believing that the brain secretes thought *in the same way* as the liver secretes bile. But Mach, who constantly sets up his views in opposition to materialism, ignores, of course, all the great materialists—Diderot, Feuerbach, Marx and Engels—just as all other official professors of official philosophy do.

In order to characterise Avenarius' earliest and basic view, let us take his first independent philosophical work, *Philosophie als Denken der Welt gemäß dem Prinzip des kleinsten Kraftmaßes. Prolegomena zu einer Kritik der reinen Erfahrung,* which appeared in 1876. Bogdanov in his *Empirio-Monism* (Book 1, 2nd ed., 1905, p. 12, note) says that "in the development of Mach's views, the starting point was philosophical idealism, while a realistic tinge was characteristic of Avenarius from the very beginning." Bogdanov said so because he believed what Mach said (see *Analyse der Empfindungen,* S. 295). Bogdanov should not have believed Mach, and his assertion is diametrically opposed to the truth. On the contrary, Avenarius' idealism emerges so clearly in his work of 1876 that Avenarius himself in 1891 was obliged to admit it. In the introduction to *Der menschliche Weltbegriff* Avenarius says:[7] "He who has read my first systematic work, *Philosophie, etc.,* will at once have presumed that I would have attempted to treat the problems of a criticism of pure experience from the 'idealist' standpoint . . . [but] the sterility of . . . idealism compelled me to doubt the correctness of my previous path." This idealist starting point of Avenarius' is universally acknowledged in

[7] *Der menschliche Weltbegriff,* 1891, Vorwort, S. IX u. X.

philosophical literature. Of the French writers I shall refer to Couwelaert, who says that Avenarius' philosophical standpoint in the *Prolegomena* is "monistic idealism." [8] Of the German writers, I shall name Rudolph Willy, Avenarius' disciple, who says that "Avenarius in his youth—and particularly in his work of 1876—was totally under the spell (*ganz im Banne*) of so-called epistemological idealism." [9]

And, indeed, it would be ridiculous to deny the idealism in Avenarius' *Prolegomena,* where he explicitly states that *"only sensation can be thought of as the existing"* (pp. 10 and 65 of the second German edition; all italics in quotations are ours). This is how Avenarius himself presents the contents of § 116 of his work. Here is the paragraph in full: "We have recognised that the existing (*das Seiende*) is substance endowed with sensation; the substance falls away . . . [it is "more economical," don't you see, there is "a lesser expenditure of effort" in thinking that there is no "substance" and that no external world exists!], sensation remains; we must then regard the existing as sensation, at the basis of which there is nothing which does not possess sensation (*nichts Empfindungsloses*)."

Sensation, then, exists without "substance," *i.e.,* thought exists without brain! Are there really philosophers capable of defending this brainless philosophy? There are! And Professor Richard Avenarius is one of them. And we must pause for a while to consider this defence, difficult though it be for a normal person to take it seriously. Here, in §§ 89 and 90 of this same work, is Avenarius' argument:

". . . And so the proposition that motion produces sensation is based on apparent experience only. This experience, which includes the act of perception, consists, presumably, in the fact that sensation is generated in a certain kind of substance (brain) as a result of transmitted motion (excitation) and with the help of other material conditions (*e.g.,* blood). However—apart from the fact that such generation has never itself been observed—in order to construct the supposed experience, as an experience which is real in all its component parts, empirical proof, at least, is required to show that sensation, which assumedly is caused in a certain substance by transmitted motion, did not already exist in that substance in one way or another; so that the appearance of sensation cannot be conceived of in any other way than as a creative act on the part of the transmitted motion. Thus only by proving that where a sensation now appears there was none previously, not even a minimal one, would it be possible to establish a fact which, denoting as it does some act of creation, contradicts the rest of experience and radically changes our conception of nature (*Naturanschauung*). But such proof is not furnished by any experience, and

[8] F. van Couwelaert, *"L'Empiriocriticisme"* in *Revue néo-scholastique,* 1907, Feb., p. 51.
[9] Rudolph Willy, *Gegen die Schulweisheit. Eine Kritik der Philosophie,* München 1905, S. 170.

cannot be furnished by any experience; on the contrary, the notion of a state of a substance totally devoid of sensation which subsequently begins to experience sensation is only a hypothesis. But such a hypothesis merely complicates and obscures our understanding instead of simplifying and clarifying it.

"Should the so-called experience, *viz.*, that the sensation is *caused* by a transmitted motion in a substance that begins to perceive from this moment, prove upon closer examination to be only apparent, there still remains sufficient material in the content of the experience to ascertain at least the relative origin of sensation from conditions of motion, namely, to ascertain that the sensation which is present, although latent or minimal, or for some reason not manifest to the consciousness, becomes, owing to transmitted motion, released or enhanced or made manifest to the consciousness. However, even this bit of the remaining content of experience is only an appearance. Were we even by an ideal observation to trace the motion proceeding from the moving substance A, transmitted through a series of intermediate centres and reaching the substance B, which is endowed with sensation, we should at best find that sensation in substance B becomes developed or enhanced simultaneously with the reception of the incoming motion— but we should not find that this occurred as a *consequence* of the motion. . . ."

We have purposely quoted this refutation of materialism by Avenarius in full, in order that the reader may see to what truly pitiful sophistries "recent" empirio-critical philosophy resorts. We shall compare with the argument of the idealist Avenarius the *materialist* argument of—Bogdanov, if only to punish Bogdanov for his betrayal of materialism!

In long bygone days, fully nine years ago, when Bogdanov was half "a natural-historical materialist" (that is, an adherent of the materialist theory of knowledge, to which the overwhelming majority of contemporary scientists instinctively hold), when he was only half led astray by the muddled Ostwald, he wrote: "From ancient times to the present day, descriptive psychology has adhered to the classification of the facts of consciousness into three categories: the domain of sensations and ideas, the domain of emotions and the domain of impulses. . . . To the first category belong the *images* of phenomena of the outer or inner world, as taken by themselves in consciousness. . . . Such an image is called a 'sensation' if it is directly produced through the sense-organs by its corresponding external phenomenon." [10] And a little farther on he says: "Sensation . . . arises in consciousness as a result of a certain impulse from the external environment transmitted by the external sense-organs" (p. 222). And further: "Sensation is the foundation of mental life; it is its immediate connection with the ex-

[10] A. Bogdanov, *The Fundamental Elements of the Historical Outlook on Nature*, St. Petersburg, 1899, p. 216.

ternal world" (p. 240). "At each step in the process of sensation a transformation of the energy of external excitation into a fact of consciousness takes place" (p. 133). And even in 1905, when with the gracious assistance of Ostwald and Mach, Bogdanov had abandoned the materialist standpoint in philosophy for the idealist standpoint, he wrote (from forgetfulness!) in his *Empirio-Monism:* "As is known, the energy of external excitation, transformed at the nerve-ends into a 'telegraphic' form of nerve current (still insufficiently investigated but devoid of all mysticism), first reaches the neurons that are located in the so-called 'lower' centres—ganglial, cerebral-spinal, subcortical, etc." (Book 1, 2nd ed., 1905, p. 118.)

For every scientist who has not been led astray by professorial philosophy, as well as for every materialist, sensation is indeed the direct connection between consciousness and the external world; it is the transformation of the energy of external excitation into a state of consciousness. This transformation has been, and is, observed by each of us a million times on every hand. The sophism of idealist philosophy consists in the fact that it regards sensation as being not the connection between consciousness and the external world, but as a fence, a wall, separating consciousness from the external world—not as an image of the external phenomenon corresponding to the sensation, but as the "sole entity." Avenarius gave but a slightly changed form to this old sophism, which had been already worn threadbare by Bishop Berkeley. Since we do not yet know all the conditions of the connection we are constantly observing between sensation and matter organised in a definite way, we therefore acknowledge the existence of sensation alone— that is what the sophism of Avenarius reduces itself to.

To conclude our description of the fundamental idealist premises of empirio-criticism, we shall briefly refer to the English and French representatives of this philosophical trend. Mach explicitly says of Karl Pearson, the Englishman, that he (Mach) is "in agreement with his epistemological (*erkenntniskritischen*) views on all essential points" (*Mechanik*, S. IX). Pearson in turn agrees with Mach.[11] For Pearson "real things" are "sense-impressions." He declares the recognition of things outside the boundaries of sense-impressions to be metaphysics. Pearson fights materialism with great determination (although he does not know Feuerbach, or Marx, or Engels); his arguments do not differ from those analysed above. However, the desire to masquerade as a materialist is so foreign to Pearson (that is a specialty of the Russian Machians), Pearson is so incautious . . . that he invents no "new" names for his philosophy and simply declares that his views and those of Mach are *"idealist"* (*ibid.*, p. 326)! He traces his genealogy directly to Berkeley and Hume. The philosophy of Pearson, as we shall repeatedly find, excels that of Mach in integrity and consistency.

11 Karl Pearson, *The Grammar of Science*, 2nd ed., London, 1900, p. 326.

Mach explicitly declares his solidarity with the French physicists, Pierre Duhem and Henri Poincaré.[12] We shall have occasion to deal with the particularly confused and inconsistent philosophical views of these writers in the chapter on the new physics. Here we shall content ourselves with noting that for Poincaré things are "groups of sensations" [13] and that a similar view is casually expressed by Duhem.[14]

We shall now proceed to examine how Mach and Avenarius, who admitted the idealist character of their original views, *corrected* them in their subsequent works.

2. *"The discovery of the world-elements"*

Such is the title under which Friedrich Adler, lecturer at the University of Zürich, probably the only German author also anxious to supplement Marx by Machism, writes of Mach.[15] And this naïve university lecturer must be given his due: in his simplicity of heart he does Machism more harm than good. At least, he puts the question point-blank—did Mach really "discover the world-elements"? If so, then, only very backward and ignorant people, of course, can still remain materialists. Or is this discovery a return on the part of Mach to the old philosophical errors?

We saw that Mach in 1872 and Avenarius in 1876 held a purely idealist view; for them the world is our sensation. In 1883 Mach's *Mechanik* appeared, and in the preface to the first edition Mach refers to Avenarius' *Prolegomena,* and greets his ideas as being "very close" (*sehr verwandte*) to his own philosophy. Here are the arguments in the *Mechanik* concerning the elements: "All natural science can only picture and represent (*nachbilden und vorbilden*) complexes of those *elements* which we ordinarily call sensations. It is a matter of the connection of these elements. . . . The connection of A (heat) with B (flame) is a problem of *physics,* that of A and N (nerves) a problem of *physiology.* Neither exists alone; both exist simultaneously. Only temporarily can we neglect either. Even processes that are apparently purely mechanical, are thus . . . always physiological" (*op. cit.,* p. 498). We find the same in the *Analyse der Empfindungen:* "Wherever . . . the terms 'sensation,' 'complex of sensations,' are used alongside of or in place of the terms 'element,' 'complex of elements,' it must be borne in mind that it is *only* in this *connection*

[12] *Analyse der Empfindungen,* S. 4; Vgl. *Erkenntnis und Irrtum,* Vorwort, 2. Auflage.
[13] Henri Poincaré, *La valeur de la science,* Paris, 1905.
[14] P. Duhem, *La théorie physique, son objet et sa structure,* Paris, 1906, pp. 6, 10.
[15] Friedrich W. Adler, *"Die Entdeckung der Weltelemente (zu Ernst Mach 70. Geburtstag),"* Der Kampf 1908, Nr. 5 (Februar). Translated in the *International Socialist Review.* 1908, No. 10 (April).

[namely, in the connection of A, B, C with K, L, M, that is, in the connection of "complexes which we ordinarily call bodies" with "the complex which we call our body"] and relation, only in this functional dependence that the elements are *sensations*. In another functional dependence they are at the same time physical objects" (p. 13). "A colour is a physical object when we consider its dependence, for instance, upon the source of illumination (other colours, temperatures, spaces and so forth). When we, however, consider its *dependence* upon the *retina* (the elements K, L, M), it is a *psychological* object, a *sensation*" (p. 14).

Thus the discovery of the world-elements amounts to this:

1) all that exists is declared to be sensation,

2) the sensations are called elements,

3) elements are divided into the physical and the psychical; the latter is that which depends on the human nerves and the human organism generally; the former does not depend on them;

4) the connection of physical elements and the connection of psychical elements, it is declared, do not exist separately from each other; they exist only in conjunction;

5) it is possible only temporarily to leave one or the other connection out of account;

6) the "new" theory is declared to be free from "one-sidedness." [16]

Indeed, it is not one-sidedness we have here, but an incoherent jumble of antithetical philosophical points of view. Since you base yourself *only* on sensations you do not correct the "one-sidedness" of your idealism by the term "element," but only confuse the issue and cravenly hide from your own theory. In word, you eliminate the antithesis between the physical and psychical,[17] between materialism (which regards nature, matter, as primary) and idealism (which regards spirit, mind, sensation as primary); in deed, you promptly restore this antithesis; you restore it surreptitiously, retreating from your own fundamental premises! For, if elements are sensations, you have no right even for a moment to accept the existence of "elements" *independently* of my nerves and my mind. But if you do admit physical objects that are independent of my nerves and my sensations and that cause sensation only by acting upon my retina—you are disgracefully abandoning your "one-sided" idealism and adopting the standpoint of "one-sided" materialism! If colour is a sensation only depending upon the retina (as natural science compels you to admit), then light rays, falling upon the retina, produce the sensation of colour. This means that

[16] Mach says in the *Analyse der Empfindungen:* "These elements are usually called sensations. But as that term already implies a one-sided theory, we prefer to speak simply of elements" (pp. 17-18).

[17] *"The antithesis between the Ego and the world, sensation or appearance and the thing, then vanishes,* and everything reduces itself to *a complex of elements"* (*ibid.,* p. 11).

outside us, independently of us and of our minds, there exists a movement of matter, let us say of ether waves of a definite length and of a
definite velocity, which, acting upon the retina, produce in man the sensation of a particular colour. This is precisely how natural science regards it. It explains the sensations of various colours by the various
lengths of light-waves existing outside the human retina, outside man
and independently of him. This is materialism: matter acting upon
our sense-organs produces sensation. Sensation depends on the brain,
nerves, retina, etc., *i.e.*, on matter organised in a definite way. The
existence of matter does not depend on sensation. Matter is primary.
Sensation, thought, consciousness are the supreme product of matter organised in a particular way. Such are the views of materialism
in general, and of Marx and Engels in particular. Mach and Avenarius
secretly smuggle in materialism by means of the word "element,"
which *supposedly* frees their theory of the "one-sidedness" of subjective idealism, *supposedly* permits the assumption that the psychical
is dependent on the retina, nerves and so forth, and the assumption
that the physical is independent of the human organism. In fact, of
course, the trick with the word "element" is a wretched sophistry, for a
materialist who reads Mach and Avenarius will immediately ask: what
are the "elements"? It would, indeed, be childish to think that one can
dispose of the fundamental philosophical trends by inventing a new
word. Either the "element" is a *sensation,* as all empirio-criticists,
Mach, Avenarius, Petzoldt,[18] etc., maintain—in which case your philosophy, gentlemen, is *idealism* vainly seeking to hide the nakedness of
its solipsism under the cloak of a more "objective" terminology; or the
"element" is not a sensation—in which case *absolutely no thought
whatever* is attached to the "new" term; it is merely an empty bauble.

Take Petzoldt, for instance, the last word in empirio-criticism, as
V. Lessevich, the first and most outstanding Russian empirio-criticist
describes him.[19] Having defined elements as sensations, he says in the
second volume of the work mentioned: "In the statement that 'sensations are the elements of the world' one must guard against taking the
term 'sensation' as denoting something only subjective and therefore
ethereal, transforming the ordinary picture of the world into an illusion (*Verflüchtigendes*)." [20]

One speaks of what hurts one most! Petzoldt feels that the world
"evaporates" (*verflüchtigt sich*), or becomes transformed into an illusion, when the world-elements are regarded as sensations. And the
good Petzoldt imagines that he helps matters by the reservation that

---

[18] Joseph Petzoldt, *Einführung in die Philosophie der reinen Erfahrung,* Bd. I, Leipzig, 1900, S. 113: "Elements are sensations in the ordinary sense of simple, irreducible perceptions (*Wahrnehmungen*)."
[19] V. Lessevich, *What is Scientific* [read: fashionable, professorial, eclectic] *Philosophy?,* St. Petersburg, 1891, pp. 229, 247.
[20] Petzoldt, *op. cit.,* Bd. II, 1904, S. 329.

sensation must not be taken as something only subjective! Is this not a ridiculous sophism? Does it make any difference whether we "take" sensation as sensation or whether we try to stretch the meaning of the term? Does this do away with the fact that sensations in man are connected with normally functioning nerves, retina, brain, etc., that the external world exists independently of our sensations? If you are not trying to evade the issue by a subterfuge, if you are really in earnest in wanting to "guard" against subjectivism and solipsism, you must above all guard against the fundamental idealist premises of your philosophy; you must replace the idealist line of your philosophy (from sensations to the external world) by the materialist line (from the external world to sensations); you must abandon that empty and muddled verbal embellishment, "element," and simply say that colour is the result of the action of a physical object on the retina, which is the same as saying that sensation is a result of the action of matter on our sense-organs.

Let us take Avenarius. The most valuable material on the question of the "elements" is to be found in his last work (and, it might be said, the most important for the comprehension of his philosophy), *Notes on the Concept of the Subject of Psychology*.[21] The author, by the way, here gives a very "graphic" table (Vol. XVIII, p. 410), the main part of which we reproduce here:

I. Things, or the substantial (*Sachhaftes*)	Elements, complexes of elements Corporeal things
II. Thoughts, or the mental (*Gedankenhaftes*)	Incorporeal things, recollections and fantasies

Compare this with what Mach says after all his elucidation of the "elements" (*Analyse der Empfindungen,* S. 23): "It is not bodies that produce sensations, but complexes of elements (complexes of sensations) that make up bodies." Here you have the "discovery of the world-elements" that overcomes the one-sidedness of idealism and materialism! At first we are assured that the "elements" are something new, both physical and psychical at the same time; then a little correction is surreptitiously inserted: instead of the crude, materialist differentiation of matter (bodies, things) and the psychical (sensations, recollections, fantasies) we are presented with the doctrine of "recent positivism" regarding elements substantial and elements mental. Adler (Fritz) did not gain very much from "the discovery of the world-elements"!

Bogdanov, arguing against Plekhanov in 1906, wrote: ". . . I can-

21 R. Avenarius, *"Bemerkungen zum Begriff des Gegenstandes der Psychologie"* in *Vierteljahrsschrift für wissenschaftliche Philosophie,* Bd. 18, 1894, und Bd. 19, 1895.

532   MARXISM AND THE PHILOSOPHY OF HISTORY

not own myself a Machian in philosophy. In the general philosophical conception there is only one thing I borrowed from Mach—the idea of the neutrality of the elements of experience in relation to the 'physical' and 'psychical,' and the dependence of these characteristics solely on the *connection* of experience." [22] This is as though a religious man were to say—I cannot own myself a believer in religion, for there is "only one thing" I have borrowed from the believers—the belief in God. This "one thing" which Bogdanov borrowed from Mach is the *basic error* of Machism, the basic falsity of its entire philosophy. Those deviations of Bogdanov's from empirio-criticism to which he himself attaches great significance are in fact of entirely secondary importance and amount to nothing more than inconsiderable private and individual differences between the various empirio-criticists who are approved by Mach and who approve Mach (we shall speak of this in greater detail later). Hence when Bogdanov was annoyed at being confused with the Machians he only revealed his failure to understand what *radically* distinguishes materialism from what is common to Bogdanov and to all other Machians. How Bogdanov developed, improved or worsened Machism is not important. What is important is that he has abandoned the materialist standpoint and has thereby inevitably condemned himself to confusion and idealist aberrations.

In 1899, as we saw, Bogdanov had the correct standpoint when he wrote: "The image of the man before me, directly given to me by vision, is a sensation." [23] Bogdanov did not trouble to give a criticism of this earlier position of his. He blindly believed Mach and began to repeat after him that the "elements" of experience are neutral in relation to the physical and psychical. "As has been established by recent positivist philosophy," wrote Bogdanov in Book I of *Empirio-Monism* (2nd ed., p. 90), "the elements of psychic experience are identical with the elements of experience in general, as they are with the elements of physical experience." Or in 1906 (Bk. III, p. xx): "as to 'idealism,' can it be called idealism merely on the grounds that the elements of 'physical experience' are regarded as identical with the elements of 'psychic experience,' or with elementary sensations—when this is simply an indubitable fact?"

Here we have the true source of all Bogdanov's philosophical misadventures, a source which he shares with the rest of the Machians. We can and must call it idealism when "the elements of physical experience" (*i.e.,* the physical, the external world, matter) are regarded as identical with sensations, for this is sheer Berkeleianism. There is not a trace here of recent philosophy, or positivist philosophy, or of indubitable fact. It is merely an old, old idealist sophism. And were one to ask Bogdanov how he would prove the "indubitable fact" that the physical is identical with sensations, one would get no other argument save the

[22] *Empirio-Monism,* Bk. III, St. Petersburg, 1906, p. xli.
[23] *The Fundamental Elements,* etc., p. 216; *cf.* the quotations cited above.

eternal refrain of the idealists: I am aware only of my sensations; the "testimony of self-consciousness" (*die Aussage des Selbstbewußtseins*) of Avenarius in his *Prolegomena* (2nd German ed., § 93, p. 56); or: "in our experience [which testifies that "we are sentient substance"] sensation is given us with more certainty that is substantiality" (*ibid.,* § 91, p. 55), and so on and so forth. Bogdanov (trusting Mach) accepted a reactionary philosophical trick as an "indubitable fact." For, indeed, not a single fact was or could be cited which would refute the view that sensation is an image of the external world—a view which was shared by Bogdanov in 1899 and which is shared by science to this day. In his idealist wanderings the physicist Mach has completely strayed from the path of "modern science." Regarding this important circumstance, which Bogdanov overlooked, we shall have much to say later.

One of the circumstances which helped Bogdanov to jump so quickly from the materialism of the natural scientists to the muddled idealism of Mach was (apart from the influence of Ostwald) Avenarius' doctrine of the dependent and independent series of experience. Bogdanov himself expounds the matter in Book I of his *Empirio-Monism* thus: "In so far as the data of experience appear in *dependence upon the state of the particular nervous system,* they form the *psychical world* of the particular person; in so far as the data of experience are taken *outside of such a dependence,* we have before us the *physical world.* Avenarius therefore characterises these two realms of experience respectively as the *dependent series* and the *independent series* of experience" (p. 18).

That is just the whole trouble, the doctrine of the *independent* (*i.e.,* independent of human sensation) "series" is a surreptitious importation of materialism, which, from the standpoint of a philosophy that maintains that bodies are complexes of sensations, that sensations are "identical" with physical "elements," is illegitimate, arbitrary, and eclectic. For once you have recognised that the source of light and light-waves exists *independently* of man and the human consciousness, that colour is dependent on the action of these waves upon the retina, you have in fact adopted the materialist standpoint and have *completely destroyed* all the "indubitable facts" of idealism, together with all "the complexes of sensations," the elements discovered by recent positivism, and similar nonsense.

That is just the whole trouble. Bogdanov (like the rest of the Russian Machians) has never looked into the idealist views originally held by Mach and Avenarius, has never examined their fundamental idealist premises, and has therefore failed to discover the illegitimacy and eclecticism of their subsequent attempts to smuggle in materialism surreptitiously. Yet, just as the initial idealism of Mach and Avenarius is generally acknowledged in philosophical literature, so is it generally acknowledged that subsequently empirio-criticism endeavoured to swing towards materialism. Couwelaert, the French writer quoted above, asserts that Avenarius' *Prolegomena* is "monistic idealism," the *Kritik der reinen Erfahrung* (1888-90) is "absolute realism," while *Der menschliche Weltbegriff* (1891) is an attempt "to explain" the change. Let us note that the term realism is here employed as the antithesis of idealism. Following Engels, I use *only* the term materialism in this sense, and consider it the sole correct terminology, especially since the term "realism" has been bedraggled by the positivists and the other muddleheads who vacillate between materialism and idealism. For the present it will suffice to note that Couwelaert had the indisputable fact in mind that in the *Prolegomena* (1876) sensation, according to Avenarius, is the only entity, while "substance"—in accordance with the principle of "the economy of thought"!—is eliminated, and that in the *Kritik der reinen Erfahrung* the physical is taken as the *independent series,* while the psychical and, consequently, sensations, are taken as the dependent series.

Avenarius' disciple Rudolph Willy likewise admits that Avenarius was a "complete" idealist in 1876, but subsequently "reconciled" (*Ausgleich*) "naïve realism" (*i.e.,* the instinctive, unconscious materialist standpoint adopted by humanity, which regards the external world as existing independently of our minds) with this teaching (*loc. cit.*).

Oskar Ewald, the author of the book *Avenarius as the Founder of Empirio-Criticism,* says that this philosophy combines contradictory idealist and "realist" (he should have said materialist) elements (not in Mach's sense, but in the human sense of the term element). For example, "the absolute [method of consideration] would perpetuate naïve realism, the relative would declare exclusive idealism as permanent." [24] Avenarius calls the absolute method of consideration that which corresponds to Mach's connection of "elements" outside our body, and the relative that which corresponds to Mach's connection of "elements" dependent on our body.

But of particular interest to us in this respect is the opinion of Wundt, who himself, like the majority of the above-mentioned writers, adheres to the confused idealist standpoint, but who has analysed empirio-criticism perhaps more attentively than all the others. P. Yushkevich has the following to say in this connection: "It is interesting to note that Wundt regards empirio-criticism as the most scientific form of the latest type of materialism," [25] *i.e.,* the type of those materialists who regard the spiritual as a function of corporeal processes (and whom—we would add—Wundt defines as standing midway between Spinozism and absolute materialism).[26]

True, this opinion of Wundt's is extremely interesting. But what is

[24] Oskar Ewald, *Richard Avenarius als Begründer des Empiriokritzismus,* Berlin, 1905, S. 66.
[25] P. Yushkevich, *Materialism and Critical Realism,* St. Petersburg, 1908, p. 15.
[26] W. Wundt, *"Ueber naiven und kritischen Realismus"* in *Philosophische Studien,* Bd. XIII, 1898, S. 334.

even more "interesting" is Mr. Yushkevich's attitude towards the books and articles on philosophy of which he treats. This is a typical example of the attitude of our Machians to such matters. Gogol's Petrushka[27] used to read and find it interesting that letters always combined to make words. Mr. Yushkevich read Wundt and found it "interesting" that Wundt accused Avenarius of materialism. If Wundt is wrong, why not refute him? If he is right, why not explain the antithesis between materialism and empirio-criticism? Mr. Yushkevich finds what the idealist Wundt says "interesting," but this Machian regards it as a waste of effort to endeavour to go to the root of the matter (probably on the principle of "the economy of thought"). . . .

The point is that by informing the reader that Wundt accuses Avenarius of materialism, and by not informing him that Wundt regards some aspects of empirio-criticism as materialism and others as idealism and holds that the connection between the two is artificial, Yushkevich entirely *distorted the matter*. Either this gentleman absolutely does not understand what he reads, or he was prompted by a desire to indulge in false self-praise with the help of Wundt, as if to say: you see, the official professors regard us, too, as materialists, and not as muddleheads.

The above-mentioned article by Wundt constitutes a large book (more than 300 pages), devoted to a detailed analysis first of the immanentist school, and then of the empirio-criticists. Why did Wundt connect these two schools? Because he considers them *closely akin;* and this opinion, which is shared by Mach, Avenarius, Petzoldt and the immanentists is, as we shall see later, entirely correct. Wundt shows in the first part of this article that the immanentists are idealists, subjectivists and adherents of fideism. This, too, as we shall see later, is a perfectly correct opinion, although Wundt expounds it with a superfluous ballast of professorial erudition, with superfluous niceties and reservations, which is to be explained by the fact that Wundt himself is an idealist and fideist. He reproaches the immanentists not because they are idealists and adherents of fideism, but because, in his opinion, they arrive at these great principles by incorrect methods. Further, the second and third parts of Wundt's article are devoted to empirio-criticism. There he quite definitely points out that very important theoretical propositions of empiro-criticism (*e.g.,* the interpretation of "experience" and the "principal co-ordination," of which we shall speak later) are *identical* with those held by the immanentists (*die empiriokritische in Uebereinstimmung mit der immanenten Philosophie annimmt, S.* 382). Other of Avenarius' theoretical propositions are borrowed from materialism, and in general empirio-criticism is a *"motley"* (*bunte Mischung, ibid., S.* 57), in which the "various component elements *are entirely heterogeneous"* (*an sich einander völlig heterogen sind, S.* 56).

Wundt regards Avenarius' doctrine of the *"independent vital series,"*

27 In *Dead Souls.—Trans.*

in particular, as one of the materialist morsels of the Avenarius-Mach hotchpotch. If you start from the "system C" (that is how Avenarius—who was very fond of making erudite play of new terms—designates the human brain or the nervous system in general), and if the psychical is for you a function of the brain, then this "system C" is a "metaphysical substance"—says Wundt (*ibid.,* p. 64), and your doctrine is materialism. It should be said that many idealists and all agnostics (Kantians and Humeans included) call the materialists metaphysicians, because it seems to them that to recognise the existence of an external world independent of the human mind is to transcend the bounds of experience. As to this terminology and its utter incorrectness from the point of view of Marxism, we shall speak in its proper place. Here it is important to note that the recognition of the "independent" series by Avenarius (and also by Mach, who expresses the same idea in different words), is according to the general opinion of philosophers of various parties, *i.e.,* of various trends in philosophy, an *appropriation from materialism*. If you assume that everything that exists is sensation, or that bodies are complexes of sensations, you cannot, without violating all your fundamental premises, all "your" philosophy, arrive at the conclusion that the *physical* exists *independently* of our minds, and that sensation is a *function* of matter organised in a definite way. Mach and Avenarius, in their philosophy, combine fundamental idealist premises with individual materialist deductions for the very reason that their theory is an example of that "pauper's broth of eclecticism" of which Engels speaks with just contempt.[28]

This eclecticism is particularly marked in Mach's latest philosophical work *Erkenntnis und Irrtum,* 2nd edition, 1906. We have already seen that Mach there declared that "there is no difficulty in constructing every physical element out of sensation, *i.e.,* out of psychical elements," and in the same book we read: "Dependencies outside the boundary of U [= *Umgrenzung, i.e.,* "the spatial boundary of our body," p. 8] are *physics in the broadest sense*" (p. 323, § 4). "To obtain those dependencies in a pure state (*rein erhalten*) it is necessary as much as possible to eliminate the influence of the observer, that is, of those elements that lie within U" (*loc. cit.*). Well, well, the titmouse first promised to set the sea on fire . . . *i.e.,* to construct physical elements from psychical elements, and then it turns out that physical elements

[28] The foreword to *Ludwig Feuerbach,* dated February 1888. These words of Engels' refer to German professorial philosophy in general. The Machians who would like to be Marxists, being unable to grasp the significance and meaning of this thought of Engels', sometimes take refuge in a wretched evasion: "Engels did not yet know Mach" (Fritz Adler). On what is this opinion based? On the fact that Engels does not quote Mach and Avenarius? There are no other grounds, and these grounds are worthless, for Engels does not name *any* of the eclectics by name, and it is hardly likely that Engels did not know Avenarius, who had been editing a quarterly of "scientific" philosophy ever since 1876.

lie beyond the boundary of psychical elements, "which lie within our body"! A remarkable philosophy!

Another example: "A perfect (*vollkommenes*) gas, a perfect liquid, a perfect elastic body, does not exist; the physicist knows that his fictions only approximate to the facts and arbitrarily simplify them; he is aware of the divergence, which cannot be eliminated" (p. 418, § 30).

What divergence (*Abweichung*) is meant here? The divergence of what from what? Of thought (physical theory) from the facts. And what are thoughts, ideas? Ideas are the "tracks of sensations" (p. 9). And what are facts? Facts are "complexes of sensations." And so, the divergence of the tracks of sensations from complexes of sensations cannot be eliminated.

What does this mean? It means that Mach *forgets* his own theory and, when treating of various problems of physics, speaks plainly, without idealist twists, *i.e.*, materialistically. All the "complexes of sensations" and the entire stock of Berkeleian wisdom vanish. The physicists' theory proves to be a reflection of bodies, liquids, gases existing outside us and independently of us, a reflection which is, of course, approximate; but to call this approximation or simplification "arbitrary" is wrong. *In fact,* sensation is here regarded by Mach just as it is regarded by all science which has not been "purified" by the disciples of Berkeley and Hume, *viz.*, as an *image of the external world.* Mach's own theory is subjective idealism; but when the factor of objectivity is required, Mach unceremoniously inserts into his arguments the premises of the contrary, *i.e.*, the materialist, theory of knowledge. Eduard von Hartmann, a consistent idealist and consistent reactionary in philosophy, *who sympathises with the Machian's fight against materialism,* comes very close to the truth when he says that Mach's philosophical position is a "mixture (*Nichtunterscheidung*) of naïve realism and absolute illusionism." [29] That is true. The doctrine that bodies are complexes of sensations, etc., is absolute illusionism, *i.e.*, solipsism; for from this standpoint the world is nothing but my illusion. On the other hand, Mach's aforementioned arguments, as well as many other of his fragmentary arguments, are what is known as "naïve realism," *i.e.*, the materialist theory of knowledge unconsciously and instinctively taken over from the scientists.

Avenarius and the professors who follow in his footsteps attempt to disguise this mixture by the theory of the "principal co-ordination." We shall proceed to examine this theory presently, but let us first finish with the charge that Avenarius is a materialist. Mr. Yushkevich, to whom Wundt's opinion which he failed to understand seemed so interesting, was either himself not enough interested to learn, or else did not condescend to inform the reader, how Avenarius' nearest disciples and successors reacted to this charge. Yet this is necessary to clarify the mat-

[29] Eduard von Hartmann, *Die Weltanschauung der modernen Physik,* Leipzig 1902, S. 219.

ter if we are interested in the relation of Marx's philosophy, *i.e.,* materialism, to the philosophy of empirio-criticism. Moreover, if Machism is a muddle, a mixture of materialism and idealism, it is important to know whither this current turned—if we may so express it—after the official idealists began to disown it because of its concessions to materialism.

Wundt was answered, among others, by two of Avenarius' purest and most orthodox disciples, J. Petzoldt and Fr. Carstanjen. Petzoldt, with haughty resentment, repudiated the charge of materialism, which is so degrading to a German professor, and in support referred to—what do you think?—Avenarius' *Prolegomena,* where, forsooth, the concept of substance has been annihilated! A convenient theory, indeed, that can be made to embrace both purely idealist works and arbitrarily assumed materialist premises! Avenarius' *Kritik der reinen Erfahrung,* of course, does not contradict this teaching, *i.e.,* materialism, writes Petzoldt, but neither does it contradict the directly opposite spiritualist doctrine.[30] An excellent defence! This is exactly what Engels called "a pauper's broth of eclecticism." Bogdanov, who refuses to own himself a Machian and who wants to be considered a Marxist (*in philosophy*), follows Petzoldt. He asserts that "empirio-criticism is not . . . concerned with materialism, or with spiritualism, or with metaphysics in general," [31] that "truth . . . does not lie in the 'golden mean' between the conflicting trends (materialism and spiritualism), but lies outside of both." [32] What appeared to Bogdanov to be truth is, as a matter of fact, confusion, a wavering between materialism and idealism.

Carstanjen, rebutting Wundt, said that he absolutely repudiated this "importation (*Unterschiebung*) of a materialist element which is utterly foreign to the critique of pure experience." [33] "Empirio-criticism is scepticism κατ' ἐξοχήʼν (pre-eminently) in relation to the content of the concepts." There is a grain of truth in this insistent emphasis on the neutrality of Machism; the amendment made by Mach and Avenarius to their original idealism amounts to an admission of partial concessions to materialism. Instead of the consistent standpoint of Berkeley— the external world is my sensation—we sometimes get the Humean standpoint—I exclude the question whether or not there is anything beyond my sensations. And this agnostic standpoint inevitably condemns one to vacillate between materialism and idealism.

---

[30] J. Petzoldt, *Einführung in die Philosophie der reinen Erfahrung,* Bd. I, S. 351-52.

[31] Bogdanov, *Empirio-Monism,* Bk. I, 2nd ed., p. 21.

[32] *Ibid.,* p. 93.

[33] Fr. Carstanjen, *"Der Empiriokritizismus, zugleich eine Erwiderung auf. W. Wundts Aufsätze," Vierteljahrsschrift für wissenschaftliche Philosophie,* Jahrg. 22 (1898), S. 73 u. 213.

3. *The principal co-ordination and "naïve realism"*

Avenarius' doctrine of the principal co-ordination is expounded in *Der menschliche Weltbegriff* and in the *Bemerkungen*. The second was written later, and in it Avenarius emphasises that he is expounding, it is true in a somewhat altered form, something that is not different from the *Kritik der reinen Erfahrung* and *Der menschliche Weltbegriff,* but *exactly the same* (*Bemerkungen,* 1894, S. 137 in the journal quoted above). The essence of this doctrine is the thesis of "the *indissoluble* (*unauflösliche*) co-ordination [*i.e.,* the correlative connection] of the self and the environment" (S. 146). "Expressed philosophically," Avenarius says here, one can say the *"self* and *not-self."* We *"always* find together" (*immer ein Zusammenvorgefundenes*) the one and the other, the *self* and the environment. "No full description of what we find (*von Vorgefundenem*) can contain an 'environment' without some self (*ohne ein Ich*) *whose* environment it is, even though it be only the *self* that is describing what is found (*das Vorgefundene*)" (p. 146). The *self* is called the *central term* of the co-ordination, the environment the *counter-term* (*Gegenglied*). (*Cf. Der menschliche Weltbegriff,* 2. Auflage, 1905, S. 83-84, § 148 ff.)

Avenarius claims that by this doctrine he recognises the full value of what is known as *naïve realism,* that is, the ordinary non-philosophical, naïve view which is entertained by all people who do not trouble themselves as to whether they themselves exist and whether the environment, the external world, exists. Expressing his solidarity with Avenarius, Mach also tries to represent himself as a defender of "naïve realism" (*Analyse der Empfindungen,* S. 39). The Russian Machians, without exception, believed Mach's and Avenarius' claim that this was indeed a defence of "naïve realism": the *self* is acknowledged, the environment is acknowledged—what more do you want?

In order to decide who actually possesses the greatest degree of *naïveté,* let us proceed from a somewhat remote starting point. Here is a popular dialogue between a certain philosopher and his reader:

"Reader: The existence of a system of things [according to ordinary philosophy] is required and from this only is consciousness to be derived.

"Author: Now you are speaking in the spirit of a professional philosopher . . . and not according to human common sense and actual consciousness. . . .

"Tell me, and reflect well before you answer: Does a thing appear in you and become present in you and for you otherwise than simultaneously with and through your consciousness of the thing? . . .

"Reader: Upon sufficient reflection, I must grant you this.

"Author: Now you are speaking from yourself, from your heart. Take care, therefore, not to jump out of yourself and to apprehend any-

thing otherwise than you are able to apprehend it, as consciousness *and* [the italics are the philosopher's] the thing, the thing *and* consciousness; or, more precisely, neither the one nor the other, but that which only subsequently becomes resolved into the two, that which is the absolute subjective-objective and objective-subjective."

Here you have the whole essence of the empirio-critical principal co-ordination, the latest defence of "naïve realism" by the latest positivism! The idea of "indissoluble" co-ordination is here stated very clearly and as though it were a genuine defence of the point of view of the common man, uncorrupted by the subtleties of "the professional philosophers." But, as a matter of fact, this dialogue is taken from the work of a classical representative of *subjective idealism,* Johann Gottlieb Fichte, *published in 1801.*[34]

There is nothing but a paraphrase of subjective idealism in the teachings of Mach and Avenarius we are examining. The claim that they have risen above materialism and idealism, that they have eliminated the opposition between the point of view that proceeds from the thing *to* consciousness and the contrary point of view—is but the empty claim of a renovated Fichteanism. Fichte too imagined that he had "indissolubly" connected the "self" and the "environment," the mind and the thing; that he had "solved" the problem by the assertion that a man cannot jump out of himself. In other words, the Berkeleian argument is repeated: I perceive only my perceptions, I have no right to assume "objects in themselves" outside of my sensation. The different methods of expression used by Berkeley in 1710, by Fichte in 1801, and by Avenarius in 1891-94 do not in the least change the essence of the matter, *viz.,* the fundamental philosophical line of subjective idealism. The world is my sensation; the non-*self* is "postulated" (is created, produced) by the self; the thing is indissolubly connected with the consciousness; the indissoluble co-ordination of the *self* and the environment is the empirio-critical principal co-ordination;—this is all one and the same proposition, the same old trash with a slightly refurbished, or repainted signboard.

The reference to "naïve realism," supposedly defended by this philosophy, is *sophistry* of the cheapest kind. The "naïve realism" of any healthy person who has not been an inmate of a lunatic asylum or a pupil of the idealist philosophers consists in the view that things, the environment, the world, exist *independently* of our sensation, of our consciousness, of our *Self* and of man in general. The same *experience* (not in the Machian sense, but in the human sense of the term) that has produced in us the firm conviction that *independently* of us there exist other people, and not mere complexes of my sensations of high, short, yellow, hard, etc.—this same *experience* produces in us the conviction

---

[34] Johann Gottlieb Fichte, *Sonnenklarer Bericht an das gröbere Publikum über das eigentliche Wesen der neuesten Philosophie. Ein Versuch, die Leser zum Verstehen zu zwingen.* Berlin, 1801, S. 178-80.

that things, the world, the environment exist independently of us. Our sensation, our consciousness is only *an image* of the external world, and it is obvious that an image cannot exist without the thing imaged, and that the latter exists independently of that which images it. Materialism *deliberately* makes the "naïve" belief of mankind the foundation of its theory of knowledge.

Is not the foregoing evaluation of the "principal co-ordination" a product of the materialist prejudice against Machism? Not at all. Specialists in philosophy who cannot be accused of partiality towards materialism, who even detest it and who accept one or other of the idealist systems, agree that the principal co-ordination of Avenarius and Co. is subjective idealism. Wundt, for instance, whose interesting opinion was not understood by Mr. Yushkevich, explicitly states that Avenarius' theory, according to which a full description of the given or the found is impossible without some Self, an observer or describer, is "a false confusion of the content of real experience with reflections about it." Natural science, says Wundt, completely abstracts from every observer. "Such abstraction is possible only because the attribution (*Hinzuden-ken*) of an experiencing individual to every content of experience, which the empirio-critical philosophy, in agreement with the immanent-ist philosophy, assumes, is an entirely empirical and unfounded assumption arising from a false confusion of the content of real experience with reflections about it" (*loc. cit.,* p. 382). For the immanentists (Schuppe, Rehmke, Leclair, Schubert-Soldern), who themselves voice —as we shall see later—their hearty sympathy with Avenarius, proceed from *this very* idea of the "indissoluble" connection between subject and object. And W. Wundt, before analysing Avenarius, demonstrated in detail that the immanentist philosophy is only a "modification" of Berkeleianism, that however much the immanentists may deny their kinship with Berkeley we should not allow verbal differences to conceal from us the "deeper content of these philosophical doctrines," *viz.,* Berkeleianism or Fichteanism.[35]

The English writer Norman Smith, analysing Avenarius' "Philosophy of Pure Experience," puts this criticism in an even more straightforward and emphatic form:

"Most readers of Avenarius' *Der Menschliche Weltbegriff* will probably agree that, however convincing as criticism [of idealism], it is tantalisingly illusive in its positive teaching. So long as we seek to interpret his theory of experience in the form in which it is avowedly presented, namely, as genuinely realistic, it eludes all clear comprehension: its whole meaning seems to be exhausted in negation of the subjectivism which it overthrows. It is only when we translate Avenarius' technical terms into more familiar language that we discover where the

[35] *Loc. cit.,* § C: *Die immanente Philosophie und der Berkeleysche Idealismus,* S. 373 u. 375; vgl. S. 386 u. 407. *Ueber die Unvermeidlichkeit des Solipsismus von diesem Standpunkt,* S. 381.

real source of the mystification lies. Avenarius has diverted attention from the defects of his position by directing his main attack against the very weakness [*i.e.,* of the idealist position] which is fatal to his own theory." [36] "Throughout the whole discussion the vagueness of the term experience stands him in good stead. Sometimes it means experiencing and at other times the experienced, the latter meaning being emphasised when the nature of the self is in question. These two meanings of the term experience practically coincide with his important distinction between the absolute and the relative standpoints [I have examined above what significance this distinction has for Avenarius]; and these two points of view are not in his philosophy really reconciled. For when he allows as legitimate the demand that experience be ideally completed in thought [the full description of the environment is ideally completed by thinking of an observing self], he makes an admission which he cannot successfully combine with his assertion that nothing exists save in relation to the self. The ideal completion of given reality which results from the analysis of material bodies into elements which no human senses can apprehend, [here are meant the material elements discovered by natural science, the atoms, electrons, etc., and not the fictitious elements invented by Mach and Avenarius] or from following the earth back to a time when no human being existed upon it, is, strictly, not a completion of experience but only of what is experienced. It completes only one of the two aspects which Avenarius has asserted to be inseparable. It leads us not only to what has not been experienced but to what can never by any possibility be experienced by beings like ourselves. But here again the ambiguities of the term experience come to Avenarius' rescue. He argues that thought is as genuine a form of experience as sense-perception, and so in the end falls back on the time-worn argument of subjective idealism, that thought and reality are inseparable, because reality can only be conceived in thought, and thought involves the presence of the thinker. Not, therefore, any original and profound re-establishment of realism, but only the restatement in its crudest form of the familiar position of subjective idealism is the final outcome of Avenarius' positive speculations" (p. 29).

The mystification wrought by Avenarius, who completely duplicates Fichte's error, is here excellently exposed. The much-vaunted elimination of the antithesis between materialism (Norman Smith erroneously uses the term realism) and idealism by means of the term "experience" instantly proves to be a myth as soon as we proceed to definite and concrete problems. Such, for instance, is the problem of the existence of the earth *prior* to man, *prior* to any sentient being. We shall presently speak of this point in detail. Here we will note that not only Norman Smith, an opponent of his theory, but also W. Schuppe, the immanentist, who warmly greeted the appearance of *Der menschliche Weltbegriff* as *a*

[36] Norman Smith, "Avenarius' Philosophy of Pure Experience," *Mind,* Vol. XV, 1906, pp. 27-28.

confirmation of naïve realism[37] unmasks Avenarius and his fictitious "realism." The fact of the matter is that Schuppe *fully* agrees with *such* "realism," *i.e.,* the mystification of materialism dished out by Avenarius. Such "realism," he wrote to Avenarius, I, the immanentist philosopher who have been slandered as a subjective idealist, have always claimed with as much right as yourself, *hochverehrter Herr Kollege.* "My conception of thought . . . excellently harmonises (*verträgt sich-vortrefflich*) with your 'pure experience' " (p. 384). "The connection and inseparability of the two terms of the co-ordination" are provided only by the *self* (*das Ich,* the abstract, Fichtean self-consciousness, a thought divorced from the brain). "That which you desired to eliminate you have tacitly assumed"—so Schuppe wrote to Avenarius (p. 388). And it is difficult to say who more rudely unmasks Avenarius the mystifier—Smith by his straightforward and clear refutation, or Schuppe by his enthusiastic opinion of Avenarius' crowning work. The kiss of Wilhelm Schuppe in philosophy is no better than the kiss of Peter Struve or Menshikov[38] in politics.

O. Ewald, who praises Mach for not succumbing to materialism, speaks of the principal co-ordination in a similar manner: "If one declares the correlation of central term and counter-term to be an epistemological necessity which cannot be avoided, then, even though the word 'empirio-criticism' be inscribed on the signboard in shrieking letters, one is adopting a standpoint that differs in no way from absolute idealism. [The term is incorrect; he should have said subjective idealism, for Hegel's absolute idealism is reconcilable with the existence of the earth, nature, and the physical universe without man, since nature is regarded as the "otherness" of the absolute idea.] On the other hand, if we do not hold fast to this co-ordination and grant the counter-terms their independence, then the way is at once opened for every metaphysical possibility, especially in the direction of transcendental realism" (*op. cit.,* pp. 56-57).

By metaphysics and transcendental realism, Herr Friedlander, who is disguised under the pseudonym Ewald, means *materialism.* Himself professing one of the varieties of idealism, he fully agrees with the Machians and the Kantians that materialism is metaphysics—"from beginning to end the wildest metaphysics" (p. 134). On the question of the "transcendence" and the metaphysical character of materialism he is in agreement with Bazarov and all our Machians, and of this we shall have occasion to say more later. Here again it is important to note

[37] See Schuppe's letter to Avenarius in *Vierteljahrsschrift für wissenschaftliche Philosophie,* Bd. XVII, 1893, S. 364-88.
[38] P. B. Struve, formerly a "legal Marxist," and later a member of the liberal-monarchist Constitutional Democratic Party, at this period had definitely joined the counter-revolutionary camp.
M. O. Menshikov, contributor to the reactionary newspaper *Novoye Vremya.*—*Trans.*

how *in fact* the shallow and pedantic claim to have transcended idealism and materialism vanishes, and how the question arises inexorably and irreconcilably. "To grant the counter-terms their independence" means (if one translates the pretentious language of the affected Avenarius into common parlance) to regard nature and the external world as independent of human consciousness and sensation. And that is materialism. To build a theory of knowledge on the hypothesis of the indissoluble connection between the object and human sensation ("complexes of sensations" as identical with bodies; "world-elements" that are identical both psychically and physically; Avenarius' co-ordination, and so forth) is to land inevitably into idealism. Such is the simple and unavoidable truth that with a little attention may be easily detected beneath the piles of distorted and quasi-erudite terminology of Avenarius, Schuppe, Ewald and the others, which deliberately obscures matters and frightens the general public away from philosophy.

The "reconciliation" of Avenarius' theory with "naïve realism" in the end aroused misgivings even among his own disciples. For instance, R. Willy says that the common assertion that Avenarius came to adopt "naïve realism" should be taken *cum grano salis*. "As a dogma, naïve realism would be nothing but the belief in things-in-themselves existing outside man (*außerpersönliche*) in their perceptible form." [39] In other words, the only theory of knowledge that is really created by an actual and not fictitious agreement with "naïve realism" is, according to Willy, materialism! And Willy, of course, rejects materialism. But he is compelled to admit that Avenarius in *Der menschliche Weltbegriff* restores the unity of "experience," the unity of the "self" and the environment "by means of a series of complicated and extremely artificial subsidiary and intermediary conceptions" (p. 171). *Der menschliche Weltbegriff*, being a reaction against the original idealism of Avenarius, "entirely bears the character of a *reconciliation (eines Ausgleiches)* between the naïve realism of common sense and the epistemological idealism of school philosophy. But that such a reconciliation could restore the unity and integrity of experience [Willy calls it *Grunderfahrung,* that is, a basic experience—another new word!], I would not assert" (p. 170).

A valuable admission! Avenarius' "experience" failed to reconcile idealism and materialism. Willy, it seems, repudiates the *school philosophy* of experience in order to replace it by a philosophy of "basic" experience, which is confusion thrice confounded. . . .

4.   *Did nature exist prior to man?*

We have already seen that this question is particularly repugnant to the philosophy of Mach and Avenarius. Natural science positively asserts

[39] Rudolph Willy, *Gegen die Schulweisheit,* S. 170.

that the earth once existed in such a state that no man or any other creature existed or could have existed on it. Organic matter is a later phenomenon, the fruit of a long evolution. It follows that there was no sentient matter, no "complexes of sensations," no *self* that was supposedly "indissolubly" connected with the environment in accordance with Avenarius' doctrine. Matter is primary, and thought, consciousness, sensation are products of a very high development. Such is the materialist theory of knowledge, to which natural science instinctively prescribes.

The question arises, have the eminent representatives of empirio-criticism observed this contradiction between their theory and natural science? They have observed it, and they have definitely asked themselves by what arguments this contradiction can be removed. Three attitudes to this question are of particular interest from the point of view of materialism, that of Avenarius himself and those of his disciples J. Petzoldt and R. Willy.

Avenarius tries to eliminate the contradiction to natural science by means of the theory of the "potential" central term in the co-ordination. As we know, co-ordination is the "indissoluble" connection between *self* and environment. In order to eliminate the obvious absurdity of this theory the concept of the "potential" central term is introduced. For instance, what about man's development from the embryo? Does the environment (the "counter-term") exist if the "central term" is represented by an embryo? The embryonic system C—Avenarius replies— is the "potential central term in relation to the future individual environment" (*Bemerkungen,* S. 140). The potential central term is never equal to zero, even when there are as yet no parents (*elterliche Bestandteile*), but only the "integral parts of the environment" capable of becoming parents (p. 141).

The co-ordination then is indissoluble. It is essential for the empiriocriticist to assert this in order to save the fundamentals of his philosophy—sensations and their complexes. Man is the central term of this co-ordination. But when there is no man, when he has not yet been born, the central term is nevertheless not equal to zero; it has only become a *potential* central term! It is astonishing that there are people who can take seriously a philosopher who advances such arguments! Even Wundt, who stipulates that he is not an enemy of every form of metaphysics (*i.e.,* of fideism), was compelled to admit "the mystical obscuration of the concept experience" by the word "potential," which destroys co-ordination entirely (*op. cit.,* p. 379).

And, indeed, how can one seriously speak of a co-ordination the indissolubility of which consists in one of its terms being potential?

Is this not mysticism, the very antechamber of fideism? If it is possible to think of the potential central term in relation to a future environment, why not think of it in relation to a *past* environment, that is, *after man's death?* You will say that Avenarius did not draw this conclusion from his theory? Granted, but that absurd and reactionary theory became the more cowardly and not any the better for that. Avenarius, in 1894, did not carry this theory to its logical conclusion, or perhaps feared to do so. But R. Schubert-Soldern, as we shall see, resorted in 1896 to *this very theory* to arrive at theological conclusions, which in 1906 earned the *approval* of Mach, who said that Schubert-Soldern was following *"very close paths"* (to Machism).[40] Engels was quite right in attacking Dühring, an avowed atheist, for inconsistently *leaving loopholes* for fideism in his philosophy. Engels several times, and justly, brought this accusation against the materialist Dühring, although the latter had not drawn any theological conclusions, in the 'seventies at least. But we have among us people who would have us regard them as Marxists, yet who bring to the masses a philosophy which comes very close to fideism.

". . . It would seem," Avenarius wrote in the *Bemerkungen,* "that from the empirio-critical standpoint natural science is not entitled to enquire about periods of our present environment which in time preceded the existence of man" (S. 144). Avenarius answers: "The enquirer cannot avoid mentally projecting himself" (*sich hinzuzudenken, i.e.,* imagining oneself to be present). For—Avenarius continues—"what the scientist wants (although he may not be clearly aware of it) is essentially only this: how is the earth . . . to be defined prior to the appearance of living beings or men if I were mentally to project myself in the role of a spectator—in much the same way as though it were thinkable that we could from our earth follow the history of another star or of another solar system with the help of perfected instruments."

An object cannot exist independently of our consciousness. "We always mentally project ourselves as the intelligence endeavouring to apprehend the object."

This theory of the necessity of "mentally projecting" the human mind to every object and to nature prior to man is given by me in the first paragraph in the words of the "recent positivist," R. Avenarius, and in the second, in the words of the subjective idealist, J. G. Fichte.[41] The sophistry of this theory is so manifest that one feels reluctant to analyse it. If we "mentally project" ourselves, our presence will be *imaginary*—but the existence of the earth prior to man is *real.* Man *could not* in practice be an observer, for instance, of the earth in an incandescent state, and to "imagine" his being present at the time is *obscurantism,* exactly as though I were to endeavour to prove the existence of hell by the argument that if I "mentally projected" myself thither as an observer I could observe hell. The "reconciliation" of empirio-criticism and natural science amounts to this, that Avenarius graciously consents to "mentally project" something the possibility of admitting which is *excluded* by natural science. No man in the least educated or in the

[40] *Analyse der Empfindungen,* S. 4.
[41] J. G. Fichte, *Recension des Aenesidemus,* 1794, *Sämtliche Werke,* Bd. I, S. 19.

least healthy doubts that the earth existed at a time when there *could not* have been any life on it, any sensation or any "central term," and consequently the whole theory of Mach and Avenarius, from which it follows that the earth is a complex of sensations ("bodies are complexes of sensations") or "complexes of elements in which the psychical and physical are identical," or "a counter-term of which the central term can never be equal to zero," is *philosophical obscurantism,* the reduction of subjective idealism to absurdity.

J. Petzoldt perceived the absurdity of the position into which Avenarius had fallen and felt ashamed. In his *Einführung in die Philosophie der reinen Erfahrung* (Vol. II) he devotes a whole paragraph (§ 65) "to the question of the reality of earlier (*frühere*) periods of the earth."

"In the teaching of Avenarius," says Petzoldt, "the self (*das Ich*) plays a role different from that which it plays in the teaching of Schuppe [let us note that Petzoldt openly and repeatedly declares: our philosophy was founded by *three* persons—Avenarius, Mach and Schuppe], yet it is a role which, perhaps, possesses too much importance for his theory." (Petzoldt was evidently influenced by the fact that Schuppe had unmasked Avenarius by showing that with him too everything rests entirely on the *self;* and Petzoldt wishes to make a correction.) "Avenarius said on one occasion," Petzoldt continues, "that we can think of a 'region' where no human foot has yet trodden, but to be able *to think* (italicised by Avenarius) of such an environment there is required 'what we designate by the term self (*Ich-Bezeichnetes*), *whose* (italicised by Avenarius) thought the thinking is' (*V. f. wiss. Ph.,* 18 Bd., 1894, S. 146, Anm.)."

Petzoldt replies:

"The epistemologically important question, however, is not whether we can think of such a region at all, but whether we are entitled to think of it as existing, or as having existed, independently of any individual mind."

Right is right! People can think and "mentally project" for themselves any kind of hell and any kind of hobgoblin. Lunacharsky even "mentally projected" for himself—well, to use a mild expression—religious conceptions. But it is precisely the purpose of the theory of knowledge to show the unreal, fantastic and reactionary character of such projections.

". . . For, that the system C (*i.e.,* the brain) is necessary for thought is obvious both for Avenarius and for the philosophy which is here presented. . . ."

That is not true. Avenarius' theory of 1876 is a theory of thought without brain. And even in his theory of 1891-94, as we shall presently see, there is a similar element of idealist nonsense.

". . . But is this system C a condition of *existence* [italicised by Petzoldt] of, say, the Mesozoic period of the earth?" And Petzoldt, presenting the argument of Avenarius I have already cited on the subject of what science actually wants and how we can "mentally project" the spectator, objects:

"No, we wish to know whether I have the right to think that the earth at that remote epoch existed in the same way as I think of it as having existed yesterday or a minute ago. Or must the existence of the earth be really made conditional, as Willy claimed, on our right at least to assume that at the given period there co-existed some system C, even though at the lowest stage of its development?" Of this idea of Willy's we shall speak presently.

"Avenarius evades Willy's strange conclusion by the argument that the person who puts the question cannot mentally remove himself (*sich wegdenken, i.e.,* think himself as absent), nor can he avoid mentally projecting himself (*sich hinzuzudenken,* see Avenarius, *Der menschliche Weltbegriff,* S. 130). But then Avenarius makes the individual self of the person who puts the question, or the thought of such a self, the condition not only of the act of thought regarding the uninhabitable earth, but also of the justification for believing in the existence of the earth at that time.

"These false paths are easily avoided if we do not ascribe so much theoretical importance to the self. The only thing the theory of knowledge should demand of the various conceptions of that which is remote in space or time is that it be conceivable and uniquely (*eindeutig*) determined; the rest is the affair of the special sciences" (Vol. II, p. 325).

Petzoldt rechristened the law of causality the law of unique determination and imported into his theory, as we shall se later, the *apriority* of this law. This means that Petzoldt saves himself from Avenarius' subjective idealism and solipsism ("he attributes an exaggerated importance to the self," as the professorial jargon has it) with the help of *Kantian* ideas. The absence of the objective element in Avenarius' doctrine, the impossibility of reconciling it with the demands of natural science, which declares the earth (object) to have existed long before the appearance of living beings (subject), compelled Petzoldt to resort to causality (unique determination). The earth existed, for its existence prior to man is causally connected with the present existence of the earth. Firstly, where does causality come from? *A priori,* says Petzoldt. Secondly, are not the ideas of hell, devils, and Lunacharsky's "mental projections" also connected by causality? Thirdly, the theory "of the complexes of sensations" in any case turns out to be destroyed by Petzoldt. Petzoldt failed to resolve the contradiction he observed in Avenarius, and only entangled himself still more, for only one solution is possible, *viz.,* the recognition that the external world reflected by our mind exists independently of our mind. This materialist solution alone is really compatible with natural science, and it alone eliminates both Petzoldt's and Mach's idealist solution of the question of causality, which we shall speak of separately.

The third empirio-criticist, R. Willy, first raised the question of this difficulty in Avenarius' philosophy in 1896, in an article entitled *"Der Empiriokritizismus als einzig wissenschaftlicher Standpunkt"* ("Empirio-criticism as the Only Scientific Standpoint"). What about the world prior to man?—Willy asks here,[42] and at first answers according to Ave-narius: "we project ourselves *mentally* into the past." But then he goes on to say that we are not necessarily obliged to regard *experience* as human experience. "For we must simply regard the animal kingdom —be it the most insignificant worm—as primitive fellow-men (*Mit-menschen*) if . . . we regard animal life in connection with general experience" (pp. 73-74). Thus, prior to man the earth was the "experi-ence" of a worm, which discharged the functions of the "central term" in order to save Avenarius' "co-ordination" and Avenarius' philosophy! No wonder Petzoldt tried to dissociate himself from an argument which is not only the height of absurdity (ideas of the earth correspond-ing to the theories of the geologists attributed to a worm), but which does not in any way help our philosopher, for the earth existed not only before man but before any living being generally.

Willy returned to the question in 1905. The worm was now re-moved.[43] But Petzoldt's "law of unique determination" could not, of course, satisfy Willy, who regarded it merely as "logical formalism." The author says—will not the question of the world prior to man, as Petzoldt puts it, lead us "back again to the things-in-themselves of common sense"? (*i.e.,* to materialism! How terrible indeed!). What does millions of years without life mean? "Is time perhaps a thing-in-itself? Of course not! [44] And that means that things outside men are only impressions, bits of fantasy fabricated by men with the help of a few fragments we find about us. And why not? Need the philosopher fear the stream of life? . . . And so I say to myself: abandon all this love of systems and grasp the moment (*ergreife den Augenblick*), the moment you are liv-ing in, the moment which alone brings happiness" (pp. 177-78).

Well, well! Either materialism or solipsism—this, in spite of his vocif-erous phrases, is what Willy arrives at when he analyses the question of the existence of nature before man.

To summarise. Three augurs of empirio-criticism have appeared be-fore us and have laboured in the sweat of their brow to reconcile their philosophy with natural science, to patch up the holes in their solipsism. Avenarius repeated Fichte's argument and substituted an imaginary world for the real world. Petzoldt withdrew from Fichtean idealism and moved towards Kantian idealism. Willy, having suffered a fiasco with the "worm," threw up the sponge and inadvertently blurted out the truth: either materialism or solipsism, or even the recognition of noth-ing but the present moment.

It only remains for us to show the reader *how* this problem was un-

---

[42] *Vierteljahrsschrift für wissenschaftliche Philosophie, Jahrg.* XX, 1896, S. 72.
[43] R. Willy, *Gegen die Schulweisheit,* 1905, S. 173-78.
[44] We shall discuss this point with the Machians later.

550 MARXISM AND THE PHILOSOPHY OF HISTORY

derstood and treated by our own native Machians. Here is Bazarov in the *Studies "in" the Philosophy of Marxism* (p. 11):

"It remains for us now, under the guidance of our faithful *vademecum* [*i.e.,* Plekhanov], to descend into the last and most horrible circle of the solipsist inferno, into that circle where, as Plekhanov assures us, every subjective idealism is menaced with the necessity of conceiving the world as it was contemplated by the ichthyosauruses and archaeopteryxes. 'Let us mentally transport ourselves,' writes Plekhanov, 'to that epoch when only very remote ancestors of man existed on the earth, for instance, to the Mesozoic epoch. The question arises, what was the status of space, time and causality *then? Whose* subjective forms were they then? Were they the subjective forms of the ichthyosauruses? And *whose intelligence* at the time dictated its laws to nature? The intelligence of the archaeopteryx? To these queries the Kantian philosophy *can give no answer.* And it must be rejected as absolutely incompatible with modern science' (*L. Feuerbach,* p. 117)."

Here Bazarov breaks the quotation from Plekhanov just before a very important passage—as we shall soon see—namely: "Idealism says that without subject there is no object. The history of the earth shows that the object existed long before the subject appeared, *i.e.,* long before the appearance of organisms possessing a perceptible degree of consciousness. . . . The history of development reveals the truth of materialism."

We continue the quotation from Bazarov:

". . . But does Plekhanov's thing-in-itself provide the desired solution? Let us remember that even according to Plekhanov we can have no idea of things as they are in themselves; we know only their phenomena, only the results of their actions on our sense-organs. Apart from this action they possess no aspect (*L. Feuerbach,* p. 112). What sense-organs existed in the period of the ichthyosauruses? Evidently, only the sense-organs of the ichthyosauruses and their like. Only the ideas of the ichthyosauruses were then the actual, the real manifestations of things-in-themsleves. Hence, according to Plekhanov also, if the paleontologist desires to remain on 'real' ground he must write the story of the Mesozoic epoch in the light of the contemplations of the ichthyosaurus. And, consequently, not a single step forward is made in comparison with solipsism."

Such is the complete argument (the reader must pardon the lengthy quotation—we could not avoid it) of a Machian, an argument worthy of perpetuation as a first-class example of muddleheadedness.

Bazarov imagines that Plekhanov gave himself away. If things-in-themselves, apart from their action on our sense-organs, have no aspect of their own, then in the Mesozoic epoch they did not exist except as the "aspect" of the sense-organs of the ichthyosaurus. And this is the argument of a materialist! If an "aspect" is the result of the action of "things-in-themselves" on sense-organs—it follows that things *do not exist independently* of sense-organs of one kind or another!

Let us assume for a moment that Bazarov indeed "misunderstood" Plekhanov's words (improbable as such an assumption may seem), that they did appear obscure to him. Be it so. We ask: is Bazarov engaged in a fencing bout with Plekhanov (whom the Machians exalt to the position of the only representative of materialism!), or is he endeavouring to clear up the problem *of materialism?* If Plekhanov seemed obscure to you, or contradictory, and so forth, why did you not turn to other materialists? Is it because you do not know them? But ignorance is no argument.

If Bazarov indeed does not know that the fundamental premise of materialism is the recognition of the external world, of the existence of *things* outside and independent of our mind, this is truly a striking case of crass ignorance. We would remind the reader of Berkeley, who in 1710 rebuked the materialists for their recognition of "objects in themselves" existing independently of our mind and reflected by our mind. Of course, everybody is free to side with Berkeley or anyone else *against* the materialists; that is unquestionable. But it is equally unquestionable that to speak of the materialists and distort or ignore the fundamental premise of *all* materialism is to import preposterous confusion into the problem.

Was Plekhanov right when he said that for idealism there is no object without a subject, while for materialism the object exists independently of the subject and is reflected more or less adequately in the subject's mind? If this is *wrong,* then any man who has the slightest respect for Marxism should have pointed out *this* error of Plekhanov's, and should have dealt *not* with him, but with someone else, with Marx, Engels, or Feuerbach, on the question of materialism and the existence of nature prior to man. But if this is right, or, at least, if you are unable to find an error here, then your attempt to shuffle the cards and to confuse in the reader's mind the most elementary conception of materialism, as distinguished from idealism, is a literary indecency.

As for the Marxists who are interested in the question *apart* from every little word uttered by Plekhanov, we shall quote the opinion of L. Feuerbach, who as is known (perhaps *not* to Bazarov?), was a materialist, and through whom Marx and Engels, as is well known, came from the idealism of Hegel to their materialist philosophy. In his rejoinder to R. Haym, Feuerbach wrote:

"Nature, which is not an object of man or mind, is for speculative philosophy, or at least for idealism, a Kantian thing-in-itself [we shall speak later in detail of the fact that our Machians confuse the Kantian thing-in-itself with the materialist thing-in-itself], an abstraction without reality, but it is nature that causes the downfall of idealism. Natural science, at least in its present state, necessarily leads us back to a point when the conditions for human existence were still absent, when nature, *i.e.,* the earth, was not yet an object of the human eye and mind, when, consequently, nature was an absolutely non-human entity (*absolut unmenschliches Wesen*). Idealism may retort: but nature also is something thought of by you (*von dir gedachte*). Certainly, but from this it does not follow that this nature did not at one time actually exist, just as from the fact that Socrates and Plato do not exist for me if I do not think of them, it does not follow that Socrates and Plato did not actually at one time exist without me." [45]

This is how Feuerbach regarded materialism and idealism from the standpoint of the existence of nature prior to the appearance of man. Avenarius' sophistry (the "mental projection of the observer") was refuted by Feuerbach, who did not know the "recent positivism" but who thoroughly knew the old idealist sophistry. And Bazarov offers us absolutely nothing new, but merely repeats this sophistry of the idealists: "Had I been there [on earth, prior to man], I would have seen the world so-and-so" (*Studies "in" the Philosophy of Marxism,* p. 29). In other words: if I make an assumption that is obviously absurd and contrary to natural science (that man can be an observer in an epoch before man existed), I shall be able to patch up the breach in my philosophy!

This gives us an idea of the extent of Bazarov's knowledge of the subject and of his literary methods. Bazarov did not even hint at the "difficulty" with which Avenarius, Petzoldt and Willy wrestled; and, moreover, he made such a hash of the whole subject, placed before the reader such an incredible hotchpotch, that there ultimately appears to be no difference between materialism and solipsism! Idealism is represented as "realism," and to materialism is ascribed the denial of the existence of things outside of their action on the sense-organs! Truly, either Feuerbach did not know the elementary difference between materialism and idealism, or else Bazarov and Co. have completely altered the elementary truths of philosophy.

Or let us take Valentinov, a philosopher who, naturally, is delighted with Bazarov: 1) "Berkeley is the founder of the correlativist theory of the relativity of subject and object" (p. 148). This is not Berkeleian idealism, oh, no! This is a "profound analysis." 2) "In the most realistic aspect, irrespective of the forms [!] of their usual idealist interpretation [only interpretation!], the fundamental premises of the theory are formulated by Avenarius" (p. 148). Infants, as we see, are taken in by the hocus pocus! 3) "His [Avenarius'] conception of the starting point of knowledge is that each individual finds himself in a definite environment, in other words, the individual and the environment are repre-

45 Ludwig Feuerbach, *Sämtliche Werke,* herausgegeben von W. Bolin und Fr. Jodl, Bd. VII, Stuttgart 1903, S. 510; or Karl Grün, *L. Feuerbach in seinem Briefwechsel und Nachlaß, sowie in seiner philosophischen Charakterentwicklung,* Bd. I, Leipzig 1874, S. 423-35.

sented as connected and inseparable [!] terms of one and the same co-ordination" (p. 148). Delightful! This is not idealism—Bazarov and Valentinov have risen above materialism and idealism—this "insepara-bility" of the subject and object is "realism" itself. 4) "Is the reverse assertion correct, namely, that there is no counter-term to which there is no corresponding central term—an individual? Naturally [!] not. . . . In the archaic period the woods were verdant . . . yet there was no man" (p. 148). That means that the inseparable *can* be separated! Is that not "natural"? 5) "Yet from the standpoint of the theory of knowledge, the question of the object in itself is absurd" (p. 148). Of course! When there were no sentient organisms objects were neverthe-less "complexes of elements" *identical* with sensations! 6) "The im-manentist school, in the person of Schubert-Soldern and Schuppe, clad these [!] thoughts in an unsatisfactory form and found itself in the *cul-de-sac* of solipsism" (p. 149). But "these thoughts" themselves, of course, contain no solipsism, and empirio-criticism, of course, is not a paraphrase of the reactionary theories of the immanentists, who lie when they declare themselves to be in sympathy with Avenarius!

This, Messrs. Machians, is not philosophy, but an incoherent jumble of words.

5.   *Does man think with the help of the brain?*

Bazarov emphatically answers this question in the affirmative. He writes: "If Plekhanov's thesis that 'consciousness is an internal [? Ba-zarov] state of matter' be given a more satisfactory form, *e.g.,* that 'every psychical process is a function of the cerebral process,' then neither Mach nor Avenarius would dispute it" (*Studies "in" the Phi-losophy of Marxism,* p. 29).

To the mouse no beast is stronger than the cat. To the Russian Mach-ians there is no materialist stronger than Plekhanov. Was Plekhanov really the *only* one, or the first, to advance the materialist thesis that consciousness is an internal state of matter? And if Bazarov did not like Plekhanov's formulation of materialism, why did he take Plekhanov and not Engels or Feuerbach?

Because the Machians are afraid to admit the truth. They are fight-ing materialism, but pretend that it is only Plekhanov they are fighting. A cowardly and unprincipled method.

But let us turn to empirio-criticism. Avenarius "would not dispute" the statement that thought is a function of the brain. These words of Bazarov's contain a direct untruth. Not only does Avenarius *dispute* the materialist thesis, but invents a whole "theory" in order to refute it. "The brain," says Avenarius in *Der menschliche Weltbegriff,* "is not the habitation, the seat, the creator, it is not the instrument or organ, the supporter or substratum, etc., of thought" (p. 76—approvingly quoted by Mach in the *Analyse der Empfindungen,* p. 22, note). "Thought is not an indweller, or commander, or the other half, or side, etc., nor is it a product or even a physiological function, or a state in general of the brain" (*ibid.*). And Avenarius expresses himself no less emphatically in his *Bemerkungen:* "presentations" are "not functions (physiological, psychical, or psycho-physical) of the brain" (*op. cit.,* § 115). Sensations are not "psychical functions of the brain" (§ 116).

Thus, according to Avenarius, the brain is not the organ of thought, and thought is not a function of the brain. Take Engels, and we immediately find directly contrary, frankly materialist formulations. "Thought and consciousness," says Engels in *Anti-Dühring,* "are products of the human brain." [46] This idea is often repeated in that work. In *Ludwig Feuerbach* we have the following exposition of the views of Feuerbach and Engels: ". . . the material (*stofflich*), sensuously perceptible world to which we ourselves belong is the only reality . . . our consciousness and thinking, however supra-sensuous they may seem, are the product (*Erzeugnis*) of a material, bodily organ, the brain. Matter is not a product of mind, but mind itself is merely the highest product of matter. This is, of course, pure materialism" (4th German ed., p. 18).[47] Or on p. 4, where he speaks of the reflection of the processes of nature in "the thinking brain," etc., etc.

Avenarius rejects this materialist standpoint and says that "the thinking brain" is a *"fetish of natural science"* (*Der menschliche Weltbegriff,* 2. Aufl., S. 70). Hence, Avenarius cherishes no illusions concerning his absolute disagreement with natural science on this point. He admits, as do Mach and all the immanentists, that natural science holds an instinctive and unconscious materialist point of view. He admits and explicitly declares that *he absolutely differs from the "prevailing psychology"* (*Bemerkungen,* S. 150, etc.). This prevailing psychology is guilty of an inadmissible "introjection"—such is the new term contrived by our philosopher—*i.e.,* the insertion of thought into the brain, or of sensations into us. These "two words" (into us—*in uns*), Avenarius goes on to say, contain the assumption (*Annahme*) that empirio-criticism disputes. "This *insertion* (*Hineinverlegung*) of the visible, etc., into man is what we call *introjection*" (p. 153, § 45).

Introjection deviates "in principle" from the "natural conception of the world" (*natürlicher Weltbegriff*) by substituting "into me" for "before me" (*vor mir,* p. 154) "by turning a component part of the (real) environment into a component part of (ideal) thought" (*ibid.*). "Out of the *amechanical* [a new word in place of "psychical"] which manifests itself freely and clearly in the experienced [or, in what is found— *im Vorgefundenen*], introjection makes something which hides itself [*Latitierendes,* says Avenarius—another new word] mysteriously in the central nervous system" (*ibid.*).

[46] See *Anti-Dühring,* English ed., 1935, p. 44.—*Trans.*
[47] F. Engels, *Ludwig Feuerbach,* English ed., 1934, p. 35—*Trans.*

Here we have the same *mystification* that we encountered in the famous defence of "naïve realism" by the empirio-criticists and immanentists. Avenarius here acts on the advice of the charlatan in Turgenev: denounce most of all those vices which you yourself possess. Avenarius tries to pretend that he is combating idealism: philosophical idealism, you see, is usually deduced from introjection, the external world is converted into sensation, into ideas, and so forth, while I defend "naïve realism," the equal reality of everything presented, both *"self"* and environment, without inserting the external world into the human brain.

The sophistry here is the same as that which we observed in the case of the famous co-ordination. While distracting the attention of the reader by attacking idealism, Avenarius is in fact defending idealism, albeit in slightly different words: thought is not a function of the brain; the brain is not the organ of thought; sensations are not functions of the nervous system, oh, no! sensations are—"elements," psychical only in one connection, while in another connection (although the elements are *"identical"*) they are physical. With his new and muddled terminology, with his new and pompous epithets, supposedly expressing a new "theory," Avenarius merely beat about the bush and returned to his fundamental idealist premise.

And if our Russian Machians (*e.g.,* Bogdanov) failed to notice the "mystification" and discerned a refutation of idealism in the "new" defence of idealism, in the analysis of empirio-criticism given by the philosophical experts we find a sober estimate of the true nature of Avenarius' ideas, which is laid bare when stripped of its pretentious terminology.

In 1903 Bogdanov wrote:[48]

"Richard Avenarius presented a most harmonious and complete philosophical picture of the development of the dualism of spirit and body. The gist of his 'doctrine of introjection' is the following: [we observe only physical bodies directly, and we infer the experiences of others, *i.e.,* the mind of another person, only by hypothesis]. . . . The hypothesis is complicated by the fact that the experiences of the other person are located within his body, are inserted (introjected) into his organism. This is already a superfluous hypothesis and even gives rise to numerous contradictions. Avenarius systematically draws attention to these contradictions by unfolding a series of successive historical facts in the development of dualism and of philosophical idealism. But here we need not follow Avenarius. . . . Introjection serves as an explanation of the dualism of mind and body."

Bogdanov swallowed the bait of professorial philosophy in believing that "introjection" was aimed against idealism. He accepted the evaluation of introjection given by Avenarius himself *at its face value* and

[48] A. Bogdanov, "Authoritative Thinking," an article in the symposium *From the Psychology of Society,* p. 119, *et seq.*

failed to notice the *barb* directed against materialism. Introjection denies that thought is a function of the brain, that sensations are functions of man's central nervous system: that is, it denies the most elementary truth of physiology in order to destroy materialism. "Dualism," it appears, is refuted *idealistically* (notwithstanding all Avenarius' diplomatic rage against idealism), for sensation and thought prove to be not secondary, not a product of matter, but *primary.* Dualism is here refuted by Avenarius only in so far as he "refutes" the existence of the object without the subject, matter without thought, the external world independent of our sensations; that is, it is refuted *idealistically.* The absurd denial of the fact that the visual image of a tree is a function of the retina, the nerves and the brain, was required by Avenarius in order to bolster up his theory of the "indissoluble" connection of the "complete" experience, which includes not only the self but also the tree, *i.e.,* the environment.

The doctrine of introjection is a muddle; it smuggles in idealistic rubbish and is contradictory to natural science, which inflexibly holds that thought is a function of the brain, that sensations, *i.e.,* the images of the *external world,* exist *within us,* produced by the action of things on our sense-organs. The materialist elimination of the "dualism of spirit and body" (*i.e.,* materialist monism) consists in the assertion that the spirit does not exist independently of the body, that spirit is secondary, a function of the brain, a reflection of the external world. The idealist elimination of the "dualism of spirit and body" (*i.e.,* idealist monism) consists in the assertion that spirit *is not* a function of the body, that, consequently, spirit is primary, that the "environment" and the "self" exist only in an inseparable connection of one and the same "complexes of elements." Apart from these two diametrically opposed methods of eliminating "the dualism of spirit and body," there can be no third method, unless it be eclecticism, which is a senseless jumble of materialism and idealism. And it was this jumble of Avenarius' that seemed to Bogdanov and Co. "the truth transcending materialism and idealism."

But the professional philosophers are not as naïve and credulous as are the Russian Machians. True, each of these professors-in-ordinary advocates his *"own"* system of refuting materialism, or, at any rate, of "reconciling" materialism and idealism. But when it comes to a competitor they unceremoniously expose the unconnected fragments of materialism and idealism that are contained in all the "recent" and "original" systems. And if a few young intellectuals swallowed Avenarius' bait, that old bird Wundt was not to be enticed so easily. The idealist Wundt tore the mask from the poseur Avenarius very unceremoniously *when he praised him for the anti-materialist tendency of the theory of introjection.*

"If empirio-criticism," Wundt wrote, "reproaches vulgar materialism because by such expressions as the brain 'has' thought, or the brain 'produces' thought, it expresses a relation which generally cannot be established by factual observation and description [evidently, for Wundt it is a "fact" that a person thinks without the help of a brain!] . . . this reproach, of course, is well-founded" (*op. cit.,* pp. 47-48).

Well, of course! The idealists will always join the halfhearted Avenarius and Mach in attacking materialism! It is only a pity, Wundt goes on to say, that this theory of introjection "does not stand in any relation to the doctrine of the independent vital series, and was, to all appearances, only tacked on to it as an afterthought and in a rather artificial fashion" (p. 365).

Introjection, says O. Ewald, "is to be regarded as nothing but a fiction of empirio-criticism, which the latter requires in order to shield its own fallacies" (*op. cit.,* p. 44). "We observe a strange contradiction: on the one hand, the elimination of introjection and the restoration of the natural world conception is intended to restore to the world the character of living reality; on the other hand, in the principal coordination empirio-criticism is leading to a purely idealist theory of an absolute correlation of the counter-term and the central term. Avenarius is thus moving in a circle. He set out to do battle against idealism but laid down his arms before it came to an open skirmish. He wanted to liberate the world of objects from the yoke of the subject, but again bound that world to the subject. What he has actually destroyed by his criticism is a caricature of idealism rather than its genuine epistemological expression" (*ibid.,* pp. 64-65).

"In his [Avenarius'] frequently quoted statement," Norman Smith says, "that the brain is not the seat, organ or supporter of thought, he rejects the only terms which we possess for defining their connection" (*op. cit.,* p. 30).

Nor is it surprising that the theory of introjection approved by Wundt appeals to the sympathy of the outspoken spiritualist, James Ward,[49] who wages systematic war on "naturalism and agnosticism," and especially on Huxley (not because he was an insufficiently outspoken and determined materialist, for which Engels reproached him, but) because his agnosticism served in fact to conceal materialism.

Let us note that Karl Pearson, the English Machian, who avoids all philosophical artifices, and who recognises neither introjection, nor coordination, nor yet "the discovery of the world-elements," arrives at the inevitable outcome of Machism when it is stripped of such "disguises," namely, pure subjective idealism. Pearson knows no "elements"; "sense impressions" are his alpha and omega. He never doubts that man thinks with the help of the brain. And the contradiction between this thesis (which alone conforms with science) and the basis of his philosophy remains naked and obvious. Pearson spares no effort in combating the concept that matter exists independently of our sense-impressions (*The Grammar of Science,* Chap. VII). Repeating all Berk-

[49] James Ward, *Naturalism and Agnosticism,* London, 1906, Vol. II, pp. 171-72.

eley's arguments, Pearson declares that matter is a nonentity. But when he comes to speak of the relation of the brain to thought, Pearson emphatically declares: "From will and consciousness associated with material machinery we can infer nothing whatever as to will and consciousness without that machinery." [50] He even advances the following thesis as a summary of his investigations in this field: "Consciousness has no meaning beyond nervous systems akin to our own; it is illogical to assert that all matter is conscious [but it is logical to assert that all matter possesses a property which is essentially akin to sensation, the property of reflection], still more that consciousness or will can exist outside matter" (*ibid.*, p. 75, 2nd thesis). Pearson's muddle is glaring! Matter is nothing but groups of sense-impressions. That is his premise, that is his philosophy. Hence, sensation and thought should be primary; matter, secondary. But no, consciousness without matter does not exist, and apparently not even without a nervous system! That is, consciousness and sensation are secondary. The waters rest on the earth, the earth rests on a whale, and the whale rests on the waters. Mach's "elements" and Avenarius' co-ordination and introjection do not clear up this muddle; all they do is to cover up traces with the help of an erudite philosophical gibberish.

Just such gibberish, and of this a word or two will suffice, is the terminology of Avenarius, who coined a plenitude of diverse "notals," "securals," "fidentials," etc., etc. Our Russian Machians for the most part shamefacedly avoid this professorial nonsense, and only now and again bombard the reader (in order to stun him) with an "existential" and such like. But if naïve people take these words for a special species of bio-mechanics, the German philosophers, who are themselves lovers of "erudite" words, laugh at Avenarius. To say "notal" (*notus* = known), or to say that this or the other thing is known to me, is absolutely one and the same, says Wundt in the section entitled *"Scholastischer Charakter des empiriokritischen Systems."* And, indeed, it is the purest and most dreary scholasticism. One of Avenarius' faithful disciples, R. Willy, had the courage to admit it. "Avenarius dreamed of a bio-mechanics," says he, ". . . but an understanding of the life of the brain can be arrived at only by actual discoveries . . . and not by the way in which Avenarius attempted to arrive at it. Avenarius' bio-mechanics is not grounded on any new observations whatever; its characteristic feature is purely schematic constructions of concepts, and, indeed, constructions that do not even bear the nature of hypotheses that open up new vistas, but rather of stereotyped speculations (*bloßen Spekulierschablonen*), which, like a wall, conceal our view." [51]

The Russian Machians will soon be like fashion-lovers who are

[50] Karl Pearson, *The Grammar of Science*, 2nd ed., London, 1900, p. 58.
[51] R. Willy, *Gegan die Schulweisheit*, p. 169. Of course, the pedant Petzoldt will not make any such admissions. With the smug satisfaction of the philistine he chews the cud of Avenarius' "biological" scholasticism (Vol. I, Chap. II).

moved to ecstasy over a hat which has already been discarded by the bourgeois philosophers of Europe.

6.   The solipsism of Mach and Avenarius

We have seen that the starting point and the fundamental premise of the philosophy of empirio-criticism is subjective idealism. The world is our sensation—this is the fundamental premise, which is obscured but in nowise altered by the word "element" and by the theories of the "independent series," "co-ordination," and "introjection." The absurdity of this philosophy lies in the fact that it leads to solipsism, to the recognition of the existence of the philosophising individual only. But our Russian Machians assure their readers that to "charge" Mach "with idealism and even solipsism" is "extreme subjectivism." So says Bogdanov in the introduction to the Russian translation of *Analyse der Empfindungen* (p. xi), and the whole Machian troop repeat it in a great variety of keys.

Having examined the methods whereby Mach and Avenarius disguise their solipsism, we have now to add only one thing: the "extreme subjectivism" of assertion lies entirely with Bogdanov and Co.; for in philosophical literature writers of the most varied trends have long since disclosed the fundamental sin of Machism beneath all its disguises. We shall confine ourselves to a mere *summary* of opinions which sufficiently indicate the "subjective" *ignorance* of our Machians. Let us note in passing that nearly every professional philosopher sympathises with one or another brand of idealism: in their eyes idealism is not a reproach, as it is with us Marxists; but they point out Mach's *actual* philosophical trend and oppose one system of idealism by another system, also idealist, but to them more consistent.

O. Ewald, in a book devoted to an analysis of Avenarius' teachings, writes: "The creator of empirio-criticism commits himself *volens nolens* to solipsism" (*loc. cit.*, pp. 61-62).

Hans Kleinpeter, a disciple of Mach with whom Mach in his preface to *Erkenntnis und Irrtum* explicitly declares his solidarity, says: "It is precisely Mach who is an example of the compatibility of epistemological idealism with the demands of natural science [for the eclectic everything is compatible], and of the fact that the latter can very well start from solipsism without stopping there" (*Archiv für systematische Philosophie,* 1900, Bd. VI, S. 87).

E. Lucka, analysing Mach's *Analyse der Empfindungen,* says: "Apart from this . . . misunderstanding (*Mißverständnis*) Mach adopts the ground of pure idealism. . . . It is incomprehensible that Mach denies that he is a Berkeleian" (*Kantstudien,* Bd. VIII, 1903, S. 416-17).

W. Jerusalem, a most reactionary Kantian with whom Mach in the above-mentioned preface expresses his solidarity ("a closer kinship" of thought than Mach had previously suspected—*Vorwort zu "Erkenntnis und Irrtum,"* S. X, 1906), says: "Consistent phenomenalism leads to solipsism." And therefore one must borrow a little from Kant! (See *Der kritische Idealismus und die reine Logik,* Wien, 1905, S. 26.)

R. Hönigswald says: ". . . the immanentists and the empirio-criticists face the alternative of solipsism or metaphysics in the spirit of Fichte, Schelling, or Hegel" (*Ueber die Lehre Humes von der Realität der Außendinge,* 1904, S. 68).

The English physicist Oliver Lodge, in his book denouncing the materialist Haeckel, speaks in passing, as though of something generally known, of "solipsists such as Mach and Karl Pearson" (*Life and Matter,* 1906, p. 8).

Nature, the organ of the English scientists, through the mouth of the geometrician E. T. Dixon, pronounced a very definite opinion of the Machian Pearson, one worth quoting, not because it is new, but because the Russian Machians have naïvely accepted Mach's philosophical muddle as the "philosophy of natural science" (A. Bogdanov, introduction to *Analyse der Empfindungen,* p. xii, *et seq.*).

"The foundation of the whole book," Dixon writes, "is the proposition that since we cannot directly apprehend anything but sense-impressions, therefore the things we commonly speak of as objective, or external to ourselves, and their variations, are nothing but groups of sense-impressions and sequences of such groups. But Professor Pearson admits the existence of other consciousness than his own, not only by implication in addressing his book to them, but explicitly in many passages." Pearson infers the existence of the consciousness of others by analogy, by observing the bodily motions of other people; but since the consciousness of others is real, the existence of people outside myself must be granted! "Of course it would be impossible thus to refute a consistent idealist, who maintained that not only external things but all other consciousness were unreal and existed only in his imagination; but to recognise the reality of other consciousnesses is to recognise the reality of the means by which we become aware of them, which . . . is the external aspect of men's bodies." The way out of the difficulty is to recognise the "hypothesis" that to our sense-impressions there corresponds an objective reality outside of us. This hypothesis satisfactorily explains our sense-impressions. "I cannot seriously doubt that Professor Pearson himself believes in them as much as anyone else. Only, if he were to acknowledge it explicitly, he would have to rewrite almost every page of *The Grammar of Science.*" [52]

Ridicule—that is the response of the thinking scientists to the idealist philosophy over which Mach waxes so enthusiastic.

And here, finally, is the opinion of a German physicist, L. Boltz-

[52] *Nature,* July 21, 1892, pp. 268-69.

mann. The Machians will perhaps say, as Friedrich Adler said, that he is a physicist of the old school. But we are concerned *now* not with theories of physics but with a fundamental philosophical problem. Writing against people who "have been carried away by the new epistemological dogmas," Boltzmann says: "Mistrust of conceptions which we can derive only from immediate sense-impressions has led to an extreme which is the direct opposite of former naïve belief. Only sense-impressions are given us, and, therefore, it is said, we have no right to go a step beyond. But to be consistent, one must further ask: are our sense-impressions of yesterday also given? What is immediately given is only the one sense-impression, or only the one thought, namely, the one we are thinking of at the present moment. Hence, to be consistent, one would have to deny not only the existence of other people outside one's self, but also all conceptions we ever had in the past." [53]

This physicist rightly regards the supposedly "new" "phenomenalist" view of Mach and Co. as the old absurdity of philosophical subjective idealism.

No, it is those who "failed to note" that solipsism is Mach's fundamental error who are stricken with "subjective" blindness.

ON DIALECTICS [1]

The division of the one and the cognition of its contradictory parts (see the quotation from Philo on Heraclitus at the beginning of Part III, "Knowledge," in Lassalle's book on Heraclitus) is the *essence* (one of the "essentials," one of the principals, if not the principal, characteristics or features) of dialectics. This is precisely how Hegel also puts the matter (Aristotle in his *Metaphysics* continually *grapples* with it and *combats* Heraclitus and Heraclitean ideas).

The correctness of this side of the content of dialectics must be tested by the history of science. This side of dialectics as a rule re-

[53] Ludwig Boltzmann, *Populäre Schriften,* Leipzig, 1905, S. 132. Vgl. S. 168, 177, 187, etc.
[1] From: Materialism and Empirio-Criticism, V. I. Lenin, pp. 377-381. International Publishers, New York, 1927.

ceives inadequate attention (*e.g.,* Plekhanov); the identity of opposites is taken as the sum total of *examples* ("for example, a seed," "for example, primitive Communism." The same is true of Engels. But with him it is "in the interests of popularisation . . .") and not as a *law of knowledge* (*and* as a law of the objective world):

In mathematics: $+$ and $-$. Differential and integral.

In mechanics: action and reaction.

In physics: positive and negative electricity.

In chemistry: the combination and dissociation of atoms.

In social science: the class struggle.

The identity of opposites (their "unity," perhaps it would be more correct to say?—although the difference between the terms identity and unity is not particularly important here. In a certain sense both are correct) is the recognition (discovery) of the contradictory, *mutually exclusive,* opposite tendencies in *all* phenomena and processes of nature (*including* mind and society). The condition for the knowledge of all processes of the world in their *"self-movement,"* in their spontaneous development, in their real life, is the knowledge of them as a unity of opposites. Development is the "struggle" of opposites. The two basic (or two possible? or two historically observable?) conceptions of development (evolution) are: development as decrease and increase, as repetition, *and* development as a unity of opposites (the division of the one into mutually exclusive opposites and their reciprocal relation).

In the first conception of motion, *self*-movement, its *driving* force, its sources, its motive, remains in the shade (or this source is made *external*—God, subject, etc.). In the second conception it is to the knowledge of the *source* of *"self"*-movement that attention is chiefly directed.

The first conception is lifeless, poor and dry. The second is vital. The second *alone* furnishes the key to the "self-movement" of everything in existence; it alone furnishes the key to the "leaps," to the "break in continuity," to the "transformation into the opposite," to the destruction of the old and the emergence of the new.

The unity (coincidence, identity, resultant) of opposites is conditional, temporary, transitory, relative. The struggle of mutually exclusive opposites is absolute, just as development and motion are absolute.

N.B. The distinction between subjectivism (scepticism, sophistry, etc.) and dialectics, incidentally, is that in (objective) dialectics the difference between the relative and the absolute is itself relative. For objective dialectics there is an absolute even *within* the relative. For subjectivism and sophistry the relative is only relative and excludes the absolute.

In his *Capital,* Marx first analyses the simplest, most ordinary, fundamental, most common and everyday *relation* of bourgeois (commodity) society, a relation that is encountered billions of times, *viz.,* the exchange of commodities. In this very simple phenomenon (in this "cell" of bourgeois society) analysis reveals *all* the contradictions (or the germs of *all* the contradictions) of modern society. The subsequent exposition shows us the development (*both* growth *and* movement) of these contradictions and of this society in the Σ^2 of its individual parts, from its beginning to its end.

Such must also be the method of exposition (or study) of dialectics in general (for with Marx the dialectics of bourgeois society is only a particular case of dialectics). To begin with the simplest, most ordinary, commonest, etc., *proposition, any* proposition one pleases: the leaves of a tree are green; John is a man; Fido is a dog, etc. Here already we have *dialectics* (as Hegel's genius recognised): the *singular* is the *general* (*cf.* Aristotle's *Metaphysics,* translated by Schwegler, Bd. II, S. 40, Buch 3, Kapitel IV, 8 und 9: *"denn natürlich kann man nicht der Meinung sein, daß es ein Haus* [a house in general] *gebe außer den sichtbaren Häusern,"* "οὐ γὰρ ἂν θείημεν εἶναί τινχ οἰκίχν παρὰ τὰς τινὰς οἰκίὰς").[3] Consequently; opposites (the singular as opposed to the general) are identical: the singular exists only in the connection that leads to the general. The general exists only in the singular and through the singular. Every singular is (in one way or another) a general. Every general is (a fragment, or a side, or the essence of) a singular. Every general only approximately comprises all the singular objects. Every singular enters into the general incompletely, etc., etc. Every singular is connected by thousands of transitions with other *kinds* of singulars (things, phenomena, processes), etc. *Here already* we have the elements, the germs, the concepts of *necessity,* of objective connection in nature, etc. Here already we have the contingent and the necessary, the appearance and the essence; for when we say: John is a man, Fido is a dog, *this* is a leaf of a tree, etc., we *disregard* a number of characteristics as *contingent;* we separate the essence from the appearance, and put one in opposition to the other.

Thus in *any* given proposition we can (and must) reveal as in a "cell" ("nucleus") the germs of *all* the elements of dialectics, and thereby show that dialectics is characteristic of all human knowledge in general. And natural science shows us (and here again it must be demonstrated in *any* given simple instance) objective nature with the same qualities, the transformation of the singular into the general, of the contingent into the necessary, transitions, modulations, and the reciprocal connection of opposites. Dialectics *is* the theory of knowledge of (Hegel and) Marxism. This is the "side" of the matter (it is not "a side" but the *essence* of the matter) to which Plekhanov not to speak of other Marxists, paid no attention.

---

2 Sum.—*Ed.*
3 For, evidently, one cannot hold the opinion that there can be a house apart from the visible houses.—*Ed.*

564   MARXISM AND THE PHILOSOPHY OF HISTORY

Knowledge is represented in the form of a series of circles both by Hegel (see his *Logik*) and by the modern "epistemologist" of natural science, the eclectic and foe of Hegelianism (which he did not understand!), Paul Volkmann (see his *Erkenntnistheoretische Grundzüge der Naturwissenschaft*).[4]

"Circles" in philosophy: (is a chronology of *persons* essential? No!).

Ancient: from Democritus to Plato and the dialectics of Heraclitus.

Renaissance: Descartes versus Gassendi (Spinoza?).

Modern: Holbach—Hegel (via Berkeley, Hume, Kant).

Hegel—Feuerbach—Marx.

Dialectics as a *living*, many-sided knowledge (with the number of sides eternally increasing) with an infinite number of shadings of every sort of approach and approximation to reality (with a philosophical system growing into a whole out of each shade)—here we have an immeasurably rich content as compared with "metaphysical" materialism, the fundamental *misfortune* of which is its inability to apply dialectics to the *Bildertheorie*,[5] to the process and development of knowledge.

Philosophical idealism is *only* nonsense from the standpoint of crude, simple, metaphysical materialism. On the other hand, from the standpoint of *dialectical* materialism, philosophical idealism is a *one-sided*, exaggerated, *überschwengliches*[6] (Dietzgen), development (inflation, distention) of one of the features, sides, facets of knowledge into an absolute, *divorced* from matter, from nature, apotheosised. Idealism is clericalism. True. But philosophical idealism is (*"more cor-*

	rectly" and *"in addition"*) a *road* to clericalism *through one*
NB:	*of the shades* of the infinitely complex *knowledge* (dialec-
this	tical) of man.
aphorism	

Human knowledge is not (or does not follow) a straight line, but a curve, which endlessly approximates to a series of circles, a spiral. Each fragment, segment, section of this curve can be transformed (transformed one-sidedly) into an independent, complete, straight line, which then (if one does not see the wood for the trees) leads into the quagmire, into clericalism (where it is *reinforced* by the class interests of the ruling classes). Rectilinearity and one-sidedness, stiffness and petrification, subjectivism and subjective blindness—*voilà*[7] the epistemological roots of idealism. And clericalism (= philosophical idealism), of course, has *epistemological* roots, it is not groundless; it is a *sterile flower* undoubtedly, but it is a sterile flower that grows on the living tree of living, fertile, genuine, powerful, omnipotent, objective, absolute human knowledge.

1915

[4] *Epistemological Foundations of Modern Science.—Ed.*
[5] Theory of reflection.—*Ed.*
[6] Extreme.—*Ed.*
[7] There you have.—*Ed.*

Karl Jaspers

THE AXIAL PERIOD[1]

In the Western World the philosophy of history was founded in the Christian faith. In a grandiose sequence of works ranging from St. Augustine to Hegel this faith visualised the movement of God through history. God's acts of revelation represent the decisive dividing lines. Thus Hegel could still say: All history goes toward and comes from Christ. The appearance of the Son of God is the axis of world history. Our chronology bears daily witness to this Christian structure of history.

But the Christian faith is only one faith, not the faith of mankind. This view of universal history therefore suffers from the defect that it can only be valid for believing Christians. But even in the West, Christians have not tied their empirical conceptions of history to their faith. An article of faith is not an article of empirical insight into the real course of history. For Christians sacred history was separated from profane history, as being different in its meaning. Even the believing Christian was able to examine the Christian tradition itself in the same way as other empirical objects of research.

An axis of world history, if such a thing exists, would have to be discovered *empirically,* as a fact capable of being accepted as such by all men, Christians included. This axis would be situated at the point in history which gave birth to everything which, since then, man has been able to be, the point most overwhelmingly fruitful in fashioning humanity; its character would have to be, if not empirically cogent and evident, yet so convincing to empirical insight as to give rise to a com-

[1] From: *The Origin and Goal of History,* Karl Jaspers, Part I, Ch. 1. Yale University Press, New Haven, 1953, and Routledge & Kegan Paul, Ltd., London, 1953. Reprinted by permission.

mon frame of historical self-comprehension for all peoples—for the West, for Asia, and for all men on earth, without regard to particular articles of faith. It would seem that this axis of history is to be found in the period around 500 B.C., in the spiritual process that occurred between 800 and 200 B.C. It is there that we meet with the most deepcut dividing line in history. Man, as we know him today, came into being. For short we may style this the 'Axial Period'.

A.   Characterisation of the Axial Period

The most extraordinary events are concentrated in this period. Confucius and Lao-tse were living in China, all the schools of Chinese philosophy came into being, including those of Mo-ti, Chuang-tse, Lieh-tsu and a host of others; India produced the Upanishads and Buddha and, like China, ran the whole gamut of philosophical possibilities down to scepticism, to materialism, sophism and nihilism; in Iran Zarathustra taught a challenging view of the world as a struggle between good and evil; in Palestine the prophets made their appearance, from Elijah, by way of Isaiah and Jeremiah to Deutero-Isaiah; Greece witnessed the appearance of Homer, of the philosophers—Parmenides, Heraclitus and Plato—of the tragedians, Thucydides and Archimedes. Everything implied by these names developed during these few centuries almost simultaneously in China, India, and the West, without any one of these regions knowing of the others.

What is new about this age, in all three areas of the world, is that man becomes conscious of Being as a whole, of himself and his limitations. He experiences the terror of the world and his own powerlessness. He asks radical questions. Face to face with the void he strives for liberation and redemption. By consciously recognising his limits he sets himself the highest goals. He experiences absoluteness in the depths of selfhood and in the lucidity of transcendence.

All this took place in reflection. Consciousness became once more conscious of itself, thinking became its own object. Spiritual conflicts arose, accompanied by attempts to convince others through the communication of thoughts, reasons and experiences. The most contradictory possibilities were essayed. Discussion, the formation of parties and the division of the spiritual realm into opposites which nonetheless remained related to one another, created unrest and movement to the very brink of spiritual chaos.

In this age were born the fundamental categories within which we still think today, and the beginnings of the world religions, by which human beings still live, were created. The step into universality was taken in every sense.

As a result of this process, hitherto unconsciously accepted ideas, customs and conditions were subjected to examination, questioned and liquidated. Everything was swept into the vortex. In so far as the traditional substance still possessed vitality and reality, its manifestations were clarified and thereby transmuted.

The *Mythical Age,* with its tranquillity and self-evidence, was at an end. The Greek, Indian and Chinese philosophers were unmythical in their decisive insights, as were the prophets in their ideas of God. Rationality and rationally clarified experience launched a struggle against the myth (*logos* against *mythos*); a further struggle developed for the transcendence of the One God against non-existent demons, and finally an ethical rebellion took place against the unreal figures of the gods. Religion was rendered ethical, and the majesty of the deity thereby increased. The myth, on the other hand, became the material of a language which expressed by it something very different from what it had originally signified: it was turned into parable. Myths were remoulded, were understood at a new depth during this transition, which was myth-creating after a new fashion, at the very moment when the myth as a whole was destroyed. The old mythical world slowly sank into oblivion, but remained as a background to the whole through the continued belief of the mass of the people (and was subsequently able to gain the upper hand over wide areas).

This overall modification of humanity may be termed *spiritualisation.* The unquestioned grasp on life is loosened, the calm of polarities becomes the disquiet of opposites and antinomies. Man is no longer enclosed within himself. He becomes uncertain of himself and thereby open to new and boundless possibilities. He can hear and understand what no one had hitherto asked or proclaimed. The unheard-of becomes manifest. Together with his world and his own self, Being becomes sensible to man, but not with finality: the question remains.

For the first time *philosophers* appeared. Human beings dared to rely on themselves as individuals. Hermits and wandering thinkers in China, ascetics in India, philosophers in Greece and prophets in Israel all belong together, however much they may differ from each other in their beliefs, the contents of their thought and their inner dispositions. Man proved capable of contrasting himself inwardly with the entire universe. He discovered within himself the origin from which to raise himself above his own self and the world.

In *speculative thought* he lifts himself up towards Being itself, which is apprehended without duality in the disappearance of subject and object, in the coincidence of opposites. That which is experienced in the loftiest flights of the spirit as a coming-to-oneself within Being, or as *unio mystica,* as becoming one with the Godhead, or as becoming a tool for the will of God is expressed in an ambiguous and easily misunderstood form in objectifying speculative thought.

It is the *specifically human in man* which, bound to and concealed within the body, fettered by instincts and only dimly aware of himself, longs for liberation and redemption and is able to attain to them already in this world—in soaring toward the idea, in the resignation of ataraxia, in the absorption of meditation, in the knowledge of his self and the world as *atman,* in the experience of *nirvana,* in concord with the *tao,* or in surrender to the will of God. These paths are widely divergent in their conviction and dogma, but common to all of them is man's reaching out beyond himself by growing aware of himself within the whole of Being and the fact that he can tread them only as an individual on his own. He may renounce all worldly goods, may withdraw into the desert, into the forest or the mountains, may discover as a hermit the creative power of solitude, and may then return into the world as the possessor of knowledge, as a sage or as a prophet. What was later called reason and personality was revealed for the first time during the Axial Period.

What the individual achieves is by no means passed on to all. The gap between the peaks of human potentiality and the crowd became exceptionally great at that time. Nonetheless, what the individual becomes indirectly changes all. The whole of humanity took a forward leap.

Corresponding to this new spiritual world, we find a *sociological* situation showing analogies in all three regions. There were a multitude of small States and cities, a struggle of all against all, which to begin with nevertheless permitted an astonishing prosperity, an unfolding of vigour and wealth. In China the small States and cities had achieved sovereign life under the powerless imperial rulers of the Chou dynasty; the political process consisted of the enlargement of small units through the subjection of other small units. In Hellas and the Near East small territorial units—even, to some extent, those subjected by Persia— enjoyed an independent existence. In India there were many States and free cities.

Reciprocal intercourse set a spiritual movement circulating within each of these three regions. The Chinese philosophers—Confucius, Mo-ti and others—wandered about the country and met in places of renown favourable to the spiritual life, founding schools which are termed academies by sinologists: the sophists and philosophers of Hellas travelled about in similar fashion and Buddha passed his entire life in wandering from place to place.

In the past, spiritual conditions had been comparatively enduring; despite catastrophes everything had repeated itself, confined within the horizons of a still, very slow spiritual movement that did not enter consciousness and was therefore not apprehended. Now, on the contrary, tension increases and causes a movement of torrential swiftness.

This movement reaches consciousness. Human existence becomes the object of meditation, as *history.* Men feel and know that something extraordinary is beginning in their own present. But this very realisation also makes men aware of the fact that this present was preceded by an infinite past. At the very commencement of this awakening of the specifically human spirit, man is sustained by memory and is conscious of belonging to a late or even a decadent age.

Men see themselves faced by *catastrophe* and feel the *desire to help* through insight, education and reform. The endeavour is made to dominate the course of events by planning, right conditions are to be re-established or brought about for the first time. History as a whole is seen as a sequence of shapes assumed by the world, either as a process of continual decline, or as a circular motion, or as an ascent. Thought is devoted to the manner in which human beings may best live together, may best be governed and administered. Practical activity is dominated by ideas of reform. Philosophers travel from State to State, become advisers and teachers, are scorned or sought after, enter into discussions and compete with one another. A sociological parallel can be drawn between Confucius' failure at the court of Wei and Plato's failure at Syracuse, between the school of Confucius, which trained future statesmen, and the academy of Plato, which served the same purpose.

The age that saw all these developments, which spanned several centuries, cannot be regarded as a simple upward movement. It was an age of simultaneous destruction and creation. No final consummation was attained. The highest potentialities of thought and practical expression realised in individuals did not become common property, because the majority of men were unable to follow in their footsteps. What began as freedom of motion finally became anarchy. When the age lost its creativeness, a process of dogmatic fixation and levelling-down took place in all three cultural realms. Out of a disorder that was growing intolerable arose a striving after new ties, through the re-establishment of enduring conditions.

The *conclusion* is at first of a political character. Mighty empires, made great by conquest, arose almost simultaneously in China (Tsin Shi hwang-ti), in India (Maurya dynasty) and in the West (the Hellenistic empires and the *Imperium Romanum*). Everywhere the first outcome of the collapse was an order of technological and organisational planning.

But the *relation to the spirit of what had gone before* remained everywhere. It became a model and an object of veneration. Its achievements and great personalities stood clearly in view and provided the content of schooling and education (Confucianism was evolved under the Han dynasty, Buddhism by Asoka, and the age of Augustus consciously established Graeco-Roman cultural education).

The universal empires which came into being at the end of the Axial Period considered themselves founded for eternity. But their stability was only apparent. Even though these empires lasted for a long time by comparison with the State-formations of the Axial Period, in the end they all decayed and fell to pieces. Subsequent millennia produced an extraordinary amount of change. From one point of view the disintegration and re-establishment of great empires has constituted history ever since the end of the Axial Period, as it had constituted it through the millennia during which the ancient civilisations were flourishing. During these millennia, however, it had possessed a different significance: it had lacked that spiritual tension which was first felt during the Axial Period and has been at work ever since, questioning all human activity and conferring upon it a new meaning.

B.   The structure of world history since the Axial Period

Reference to a few facts, such as I have made, does not suffice in itself to bring about complete conviction as to the truth of a particular view of history. Portrayal of the full wealth of historical material can alone cause the thesis either to appear in ever greater clarity or to be rejected. Such a portrayal is beyond the scope of a short book. The facts to which I have referred should be looked upon as a question and a challenge to put the thesis to the test.

Assuming this view of the Axial Period to be correct, it would seem to throw a light upon the entire history of the world, in such a way as to reveal something like a structure of world history. Let me endeavour to adumbrate this structure:

(1) The *thousands of years old ancient civilisations* are everywhere brought to an end by the Axial Period, which melts them down, assimilates them or causes them to sink from view, irrespective of whether it was the same peoples or others that became the bearers of the new cultural forms. Pre-Axial cultures, like those of Babylon, Egypt, the Indus valley and the aboriginal culture of China, may have been magnificent in their own way, but they appear in some manner unawakened. The ancient cultures only persist in those elements which enter into the Axial Period and become part of the new beginning. Measured against the lucid humanity of the Axial Period, a strange veil seems to lie over the most ancient cultures preceding it, as though man had not yet really come to himself. This fact is not obscured by isolated beginnings, moving in themselves, but without effect on the whole or on what followed (such as the Egyptian discourse of a man tired of life with his soul, the Babylonian psalms of repentence and the Gilgamesh). The monumental element in religion and religious art, and the extensive State-formations and juridical creations corresponding to it, are objects of awe and admiration to the consciousness of the Axial Period; they are even taken as models (by Confucius and Plato, for instance), but they are seen in a new light that transmutes their meaning.

Thus the imperial idea, which gains new force toward the end of the

Axial Period and terminates this era in the political domain, was a heritage from the ancient civilisations. But whereas it originally constituted a culture-creating principle, it now becomes the means by which a declining culture is stabilised by being laid in its coffin. It is as though the principle that once bore mankind upward, despite its factually despotic nature, had broken through afresh in the form of conscious despotism, but this time merely to preserve a culture in icy rigidity.

(2) *Until today* mankind has lived by what happened during the Axial Period, by what was thought and created during that period. In each new upward flight it returns in recollection to this period and is fired anew by it. Ever since then it has been the case that recollections and reawakenings of the potentialities of the Axial Period—renaissances—afford a spiritual impetus. Return to this beginning is the ever-recurrent event in China, India and the West.

(3) The Axial Period commenced within spatial limitations, but *it became historically all-embracing*. Any people that attained no part in the Axial Period remained 'primitive', continued to live that unhistorical life which had been going on for tens or even hundreds of thousands of years. Men living outside the three regions of the Axial Period either remained apart or came into contact with one of these three centres of spiritual radiation. In the latter event they were drawn into history. In the West this happened, for example, to the Germanic and Slav peoples, in the East to the Japanese, Malays and Siamese. For many primitive peoples this contact resulted in their extinction. All human beings living after the Axial Period either remained in a primitive state or took part in the new course of events, now the only one of fundamental significance. Once history had come into being, the primitive peoples represented the residue of prehistory, which occupied a continually shrinking space and has only now reached its final end.

(4) Between these three realms a *profound mutual comprehension was possible* from the moment they met. At the first encounter they recognised that they were concerned with the same problems. Despite the distance that separated them they at once became involved in one another. To be sure, they were not bound by the common possession of a single, objective truth (such a truth is only to be found in science which, methodologically conscious and compelling general assent to its propositions, is capable of spreading over the entire globe without undergoing any metamorphosis as a result and has a claim on the collaboration of all); but the authentically and absolutely true, which is lived by mankind historically from diverse origins, was seen and heard reciprocally in this encounter.

To sum up: The conception of the Axial Period furnishes the questions and standards with which to approach all preceding and subsequent developments. The outlines of the preceding civilisations dissolve. The peoples that bore them vanish from sight as they join in the movement of the Axial Period. The prehistoric peoples remain pre-historic until they merge into the historical movement that proceeds from the Axial Period, or die out. The Axial Period assimilates every-thing that remains. From it world history receives the only structure and unity that has endured—at least until our own time.

C.   Examination of the Axial Period thesis

I. DOES IT EXIST AS A FACT?

The earliest discussion of the facts of the Axial Period known to me is to be found in the works of Lasaulx and Viktor von Strauss.

Lasaulx (*Neuer Versuch einer Philosophie der Geschichte,* Munich, 1856, p. 115) writes: 'It cannot possibly be an accident that, six hun-dred years before Christ, Zarathustra in Persia, Gautama Buddha in India, Confucius in China, the prophets in Israel, King Numa in Rome and the first philosophers—Ionians, Dorians and Eleatics—in Hellas, all made their appearance pretty well simultaneously as reformers of the national religion.'

Viktor von Strauss, in his wonderful Lao-tse commentary, p. lxiv (1870), says: 'During the centuries when Lao-tse and Confucius were living in China, a strange movement of the spirit passed through all civilised peoples. In Israel Jeremiah, Habakkuk, Daniel and Ezekiel were prophesying and in a renewed generation (521-516) the second temple was erected in Jerusalem. Among the Greeks Thales was still living, Anaximander, Pythagoras, Heraclitus and Xenophanes ap-peared and Parmenides was born. In Persia an important reformation of Zarathustra's ancient teaching seems to have been carried through, and India produced Sakyamuni, the founder of Buddhism.'

Since then these facts have now and then been noted, but only mar-ginally. As far as I am aware, they have never been grasped as a whole, with the aim of demonstrating the universal parallels obtaining for the entire spiritual being of the humanity of that time. Let us consider pos-sible objections to this view.

(1) One objection might be that *the common element is only ap-parent.* The differences—differences of language and race, differences as to the types of empire and in the mode of historical recollection—are so great that, by comparison, the common element strikes us as no more than a series of coincidences. Every clear-cut formulation of the common element as a whole is refuted by the facts. Or, it is argued, it amounts to no more than the trivial maxim that fundamentally every-thing can be found everywhere amongst men, either as a beginning or as a potentiality. In the realisation of common human possibilities it is the differences which are essential, distinctive and historical; the whole

can never be apprehended as a unity, except in the unhistorical, universal characteristics of human existence.

The answer to this is: What is involved in the Axial Period is precisely the common element in an overall historical picture, the breakthrough to the principles which, right up to our own time, have been operative for humanity in borderline situations. The essential thing here is this common element, which does not stem from all over the earth, wherever man as such exists, but historically speaking solely from these three origins and the narrow area they occupy. The question is whether increasing knowledge will prove this common element to go even deeper than appeared at first, despite the differences that still remain. In that event, the temporal coincidence would become a fact, all the more astonishing the more clearly it is visualised. To demonstrate it thus convincingly would, however, demand a broader canvas.

(2) A further possible objection would be: The Axial Period is not a fact at all, but *the product of a judgement of value*. It is on the basis of a preconceived opinion that the achievements of this period are appraised so inordinately highly.

The answer to this is: In matters of the spirit, a fact can only be apprehended through the understanding of meaning. Understanding, however, is by its nature valuation. Though it rests empirically upon an accumulation of separate data, an historical construction never comes into being through these alone. Only through understanding do we arrive at our view of the Axial Period, as of the spirit of any historical period. And this view involves understanding and valuation at the same time; it includes the fact that we are emotionally moved, because we feel ourselves touched by it, because it concerns us as our own history and not merely as a past of which we can trace the effects, but as the past whose wider, more original effect, which is continually beginning afresh, is incalculable.

For this reason the whole man is the organon of historical research. 'Every man sees that which he bears within his own heart.' The source of understanding is our own present, the here and now, our sole reality. Thus the higher we ourselves ascend, the more clearly do we see the Axial Period.

If the hierarchy of the contents of history can only be grasped in the subjectivity of human existence, this subjectivity is not extinguished in the objectivity of something purely factual, but in the objectivity of communal perception—perception on the part of a community which man seeks after if he does not find himself already within it; for truth is that which links us to one another.

It is my thesis that in common understanding, which is inseparably bound up with valuation, we shall realise the significance of the Axial Period. This thesis is not, by the nature of the matter, susceptible of final proof; it can, however, be substantiated through a widening and deepening of the conception.

(3) A further objection may be: *This parallel is not historical in character*. For that which has no contact in spiritual intercourse does not share a common history.

This objection was already put forward against Hegel, who brought together China, India and the West as stages in the dialectical sequence of the development of the spirit. It was argued that here no real contact led from one stage to the next, as it did between the various stages in the development of the history of the West.

Our thesis, however, involves something altogether different. It is precisely this series of stages from China to Greece whose reality we deny; there is no such series, either in time or in meaning. The true situation was rather one of contemporaneous, side by side existence without contact. To begin with, several roads seem to lead from disparate origins toward the same goal. There is a multiplicity of the same in three shapes. There are three independent roots of one history, which later—after isolated and interrupted contacts, finally only a few centuries ago and properly speaking not until our own day—become a single unity.

The question at issue is, therefore, the nature of the parallelism involved.

II. WHAT IS THE NATURE OF THE PARALLELISM ASSERTED?

The facts of the Axial Period might represent nothing more than a number of synchronistic curiosities devoid of historical significance. Numerous strange synchronisms can be pointed to in world history. For example:

In the sixteenth century the Jesuits discovered in Japan a Buddhist sect which had flourished there since the thirteenth century. It seemed to bear (and actually did bear) an astonishing resemblance to Protestantism. According to the description given by the Japanologist Florenz (in the textbook by Chantepie de la Saussaye) their teaching was somewhat as follows: Man's own efforts contribute nothing toward his salvation. Everything depends upon faith, faith in Amida's loving kindness and aid. There are no meritorious good works. Prayer is not an achievement, but only an expression of gratitude for the redemption granted by Amida. 'If even the good shall enter into eternal life, how much more so shall sinners', said Shinran, the founder of the sect. As against traditional Buddhism it demanded: no works, no magical formulae or conjurations, no amulets, pilgrimages, atonements, fasts or other forms of asceticism. The layman has the same prospects of salvation as the priest and the monk. The priests are only a body of teachers to the laity. There is no more need for them to differ from the laity in their way of life and they wear the same clothes. Celibacy is abolished. The family is regarded as the best sphere of action for the religious life. Members of the sect are counselled to 'preserve order, obey the laws of the State and, as good citizens, to care for the wellbeing of their country'.

This example of synchronicity, which extends to identity with the basic doctrines of Lutheranism, is astonishing. Numerous other parallels occur throughout the centuries, from China to Europe. They have been tabulated on synchronistic charts.

The answer to this is:

Firstly: It can be said of many parallels in history, whether they are synchronistic or not, that they manifest a rule which holds good for single phenomena. Only in the Axial Period do we encounter a parallelism that follows no general law, but constitutes rather a specifically historical, unique fact of an all-embracing character which includes within itself all spiritual phenomena. The Axial Period is the only one that represents a total universal parallelism on the plane of world history, and not merely the chance concurrence of particular phenomena. Single phenomena or series of phenomena do not suffice to establish the kind of parallelism with which we are dealing in the Axial Period.

Secondly, the three parallel movements are close to each other only during those centuries. The attempt to prolong the parallels beyond the Axial Period—in synchronistic tables spanning millennia—becomes increasingly artificial. The lines of subsequent development do not run parallel, but rather diverge. Though originally they appeared like three roads directed toward the same goal, they finally became deeply estranged from one another. But the farther back we go toward the Axial Period, the closer our relationship becomes, the closer we feel to one another.

It seems to me continually more unlikely that this overall aspect of the Axial Period should be no more than an illusion created by historical coincidence. It seems rather to be the manifestation of some profound common element, the one primal source of humanity. What followed later in the course of increasing divergence produces occasional analogies, marks of a common origin, but never again *in toto* that real, original community of meaning.

The only comparable world historical parallelism occurs at the commencement of the ancient civilisations in Egypt, Mesopotamia, the Indus valley and China.

Within this temporal coincidence, however, there are differences of millennia. The beginnings stretch from 5000 to 3000 B.C. (Mesopotamia and Egypt; the earliest discoveries on Crete and at Troy date from the same period). The beginnings of the Chinese and Indus civilisations fall within the third millennium B.C.

Comparable to these ancient civilisations are those of Mexico and Peru, which are conjectured to have arisen during the first millennium A.D.

Their common properties are highly developed organisation and a high level of technical achievement. In Egypt, Mesopotamia, the Indus valley and in China along the banks of the Hwang-ho, analogous civilisations sprang up in the river valleys characterised by the central administration of a highly evolved mechanism for satisfying the needs of the community.

They also have in common a magical religion destitute of philosophical enlightenment, devoid of any quest for salvation and lacking any break-through into liberty in the face of extreme situations, as well as a singular apathy accompanying extraordinary stylistic achievements in art; especially, in the case of some of these civilisations, in architecture and sculpture.

However, this parallelism does not exhibit the same synchronism as does that of the Axial Period. Moreover it consists only of the similarity of an established type, not of a spiritual movement. It involves strangely stable conditions which, after destructive catastrophe, tend to reconstitute themselves in their old form. It is a world between prehistory, which is almost a closed book to us, and history proper which no longer permits things to remain constant in the realm of the spirit. It is a world which furnished the basis for the Axial Period, but was submerged in and by the latter.

III. WHAT CAUSED THE FACTS OF THE AXIAL PERIOD?

If the facts of the Axial Period are beyond dispute, we must now ask ourselves what caused them. Why did the same thing happen at three mutually independent points? The fact that these three regions were originally unknown to each other seems, at first, to be entirely extraneous—but it is an historical mystery which progressive research into the facts of the situation renders increasingly great. The Axial Period, with its overwhelming plenitude of spiritual creations, which has determined all human history down to the present day, is accompanied by the enigma of the occurrence, in these three mutually independent regions, of an analogous and inseparably connected process.

Apart from the Axial Period, the mystery of simultaneity applies, as we have shown, to perhaps only one other situation in the whole of world history: the genesis of the ancient civilisations. The question is, why did the development from the general condition of prehistoric peoples to the ancient civilisations take place more or less simultaneously —despite intervals of up to two millennia—in the river valleys of the Nile, of Mesopotamia, the Indus, and the Hwang-ho?

The usual answer is that analogous tasks (provision of irrigation and the fight against floods) had similar consequences. But in that case, why simultaneously? Why only in respect of these particular rivers? Why much later and under different conditions in America?

Commercial and cultural exchanges might have had a releasing effect. At all times civilising achievements of a craft character have slowly made their way across the earth, or at least the entire Eurasian continent. The invention of writing may possibly have taken place at a single spot and spread from there; without it the tasks of administration, and especially of river-control, would have been insuperable. But these are only possibilities. Such exchanges can be proved to have occurred in the third millennium between the Sumerian culture of Mesopotamia and the culture of the Indus valley; they existed between Egypt and Babylonia in early times, being very active during the second millennium.

But the multiple developments leading up to the ancient civilisations of the early millennia cannot be explained in terms of diffusion from a single source. E. Meyer (*Geschichte des Altertums,* I, 2, p. 935) therefore remarks: 'We must assume that around 5000 B.C. the genus *homo* had reached a stage in his evolution that opened up to all human groups or peoples, whose inherent aptitudes (i.e. the spiritual forces latent with them) rendered them capable of rising above this level at all, the way toward the genesis of a culture which would thereafter continue to advance.' The parallel phenomena would, in that event, have to be regarded as simultaneous developments in the biological evolution of human beings who are members of a similarly endowed humanity. That which, by virtue of a common origin, is dormant in all of them, manifests itself simultaneously and independently—as happens during the life-span of identical twins who have been separated from one another.

But this idea is a mere figure of speech which explains nothing. It is empty because it provides no basis for further research. The 'evolution of the genus *homo*' is not a reality that can be apprehended as such or serve as an explanation of anything. And, above all, this 'biological evolution' would only have been accomplished by a small, scattered section of mankind, not by mankind as a whole.

The mystery of the simultaneous inception of the Axial Period appears to me to be situated at a much deeper level than the problem of the birth of the ancient civilisations. In the first place, the simultaneity is much more exact and, in the second, it relates to spiritual-historical developments in the whole conscious, thinking aspect of humanity. The three regions which, from the beginnings of the ancient civilisations onward, were possessed of a unique character, brought forth creations during the millennium before Christ upon which the entire history of the human spirit has rested ever since.

These developments were originally independent of one another. Real communications and stimuli must be ruled out. Only after the penetration of Buddhism into China, which took place at the end of the Axial Period, did a profound spiritual communication between

India and China come into being. Though there had always been relations between India and the Alest, these only became extensive during Roman times, *via* Alexandria. But the origin of these developments is not affected at all by the relations between India and the West, their further course not visibly so.

Let us see how this mystery has been explained:

Lasaulx writes: 'This strange concurrence can only be founded on the inner unity of substance in the life of mankind and the life of peoples, on a vibration of the total life of humanity which passed through all peoples, and not on the particular efflorescence of the spirit of any one people.' But that is not an explanation, it is merely a paraphrase of the mystery.

V. von Strauss talks of a hidden law: 'This phenomenon, for which there is no lack of parallels in history, and from which very mysterious laws may be inferred, probably has its roots, on the one hand, in the total organism of mankind, by virtue of its homogeneous origin, while on the other it presupposes the influence of a higher spiritual power, in the same way that the urge to florescence in nature only arrives at the unfolding of its magnificence through the vivifying rays of the returning sun.' But, as with Lasaulx, such figures of speech only paraphrase the mystery. In addition they make the mistake of levelling down the uniqueness of the historical fact of the parallels of the Axial Period in the name of supposedly similar instances of shared development throughout history.

Keyserling says (*Buch vom Ursprung,* p. 151): 'From generation to generation men seem to change in the same fashion and in the same direction, and at turning-points of history a similar change embraces enormous areas and peoples who are complete strangers to one another.' But this again is simply a paraphrase of the mystery, and a bad one at that, because it sinks down completely into the realm of biology without there being the slightest basis for approaching the problem from a biological standpoint.

All these explanations overlook the clear fact that it was not mankind, not all men, who by that time had occupied the entire planet, but only a few, relatively very few, who took this step forward at three points. As in the case of the ancient civilisations not mankind as such, but only a small section was involved.

Instead, therefore, of taking as a basis a biology of mankind, something falsely supposed to be held in common and valid for the whole of humanity, the attempt has been made to trace back the few peoples amongst whom this revolution occurred to a *common historical origin* within mankind. This origin is admittedly unknown to us. It would have to be assumed to lie in prehistoric Central Asia. With their source in such a common origin the parallel developments could perhaps be considered related. But this hypothesis has so far eluded all possibility of verification. It is improbable because it would have to prove a common origin for such disparate racial groups as the Chinese, the Indo-Europeans and the Semites; furthermore, this common origin would have to be taken as only a few millennia prior to the period at which the inception of these peoples' history becomes visible to us—biologically speaking a very short space of time and hardly sufficient to allow profound racial differentiations to take place.

In response to the question, why this simultaneity? only one methodologically arguable hypothesis has so far been advanced, that put forward by Alfred Weber. The penetration of the nations of charioteers and horsemen from Central Asia—which did, in fact, reach China, India and the West and introduced the horse to the ancient civilisations—had, so he argues, analogous consequences in all three regions. The men of these equestrian peoples came to experience, thanks to the horse, the limitless vastness of the world. They took over the ancient civilisations by conquest. In hazards and disasters they experienced the problematic character of existence, as master-peoples they developed an heroico-tragic consciousness that found expression in the epic.

This turning-point of history was brought about by the Indo-European nations of horsemen. By the end of the third millennium they had reached Europe and the Mediterranean. A great new thrust carried them as far as Iran and India round about 1200. In the same way, other nations of horsemen reached China by the end of the second millennium.

Before, from Europe to China, there had been the ancient civilisations reaching back into the depths of the past and characterised variously as matriarchal, as civilisations of settled cattle-breeders, or simply as the population masses flourishing in closed self-sufficiency in the fertile regions of the belt of civilisation extending from China to Europe.

History became a conflict between these two forces: the old, stable, unawakened matriarchal powers against the new, mobile, liberating tendencies of the equestrian peoples which were rising into consciousness.

Alfred Weber's thesis demonstrates the existence of a real uniformity within the Eurasian bloc; how far the appearance of the equestrian peoples was decisive is difficult to determine, however. Geographical situations and historical constellations may have given rise to the preconditions; but what set the work of creation in motion remains the great enigma.

Weber's thesis possesses a singular power of illumination arising out of its simple, causal explanation based on the human character of the life of the horseman. But it still applies at most to a precondition. The contents of the Axial Period are so remarkable and all-embracing that one hesitates to derive them from such a cause, even if it be regarded as only a necessary precondition. Counter-evidence is afforded, for example, by China, which produced the rich contents of the Axial Period, but neither the tragic consciousness nor the epic (in China nothing comparable to the epic appears until the centuries after Christ, during the period of long-drawn-out struggles against new peoples, corresponding to our migration of the peoples). A further contradictory instance is Palestine, whose population experienced no mingling with equestrian peoples and yet, through the prophets, produced an essential factor in the spiritual creation of the Axial Period.

The credibility of the hypothesis is further impaired by the fact that movements, migrations and conquests had been precipitating themselves upon the ancient civilisations for millennia; to this is added the further fact that the period of incubation between the Indo-European invasions—themselves distributed over a period of more than a thousand years—and the inception of the spiritual development of the Axial Period was very long, while this inception, when it took place, did so with such astonishingly exact simultaneity.

That it is necessary to enquire after the historical reason for the events of the Axial Period is due to the fact that it is a question of a new departure within mankind—involving small areas only—and not of a development shared by the whole of humanity. The Axial Period does not represent a universal stage in human evolution, but a singular ramified historical process.

Whereas Alfred Weber has given an ingenious and clearcut reply to this question, that can be put to the test and rendered fruitful by further discussion, the mystery of the lack of contact between the three independent origins has usually been veiled by the vague assertion of a general Eurasian interrelationship. Perhaps, so it is meaninglessly said, influences no longer apparent to us were at work. The unity of the history of the whole Eurasian bloc, determined by constantly renewed advances, migrations and conquests from Central Asia, is pointed to, as well as the demonstrable parallels that can be observed in archaeological finds of a technological and ornamental character. These finds go back to early prehistory and permit a perpetual cultural exchange over the entire major continent to be inferred. Against this, however, it must be said that the spiritual movement of the Axial Period, in its simultaneity and the sublimity of its content, cannot be accounted for in terms of such migrations and exchanges.

In the end, the simplest explanation of the phenomena of the Axial Period seems to lie in common sociological preconditions favourable to spiritual creativeness: many small States and small towns: a politically divided age engaged in incessant conflicts; the misery caused by wars and revolutions accompanied by simultaneous prosperity elsewhere, since destruction was neither universal nor radical; questioning of previously existing conditions. These are sociological considerations which are meaningful and lead to methodical investigation, but ultimately they merely illuminate the facts and do not provide a causal explanation of them. For these conditions form part of the total spiritual phenomenon of the Axial Period. They are preconditions of which the creative result is not a necessary sequel; as part of the overall pattern their own origin remains in question.

No one can adequately comprehend what occurred here and became the axis of world history! The facts of this break-through must be seen from all sides, their many aspects must be fixed in the mind and their meaning interpreted, in order to gain a provisional conception of the Axial Period, which grows more mysterious the more closely we examine it.

It might seem as though I were out to prove direct intervention on the part of the deity, without saying so openly. By no means. For that would not only be a *salto mortale* of cognition into pseudo-knowledge, but also an importunity against the deity. I want rather to prevent the comfortable and empty conception of history as a comprehensible and necessary movement of humanity; I should like to maintain awareness of the dependence of our cognition upon current standpoints, methods and facts and, thereby, of the particularity of all cognition; I should like to hold the question open and leave room for possible new starting-points in the search for knowledge, which we cannot imagine in advance at all.

Wonder at the mystery is itself a fruitful act of understanding, in that it affords a point of departure for further research. It may even be the very goal of all understanding, since it means penetrating through the greatest possible amount of knowledge to authentic nescience, instead of allowing Being to disappear by absolutising it away into a self-enclosed object of cognition.

IV. THE MEANING OF THE AXIAL PERIOD

The problem of the meaning of the Axial Period is something quite different from that of its cause.

The fact of the threefold manifestation of the Axial Period is in the nature of a miracle, in so far as no really adequate explanation is possible within the limits of our present knowledge. The hidden meaning of this fact, however, cannot be discovered empirically at all, as a meaning somewhere intended by someone. In enquiring after it we are really only putting our own interpretation on the facts and causing something to grow out of them for us. If, in the process, we make use of terms which seem to indicate that we have in mind some plan of providence, these are only metaphors.

(*a*) Really to visualise the facts of the Axial Period and to make them the basis of our universal conception of history is to gain possession of something *common to all mankind,* beyond all differences of creed. It is one thing to see the unity of history from one's own

ground and in the light of one's own faith, another to think of it in communication with every other human ground, linking one's own consciousness to the alien consciousness. In this sense, it can be said of
the centuries between 80 and 200 B.C. that they are the empirically
evident axis of world history for all men.

The transcendental history of the revealed Christian faith is made
up out of the creation, the fall, stages of revelation, prophecies, the appearance of the Son of God, redemption and the last judgement. As
the contents of the faith of an historical human group it remains untouched. That which binds all men together, however, cannot be revelation but must be experience. Revelation is the form taken by particular historical creeds, experience is accessible to man as man. We—
all men—can share the knowledge of the reality of this universal transformation of mankind during the Axial Period. Although confined to
China, India and the West, and though there was to begin with no
contact between these three worlds, the Axial Period nonetheless
founded universal history and, spiritually, drew all men into itself.

(b) The fact of the threefold historical modification effected by the
step we call the Axial Period acts as a *challenge to boundless communication*. To see and understand others helps in the achievement of
clarity about oneself, in overcoming the potential narrowness of all
self-enclosed historicity, and in taking the leap into expanding reality.
This venture into boundless communication is once again the secret of
becoming-human, not as it occurred in the inaccessible prehistoric past,
but as it takes place within ourselves.

This demand for communication—made by the historical fact of the
threefold origin—is the best remedy against the erroneous claim to
exclusive possession of truth by any one creed. For a creed can only
be absolute in its historical existence, not universally valid for all in
its predications, like scientific truth. The claim to exclusive possession
of truth, that tool of fanaticism, of human arrogance and self-deception through the will to power, that disaster for the West—most in-
tensely so in its secularised forms, such as the dogmatic philosophies
and the so-called scientific ideologies—can be vanquished by the very
fact that God has manifested himself historically in several fashions and
has opened up many ways toward Himself. It is as though the deity
were issuing a warning, through the language of universal history,
against the claim to exclusiveness in the possession of truth.

(c) If the Axial Period gains in importance with the degree to which
we immerse ourselves in it, the question arises: *Is this period, are its
creations, the yardstick* for all that follows? If we do not consider the
quantitative aspect of its effect, nor the extent of the areas involved in
its political processes, nor the pre-eminence accorded to spiritual phenomena throughout the centuries, is it still true that the austere grandeur, the creative lucidity, the depth of meaning and the extent of
the leap toward new spiritual worlds contained in the phenomena of

the Axial Period are to be regarded as the spiritual peak of all history up to the present? Do later manifestations, in spite of the heights to which they attained and in spite of having become irreplaceable in their turn, pale before the earlier—Virgil before Homer, Augustus before Solon, Jesus before Jeremiah?

It would certainly be wrong to answer this question with a mechanical affirmative. The later manifestation invariably possesses a value of its own, which was not present in the earlier one: a maturity of its own, a sublime costliness, a depth of soul, especially in the case of the 'exception'. It is quite impossible to arrange history in a heirarchy of values following automatically from one universally applicable conception. But the manner in which this question is formulated—and also, perhaps, a prejudice against the later—does result from an understanding of the Axial Period. This in turn illumines what is specifically new and great after a different fashion and does not belong to the Axial Period. For example: Anyone studying philosophy is likely to find that after months with the Greek philosophers, St. Augustine affects him like a liberation from coldness and impersonality into questions of conscience, which have remained with us ever since the time of St. Augustine but were alien to the Greeks. Conversely, however, after spending some time on St. Augustine, he will experience an increasing desire to return to the Greeks and cleanse himself of the feeling of impurity that seems to grow with the pursuit of this type of thinking, to regain his health by immersion in the pellucid waters of Greek thought. Nowhere on earth can we find final truth, authentic salvation.

The Axial Period too ended in failure. History went on.

Only this much seems certain to me: Our present-day historical consciousness, as well as our consciousness of our present situation, is determined, down to consequences I have only been able to hint at, by the conception of the Axial Period, irrespective of whether this thesis is accepted or rejected. It is a question of the manner in which the unity of mankind becomes a concrete reality for us.

THE PRESENT SITUATION OF
THE WORLD[1]

Introduction

Of the past we have but an incomplete recollection, the future is obscure. Of the present alone we might expect to form a lucid picture. After all, we are in the midst of it. But it is precisely the present as such that is opaque to us, for it would grow clear only through complete knowledge of the past, by which it is borne, and of the future, which it conceals within it. We should like to achieve awareness of the situation of our epoch. But this situation contains hidden possibilities, which will only become visible once they have been realised.

What is historically new and, for the first time in history, decisive about our situation is the real unity of mankind on the earth. The planet has become for man a single whole dominated by the technology of communications; it is 'smaller' than the Roman Empire was formerly.

The course of development since the Age of Discovery, four hundred years ago, led up to this moment. Until the end of the nineteenth century, however, history remained for us essentially European history. To the European consciousness of that time, the rest of the world was colonial territory, of secondary importance, destined as a source of booty for Europe. It was only unintentionally that the foundations of the world history which is at present unfolding were already laid at that time by the powers that were seeking to win the great spaces of the earth for themselves. In the First World War these spaces were already brought into play. It was still a European war, however. America withdrew again. It was only in the Second World War that all of them, the whole globe, were committed to the full. The war in Eastern Asia was as grave a matter as the war in Europe. In fact it was the first real

[1] From: *The Origin and Goal of History*, Karl Jaspers, Part II, Ch. 2. Yale University Press, New Haven, 1953, and Routledge & Kegan Paul, Ltd., London, 1953. Reprinted by permission.

World War. World history, as one single history of the whole world, had begun. From our vantage point, the interlude of previous history has the appearance of an area scattered with mutually independent endeavours, as the multiple origin of the potentialities of man. Now the whole world has become the problem and task. With this a total metamorphosis of history has taken place.

The essential fact is: There is no longer anything outside. The world is closed. The unity of the earth has arrived. New perils and new opportunities are revealed. All the crucial problems have become world problems, the situation a situation of mankind.

A.   *Characterisation of the present situation*

I. THE MASSES HAVE BECOME A DECISIVE FACTOR IN THE HISTORICAL PROCESS

All previous history occurred under conditions that were relatively stable in comparison with those of today. The peasantry represented the mass of the population and remained fairly constant in its mode of life, despite catastrophic political events. It constituted the unhistorical substance of the population. The agrarian crises that occurred again and again in historical times brought upheavals, but no radical changes. The mutations of social conditions proceeded slowly and only affected individual classes and groups, within an overall condition that was felt to be permanent. As far as their consciousness was concerned men remained comparatively secure in immutable orders, even if they had to starve. They endured and submitted, and lived in a pervading religious faith.

Today things are different. Social conditions are in ceaseless flux. This flux has become conscious. The whole population of the earth has been torn out of its immemorial traditional orders and forms of consciousness. Consciousness of security is constantly diminishing. Human masses are becoming more integral. Everyone is learning to read and write. If they did not they could not come to knowledge, could not acquire a language in which to express their will, nor make their influence felt.

The masses are becoming a decisive factor. To be sure, the individual is more powerless than ever, but the individual as a member of the mass, the 'we', seems to be gaining possession of a will.

This will cannot grow originally in an anonymous mass, however. It is aroused and guided by propaganda. The masses need ideas and slogans. They have to be told what they want. But the soil for that which is told them must be ready within them. The statesman, the thinker, the artist, the poet must appeal to forces in the masses, if he wishes to have any effect. What forces these will be cannot be stated

in advance. Leaders are characterised by the impulses, value judge-
ments, and passions to which they appeal. But what they stimulate in
the masses has a retroactive effect on the leaders. The masses determine what the leaders themselves must be and what they must become
in reaction. They are exponents of the will of the masses, unless they
become dictators over masses of directed slaves.

Mass is a concept capable of several interpretations, however.
The mass means either the bulk of the population (and as such is
present at all times), or the momentary expression and comportment
of people under the influence of suggestion (and as such appears as
suddenly as it vanishes again), or it is the inferiority of the many, of
the average, whose existence determines everything by the mass pressure which it exercises (and as such is the manifestation of an historical
situation under certain conditions and by no means definitively inferior).

A distinction must be made between mass and people:

The people is subdivided into orders, is conscious of itself in ways of
life, modes of thought, and cultural heritage. A people is something
substantial and qualitative, it possesses a communal atmosphere; the
individual from the people has a personal character that is partly derived from the strength of the people by which he is borne.

The mass, on the other hand, is not subdivided, is unconscious of itself, uniform and quantitative, devoid of specific character and cultural
heritage, without foundations and empty. It is the object of propaganda, destitute of responsibility, and lives at the lowest level of consciousness.

Masses arise where men come to be without an authentic world,
without provenance or roots, disposable and exchangeable. In consequence of technology this state of affairs is growing more and more
widespread: the narrowed horizon, life that does not look ahead and is
devoid of effective recollection, the compulsion of meaningless labour,
amusement in the dissipation of leisure, excitation of the nerves mas-
querading as life, deception in the illusion of love, fidelity and trust, betrayal, especially in youth, resulting in cynicism: no one who has been
involved in this sort of thing can still respect himself. *Via* despair in the
garb of liveliness and obstinacy the road leads into oblivion and indifference, into the condition in which corporate human life is a sandheap
that can be made use of, set to work, or deported, and that is treated
in the light of qualities which can be given a number and counted by
means of tests.

The individual is both, people and mass at the same time. He feels
quite differently, however, where he is people and where he is mass.
The situation forces him into the mass, man holds fast to the people.
Illustrated by some comparative examples: As mass I thrust into the
universal, into the current fashion, into the cinema, into the mere today; as people I want corporeal, irreplaceable reality, the living theatre,

the historically present—as mass I applaud the star on the conductor's dais; as people I experience in my intimate self the music that soars above life—as mass I think in numbers, accumulate, level; as people I think in hierarchies of value and in structure.

A distinction is to be made between mass and public.

Public is the first step along the path of the transformation of people into mass. It is the echo of poetry, art, literature. When the people no longer lives comprehensively out of its community, there develops a multiplicity of separate publics, amorphous like the mass, but a forum for spiritual things in free competition. For whom does the writer write when he is free? Today he no longer writes for the people, and not yet for the mass. He woos and wins his public, if he is lucky. The people possesses enduring books that accompany its life; the public changes, is without character. But where there is public there is still a lively open forum.

The transformation of the people into public and mass can no longer be brought to a stop. The situation compels the progress of events through the medium of the masses. But mass is not something definitive. It is the mode of existence during the dissolution of humanity. Every individual in it remains a human being. The question is, to what extent is the individual and his intimate world—under the epithet 'private world' today so often the object of overweening contempt—giving birth to the new beginnings which may ultimately lead to the recovery of humanity out of the mass.

We can see the past by its pinnacles. Then it is as if, on the broad substratum of mass-existence, of which little historical information has come down to us, lofty spiritual creation made proper history. It is the life and activities of individuals, who, in the continuity that runs through the ages, call to each other as friends and foes. Every individual has his community, however, the human beings who belong to him and from whom he hears, to whom he is important, he has his circle of friends, his people in the shape of language and spiritual heritage, his public.

Now today this community is inevitably the world that is determined by the masses. That alone will remain which is assimilated by the masses. The path of history today runs inexorably *via* the masses, or seems to do so. Popular education may put the multitude on the road to spiritual nobility—a *de facto* process of natural selection, which is going on all the time, may engender a new factual aristocracy without hereditary privileges—the abolition of social repression and political terror may cause the disappearance of the rebellious and negativist way of thinking, by which the masses have, for the moment, been seized.

The school, natural selection operating in free competition, and continual improvement of the still unjust human conditions in the direction of greater social justice, may, to the accompaniment of constant tensions, blaze the trail to growing freedom.

Their failure may open the door to inconceivable horrors of abysmal mass existence. Everyone who wants to be of some account desires to go with the masses. Many thinkers presuppose that the masses are making for some particular point, and that the truth is to know this and act accordingly. Human masses as such, however, are not a person, they do not know or want anything; they are without content and a tool for anyone who flatters their universal psychological impulses and passions. Human masses are easily able to lose the power of deliberation, rush into the intoxication of change for the sake of change, and follow the Pied Piper, who leads them into the inferno. It is easy for the conditions of interaction between unreasoning masses and directing tyrants to develop. But it is also possible that the rationally striving labour of the real spirit may develop in the masses themselves, this labour that takes place in gradual changes of conditions, which no one observes in their entirety, but in which so much reason prevails that an ordered existence, free work and free creation become possible in an incalculable degree.

The world would ascend to a pinnacle of history wherever that which was formerly confined to the aristocracy became real in the masses themselves: education, disciplined moulding of the life and thought of the individual, capacity to learn and to win a part in the spirit, to reflect and deliberate and to find the rational solution historically in the most powerful tensions of men who confront one another at once critically and in solidarity.

Today, however, the monstrous peril is this: Whereas the events of all former history had little effect on the substance of humanity, this substance itself seems now to be in flux, to be threatened at its core. The instability in everything sets the problem of what man, on the basis of knowledge and technology, and out of the origin of his nature, will make of his existence. In this the situation forces us to follow the unavoidable path of the masses.

II. THE DISSOLUTION OF TRADITIONAL VALUES

Formerly, religions were bound up with the totality of social conditions. Religion was borne by these conditions, which, in turn, it justified. The conduct of everyday life was embedded in religion. The latter was taken for granted as the omnipresent breath of life. Today religion is a matter of choice. It is retained in a world which is no longer permeated by it. Not only do the various religions and confessions stand side by side and by the mere fact of doing so, cast doubt upon one another; in addition, religion itself has become a special domain, unconnected with the rest of life. The traditional religions are becoming untenable to an increasingly large number of people: almost all dogmas and revelation in its exclusive claim to absolute truth are disbelieved.

The *de facto* unchristian lives of the majority of Christians is a criticism to which it is impossible to close one's ears. A Christian life in its manifestness and unquestionable truth may perhaps still be real today as a compelling model for imitation, but it no longer exists for the masses.

In all ages in which men have thought and written since the Axial Period, there has been doubt. But now the dissolution is no longer an affair of isolated individuals and small circles. It has become a ferment in the whole population. Although men have at all times been ready to lose their faith, this apostasy never involved more than a narrow sector. Under the conditions of work and life in ages past, the population remained secure in its religious bonds. The conditions of the Age of Technology, however, have proved conducive to an outbreak of nihilistic possibilities in the whole of the population, that has degenerated into a mass.

The ever-present readiness to loss of faith is today fostered by spiritual movement as such, by misunderstood science—by misunderstanding on the part of the masses. Bacon's words have been proved right: Half knowledge leads to unbelief, whole knowledge to belief.

Our era's growing lack of faith has brought nihilism. Nietzsche is its prophet. He was the first to see it in its calamitous magnitude, to disclose it in all its manifestations, to suffer it himself as the victim of his time, to seek with a mighty effort to overcome it—in vain.

Nihilism, which was previously powerless in its sporadic beginnings, has become a dominant mode of thought. Today it seems possible that the whole of the cultural heritage since the Axial Period will be lost, that history from Homer to Goethe will sink into oblivion. This looks like a threat of the downfall of humanity; in any case, it is impossible to foresee or imagine what will happen to man under these conditions.

Today there is passing through the world the evil spell of a philosophy that finds truth in nihilism, that summons man to a strangely heroic existence without consolation and without hope, in affirmation of all harshness and mercilessness, in what is alleged to be a purely worldly humanism. This is mere repetition of the ideas of Nietzsche without his poignant tension in the will to overcome it.

Man cannot endure the fundamental attitude of nihilism, however. In the situation of universal lack of faith man succumbs rather to a blind faith. Such a faith is an immense substitute, is fragile, and suddenly discarded again; it may embrace the most singular contents; it may be, as it were, an empty faith of mere motion. It interprets itself as a feeling of oneness with nature, with world history. It takes concrete shape in programmes of salvation. It encloses itself in pseudo-scientific total conceptions, in Marxism, in psychoanalysis, in the theory of race (whose scientific elements, which seldom emerge with clarity, are at the same time beyond doubt).

The following are some typical manifestations of this dissolution of faith:

Thinking in ideologies.—An ideology is a complex of ideas or notions which represents itself to the thinker as an absolute truth for the interpretation of the world and his situation within it; it leads the thinker to accomplish an act of self-deception for the purpose of justification, obfuscation, evasion, in some sense or other to his own advantage. Hence the apprehension of a way of thinking as ideology means the unveiling of error and the unmasking of evil. Bestowal of the epithet ideology upon a way of thinking is to reproach it with untruth and untruthfulness and therefore constitutes the most violent attack.

Our era has both given birth to ideologies and seen through them. But the profound insights that have been achieved in this direction, from Hegel to Marx and Nietzsche, have become a brutal weapon in the war of words leading to the breaking off of communication. The method of this attack is directed against the opponent as such, against all views other than one's own. However, those very people who spurn everything that is believed, thought, and imagined as being ideology, are frequently themselves possessed by the most stubborn ideology consisting in this mode of interpretation.

The high daring of self-reflection, that precondition of all truthfulness, has degenerated along the path of ideological theory. Certainly an infinite number of perversions, repressions and obfuscations have taken place; they have won sociological significance as the type-view of a whole social class: for example, untruthfulness with regard to matters of sex in the bourgeois era, the self-justification of economic success, the legitimation of the *status quo* on the part of the privileged. But it is absolutely necessary to unveil the method of unveiling itself. From the heights reached by Kierkegaard and Nietzsche our age has carried the thought that unveils to the very limit of this intellectual process of unmasking; but now it has ceased to be an unveiling and has become a malicious attack; it is not critical investigation, but suggestion, not empirical exposition, but mere assertion with some degree of plausibility. Thus the method of penetrating cognition of truth has ended up as the abasements of psychoanalysis and vulgar Marxism. When the thinking that unveils becomes itself dogmatic, it completely loses the truth. Everything is ideology and this thesis itself is an ideology. Nothing is left.

But perhaps the formation of ideologies really is particularly great in its compass today. For in hopelessness there arises the need for illusion, in the aridity of personal existence the need for sensation, in powerlessness the need to violate those who are even more powerless.

The manner in which malice salves its conscience in this process is exemplified in the following arguments:

If the State commits blatant crimes, the argument runs: The State is sinful from its origin, I too am a sinner, I obey the commandments of the State, even when they are sinful, because I am no better and because national duty demands it. But this is all to the advantage of the man who speaks in these terms; he joins in the deed and enjoys its fruits, he exhibits his anguish in the contorted features that are not true anguish, but merely play-acting. He avails himself of sinfulness as a relief.

One takes part in frightful deeds and says: Life is harsh. The lofty goals of the nation, of the faith, of the finally free and just world that is coming demand harshness. One is harsh toward oneself with a safe, partial harshness which is enjoyed and which furnishes sham proof of the genuineness of one's demand for harshness, while in reality it covers up one's own unconditional will to existence and power.

One is conscious of one's own mendacity in the enjoyment of chance situations of advantage while these terrible things are happening. Now one wants to see that which one is not prepared to do oneself, does not wish to experience or suffer, is not capable of being oneself. One craves martyrs. One waxes enthusiastic about the possibility of martyrdom, as though this almost made one a martyr. One attacks others for not being martyrs. One intoxicates oneself with the destiny of men who appear to conform to the image of one's craving, but one has no desire ever to be like that oneself. This distortion of the facts goes so far that later on one sets oneself up as a pattern and becomes a fervent advocate against one's environment of that which, as a contemporary, one paid almost no attention to and, above all, did not do oneself.

We will not continue. There is no end to such illuminating instances. The dissolution of traditional contents is revealed in the mere fact that this type of intellectual unmasking is making itself universal. The age invents the theory to fit its actions. But the theory itself straightway becomes a means of intensifying the evil it is combating.

Simplification.—Simplicity is the shape of that which is true. Simplification is the violence that takes the place of lost simplicity. Simplicity is infinite in its capacity for interpretation, a world *in parvo,* replete and mobile. Simplification is finite in nature, the string by which one is guided like a puppet, incapable of development, empty and rigid.

Ours is the age of simplifications. Slogans, universal theories that explain everything, gross antitheses, meet with success. Whereas simplicity crystallised into mythical symbols, simplification adheres to pseudo-scientific absolutes.

Life out of negation.—Where faith is no longer the basis of the content of life, nothing is left but the vacuum of negation. When one is dissatisfied with oneself, the fault must be someone else's. If one is nothing, one is at least anti-. All ills are heaped onto a phantom that takes its name either from historical formations as they once presented themselves to theoretical cognition: everything is the fault of capitalism, liberalism, Marxism, Christianity, etc.—or else those unable to defend themselves are picked on in individual shapes and serve as scapegoats: everything is the fault of the Jews, the Germans, etc.

All the indissolubly intricate ramifications of causality or responsibility to which blame attaches are uncritically reduced to the blame of one single alien entity that is not oneself. All that matters is to possess the means of giving expression to its no and of attacking it in general. In this process intellectual concepts become banners and badges. Words are used like counterfeit coins, with their meaning reversed but with the emotions formerly attached to them preserved (liberty, fatherland, State, nation, empire, etc.). In the language that has been ruined by the sophistries of propaganda it is finally impossible to tell what words really do mean. Speech deteriorates into a welter of vague phrases, destined only to give expression to a perpetual no, to an anti-, that does not follow from any real pro.

B.   *What gave rise to the present situation?*

The origin of the crisis cannot be apprehended in a single cause. In the infinite web of the material and spiritual interconnexions of historical change we can only bring to mind individual threads. Every total and monocausal interpretation proves fallacious.

We cannot even visualise the fact of an age as a whole, but only more or less essential particular phenomena within this age. The more we get to know, the greater for our consciousness becomes the enigma of the whole.

Now the dividing-line that starts off the Age of Technology cuts unusually deep. It leaves no aspect of human existence undisturbed. Everything of which it is not actually the cause is modified by it. But we must avoid tracing the intricate course of human affairs back to this one solitary factor. Long before technology had these effects, movements were afoot from which the present spiritual situation springs. The fact that technology became operative and was universally adopted was due to this spiritual world, this way of thought and of life, which it found waiting for it.

The Age of Technology certainly brought about the tremendous crisis. Marx and Engels were able to gain an intrinsically illuminating piece of knowledge because they saw this new factor. This new factor was by no means a spiritually new humanity, however. That was the great mistake.

People talked about a new human consciousness, about new man, about spiritual creation, about truth and salvation, they looked into a luminous future—yet this kind of talk was nothing more than the accomplishment of the *tabula rasa,* a symptom of growing loss of consciousness. That which was devoid of any informing idea was noisily propagated as idea. Then, after great men had taken the wrong path, the world became a theatre for petty place-seekers and obedient intriguers, who knew no difference between true and false or good and evil, but were merely tools submissive to the function of power.

Or else people talked about lack of faith as being the consequence of technology. The latter was supposed to have deprived men of their roots, to have torn them out of all security, placed them, as it were, in an empty space, dispossessed them of air and with it of breath and of their souls, and to have left nothing of them over save that which can be made use of in the operation of machines.

The events of the Age of Technology, however, though they were furthered by the consequences of technology, had quite different presuppositions. The spiritual movements that led up to ourselves began long before the world was altered by technology. The great change that introduced the Enlightenment at the end of the seventeenth century, the French Revolution, the equivocal consciousness of crisis and consummation that informed German philosophical idealism, these are steps in our direction, independent of technology.

The Enlightenment. Lack of faith is deemed to be a consequence of the Enlightenment. Because men know too much, are acquainted with the dangerous books and are daily surrounded by the aura of their language in the press, they no longer believe. The discovery of the world of alien cultures and religious convictions has brought scepticism toward one's own faith through comparison. But this road need not have led to loss of faith. Only half and misconstrued enlightenment leads into nothingness, whereas total and unrestricted enlightenment renders the enigma of the origin really audible for the first time.

Carried further, this thesis propounded the view that a dialectic of spiritual evolution, impelled by Christian motives, led from Christianity to such a radical illumination of truth that this religion brought about the reversal against itself, out of its own forces. But again this road need not have led to loss of faith. To be sure, dogmatic positions were lost in this transition process of painful and perilous melting down and recasting, but the transformation of Biblical religion remained a possibility.

The French Revolution. This event, which either gave expression to the modern crisis or set it in motion, is today still an object of contradictory interpretation:

Kant, deeply moved by the attempt of reason to stand on its own feet, never reversed his high appraisal of the outset: 'That will never be forgotten.' Burke, on the other hand, was from the very first moment a critic as perspicacious as he was hostile. One saw in this event the consummation of the wonderful developments and aspirations of the eighteenth century, the other the ruin and corruption of these same tendencies which, in the French Revolution, had run off the rails—a fatality by which the eighteenth century was being not consummated, but overwhelmed.

The French Revolution grew on the soil of feudalism and absolute monarchy; as an essential phenomenon, therefore, it is not a universally European process, but confined to regions of this particular type. The soul of England or of Switzerland remained unaffected by it.

Even on the soil of feudalism, however, it was an ambiguous manifestation because although it desired liberty and reason, it made room
for despotism and violence. It determines our thinking in both directions: In the justice of the struggle against the evil of repression and
exploitation, in the name of the rights of man and the liberty of every
individual—and in the error of the opinion that the world as a whole
can be founded on reason, instead of transforming by the use of reason historical bonds, authority and the order of values, without recourse to violence.

Founded with fanaticism in boundless belief in reason, it is not the
fountainhead of modern freedom, whose roots lie rather in the continuity of genuine freedom in England, America, Holland and Switzerland.
To this extent, notwithstanding the heroic upsurge of its beginning, it is
the expression and origin of modern unbelief.

Philosophical idealism. The philosophy of German idealism—especially of Fichte and Hegel—brought about an enhancement of philosophical self-confidence, an alleged total knowledge that knows what
God is and desires, and loses all capacity for astonishment because it
fancies itself in possession of absolute truth. This kind of sham faith
was bound to swing over to lack of faith. It is true that this philosophy
unfolded in the particular, conceptions that can never be lost; it was one
of the manifestations of human thought that possessed genius, and its
speculative grandeur cannot be doubted. But the distrust of its world,
which has erroneously spread to all German philosophy, is justified.
Here the *hubris* and waywardness of genius became an unparalleled
seduction. Whoever drank of this potion became intoxicated, a pro-
moter of ruin, through the fact that a spiritual firework of a high order
caused loss of faith, which presupposes sobriety.

Even these facts, however—the Enlightenment, the French Revolution, and German philosophic idealism—are not sufficient to explain
our spiritual situation. They themselves often seem less like the cause
than the initial manifestation of the crisis. There remains the burning
and inadequately answered question as to how lack of faith came about.
The question contains the hope of mastering lack of faith through the
right answer.

This urge would be deprived of all prospect of success if certain
metaphysical interpretations of the course of history, and thereby
of the provenance of our situation, were correct. An age of consummate perplexity is supposed to be the outcome of a loss of substance.
A ceaseless total process is conceived of, that was finally put into words
by Klages in the statement that during the nineteenth century the earth-
essence deserted the plant.

Such an imprecise notion of a loss of substance seems, however, unacceptable. It is not an insight, but a metaphor for the radically pessimistic outlook. This sort of notion is more of an obfuscation than an
illumination. Yet the idea of some unrecognised total process forces

itself upon us again and again. Only it is neither a natural happening analogous to biological processes, nor in any other sense an objective, tangible happening; it is the Comprehensive, in which we are but which we do not recognise. It is the enigma of world history, which we deepen but do not dissolve, and in the excogitation of which we must not submit to any construct of thought as being supposedly necessary in its entirety; if we do we shall surrender both the openness of our possibilities of knowledge and the freedom of our inner being, of our choice and of our decision to a subordinate conception.

Preferable to any form of alleged total knowledge is the simple notion (which does not provide us with the key either): There is immutable evil in man, which has always led to the recurrence of senseless wars, but which has today brought about a quantitative increase both of their diffusion over the earth and of the measure of destruction they cause, the results of which give rise to the phenomena of both civilisational and spiritual disintegration.

No adequate answer is possible to the question of the provenance of crises and lack of faith, no matter whether it is sought along the path of empirical causality, intellectual understanding, or metaphysical interpretation.

C. *Summary*

The importance of the fact that the whole of mankind, that all the old cultures, have been drawn into this one common stream of destruction or renewal has only become conscious during the last few decades. The older ones amongst us were, as children, still living entirely within the European consciousness. India and China were alien, untouched worlds of their own that one did not learn about in history. Anyone who felt dissatisfied, or for whom things were going badly, emigrated. The world was open.

In 1918 the following sentences of de Groot's in his book on China (Universism) still affected me deeply as something absolutely new: 'The universist system represents the highest point to which the spiritual culture of China has been able to evolve. The only power capable of undermining it and bringing about its downfall is sound science. If ever the time should come when science is seriously cultivated in China, there can be no doubt that a complete revolution will take place in the whole of its spiritual life, which will either put China utterly out of joint or cause it to undergo a rebirth after which China will no longer be China and the Chinese no longer the Chinese. China herself possesses no second system with which to replace the old; consequently breakdown of the old would inevitably result in dissolution and anarchy, in short in the most complete fulfilment of their own sacred doctrine, according to which catastrophe and downfall are certain if mankind loses Tao. . . . If it should be ordained in the order of the world that the horrible work of demolition is to take its course, so that the days of China's ancient universist culture are numbered—then at least let her last day not be also the day of the corruption of a people of millions, that has been cast into misfortune by foreign influences.'

It is a remarkable world phenomenon that contemporaneously with and already prior to the emergence of the Age of Technology, a spiritual and psychical retrogression took place all over the world which has to-day become a European movement, as well. It is true that Europe continued to blossom spiritually for a short time when, after the seventeenth century, China and India were already going downhill. At the moment when these peoples were overpowered by the European technique of warfare, they were already lying at the nadir of their spiritual culture. Europe came up against a China and India that were not florescent, but very nearly oblivious of themselves.

Today, for the first time, there is a real unity of mankind which consists in the fact that nothing essential can happen anywhere that does not concern all. In this situation the technological revolution effected by the Europeans through science and discoveries is merely the material basis and precipitating cause of the spiritual catastrophe. To the success of the process of melting down and recasting that is now beginning, de Groot's remarks concerning China—once it is complete China will no longer be China, the Chinese no longer Chinese—may apply for the whole of mankind. Europe too will no longer be Europe, the Europeans will no longer be Europeans in the sense in which they felt themselves to be in de Groot's day. There will be new Chinese, new Europeans, however, whose image we cannot yet see.

Out of this experience of our historical situation as the turning-point of the ages, our gaze returns again and again. To the question: have such radical metamorphoses taken place before? our answer was: we know nothing of the events of the Promethean Age, when man first came into possession of his world through tools, fire and speech. But within history the greatest turning-point was the Axial Period, which we have discussed. If we have now entered into a new radical metamorphosis of humanity, this is no repetition of the Axial Period, but a happening that is different to its very roots.

First of all *outwardly*. Our Age of Technology is not merely relatively universal, like the events in those three mutually independent worlds of the Axial Period, but absolutely universal, because it is planetary. It is not a process that is mutually related in meaning, yet separate in fact; it is a single whole in continual mutual intercourse. Today it is taking place with consciousness of universality. It is bound to bring a different decision concerning humanity from the one that was reached then. For whereas all previous periods of crucial change were local and susceptible of being supplemented by other happenings, in other places, in other worlds, so that even if they failed the possibility of the salvation of man by other movements was left open, what is happening now is absolutely decisive. There is no longer anything outside it.

Inwardly, however, something manifestly quite different from the Axial Period is involved. Then the plentitude, now the emptiness. If we become aware of the turning-point, we know that we are only in the preparatory stage. The present age is one of real technological and political remoulding, not yet of eternal spiritual creations. We may more readily liken ourselves, with our grandiose scientific discoveries and technological inventions, to the epoch of the invention of tools and weapons, of the first use of domestic animals and horses, than with the age of Confucius, Buddha and Socrates. The fact that we are tackling the high task of reconstructing humanity from its origin, that we sense the fateful question as to how we can, in faith, become specifically human beings, is, however, evinced in the current tendency, which is becoming increasingly strong, to look back toward our origin. The deep matrix from which we sprang, the specific reality which was concealed by the veil of secondary cultural constructions, turns of phrase, conventions and institutions, is to become articulate once more. In this process of self-understanding through the knowledge of whence we come the mirror of the great Axial Period of humanity will perhaps, once more, prove one of the essential assurances.

THE UNITY OF HISTORY [1]

Introduction

Man's historicity is, from the outset, multiple historicity. But the multiple is subject to the imperative of the One. This is the exclusivity of the demand of an historicity to be the only one and to dominate all others, but it must develop for consciousness in the communication of the multiple historical as the absolute historicity of the One.

[1] From: *The Origin and Goal of History*, Karl Jaspers, Part I, Ch. 1. Yale University Press, New Haven, 1953, and Routledge & Kegan Paul, Ltd. 1953. Reprinted by permission.

It is the unity of the history of mankind, to which everything that has value and meaning seems to be related. But how are we to think of this unity of the history of mankind?

To begin with, experience seems to testify against unity. Historical phenomena are immeasurably dispersed. There are many peoples, many cultures, and in each of these again an endless multiplicity of peculiar historical facts. Everywhere on the face of the earth where there was any possibility of gaining a livelihood, man has settled and brought himself to particular manifestation. There appears to be a multiplicity which develops and passes away concurrently and successively.

To regard man in this light means to describe and classify him as is done with the multiformity of the vegetable kingdom. It is the fortuitousness of a many, which, as the genus 'man', exhibits certain typical basic features, and therein, like all living things, deviations within an area open to the play of possibilities. Any such naturalisation of man, however, causes the specifically human in man to vanish.

For in all the dispersion of the phenomenon man, the essential is that men are concerned with each other. Wherever they meet they are interested in one another, confront one another in antipathy or sympathy, learn from one another, exchange. When they meet it is as though each recognised himself in the other, and at the same time made himself independent of the other, whom he recognises as himself. In this meeting man learns that, however he may be in his particularity, he is related to all others on the basis of the one thing which, though he neither possesses nor knows it, imperceptibly guides him or, at moments, seizes him with an all-pervading enthusiasm.

Seen thus, the phenomenon of man in the dispersal of history is a movement toward the One—perhaps it is provenance from a single matrix—in any case, it is not an existence that shows its ultimate nature in the dispersion of the multiple.

A. *Facts that point to unity*

I. UNITY OF THE HUMAN MAKE-UP

We have some such trivial notion of humanity in history as this. Man is a totality of innate tendencies. At any given moment, under the particular conditions, parts of his energies, gifts and impulses are realised, whilst others slumber unawakened. Since, however, man is always the same potentially, everything remains possible at all times. The varying unfoldment of his parts does not mean a difference of nature, but a difference of manifestation. In the collation of all manifestations, as the development to varying degrees of common potentialities, the totality of humanity is first disclosed.

The question of whether man's make-up has been transformed during the few millennia of history, or whether the nature of man has remained the same throughout this period, must be answered by saying that no facts are available in evidence of any such transformation. Any changes that have taken place are rather to be understood in terms of the selection of that which was already present. That which is given in the basic make-up as permanent and unchanging appears at different times, through the agency of varying selection, in quite different directions. At any given time those men become visible, successful, and then numerically preponderant whose personal qualities satisfy the particular conditions of the current society and its situation. Conditions may be characterized by the type of human make-up they fostered. With the alteration of conditions, selection changes, and previously hidden types of make-up, which have long been suppressed and reduced to a small number by negative selection, now come to the fore. The varying manifestation of the same nature under ever diverse preconditions, with a diverse selection, is disclosed.

Nevertheless, to this train of thought the rejoinder must be made that the whole of humanity can in no wise be pictured as the totality of innate human tendencies. There is no man who is or can be everything human, neither in reality nor in the projection of an idea of him.

The further objection must be made that the essential variation of the make-up with which an individual is naturally endowed is elemental. Especially when we look at the personal qualities and character traits which already make their appearance in earliest childhood does the ineluctable course taken by the innate disposition become visible. These qualities and traits create a gulf of difference between the make-up of one man and another.

These ideas, and the objections to them, all contain an element of truth, but they do not go so far as to explain man.

To reach the unity of humanity which is revealed in history, we must pass beyond the biologico-psychological plane of consideration.

In what does the enduring nature of man consist, which alone makes understanding between us, and our solidarity, possible at all? Again and again unity is doubted. For in all history there is a mutation of human knowledge, consciousness and self-consciousness. There is a coming into being and a dying away of spiritual potentialities, an estrangement, and finally an incomprehension. Is there unity in this notwithstanding? At all events, as the unrestricted will to comprehension.

If this unity cannot be understood as being derived from the biological scaffolding, because we cannot approach its meaning in the biological sphere, it must have some other basis. What is meant by this origin is not a biological make-up, or derivation from one root, but humanity as a unity from a higher origin. This can be visually imagined only in a symbol: in the idea of the creation of man by the Deity after His image, and of the Fall.

This origin—which links all us humans together, impels us toward one another, causes us to presuppose unity as well as to seek it—cannot, as such, be either known or contemplated, nor does it stand before us as an empirical reality.

The objection to the idea of unity, based on the indication of the signal innate diversities between the make-up of individuals and peoples, which in life cause mutual repulsion and are seemingly the source of radical divisions, is fallacious if it is intended to assert the existence of a diversity of the inner being of man down to his ultimate roots, of such a kind as to create an unbridgeable gulf between man and man. Greatly as we experience, in their manifestation, the separating chasms, and great as is the conflict between those of disparate natures, or the indifference with which humans pass one another by, the factors that potentially link together, which slumber in the depths and which cannot be overlooked, are equally great. The Comprehensive remains the reality over and above all reality that has become particular. One can never foretell what may be aroused under new conditions in new situations. No one can draw a line under a man as though he could calculate what would or would not be possible for him. Still less can peoples or epochs be finally determined. The characterisation that can be made of peoples and epochs is never absolutely valid. For at all times there are other possibilities. What the individual, or small circles, succeed in doing need by no means be universally adopted and become a character of the people and its culture as a whole, and yet it forms part of it. Aristarchus' astronomy (the Copernican universe) was without effect in Greece, as were the wisdom and divine faith of Amenemhope in Egypt. So often have the highest achievements stood on one side, uncomprehended and isolated, and either attained an ineffectual prestige for particular contingent reasons of the moment or taken effect through being misunderstood and distorted. It can be doubted whether Plato had any real effect in Greece, or Kant in Germany, outside a narrow, though magnificent, spiritual current.

Thus the unity toward which man lives, if he becomes authentically historical, cannot have its basis in a unity of biological derivation, but only in the higher origin that causes man to become directly out of the hand of the Deity. This unity of origin is not the continuance of a *status quo*. It is rather historicity itself. This is evident from the following:

(1) The unity of man in the movement of his metamorphoses is not a static unity of persisting, and merely alternately realised, qualities. Man has become man in history through a movement that is not a movement of his natural make-up. As a natural being he is given his make-up in the area open to the play of its variations, as an historical being he reaches out beyond this natural datum. From this origin he must press on toward the unity that links all. This is a postulate:

Without this unity understanding would not be possible, there would be a chasm between those of disparate natures, an understanding history would be impossible.

(2) The manifestation of individual men is of a self-exclusive character in its particular reality. Man as an individual cannot unite what he realises out of essentially disparate origins, for instance, the hero and the saint.

Man, even the individual man, is from his origin potentially everything, but in reality a single thing. In this he is not a restricted part, however, but historical, an origin of his own, turned to the other historical origin in the consciousness of the one historical fundament that links all.

The individual man is never a complete, never an ideal man. The complete man cannot, in principle, exist; for everything which he is and realises, can be, and is, broken through again, is open. Man is not a finished and not a perfectible being.

(3) In history, that which is unrepeatable and irreplaceable comes to light in unique creations, break-throughs and realisations. Because these creative steps cannot be in any way conceived causally, nor deduced as necessary, they are like revelations from some other source than the mere course of happening. But once they have come into existence, they lay the foundations of the humanity that comes after. From them man acquires his knowledge and volition, his prototypes and antitypes, his criteria, his thought-patterns and his symbols, his inner world. They are steps toward unity, because they appertain to the one self-understanding spirit and address themselves to all.

II. THE UNIVERSAL

The unity of mankind is impressively evident in the fact that similar basic traits of religion, forms of thought, implements, and social forms recur all over the earth. The simplicity of man is great, despite his diversity. Psychological and sociological facts are such that comparison is possible everywhere, and a multitude of regularities can be noted, which demonstrate fundamental structures of humanity in the psychological and sociological provinces. Precisely through observation of the common element, however, does that which is divergent become clear, whether it is to be comprehended from specific types of human make-up, or from historical situations and events. If we turn our gaze upon the universal, we shall find congruence in that which is essential, and comprehend particularities as local, attaching them to place and time.

It is precisely this universal, however, which cannot constitute the true unity of mankind. Just the reverse. If we turn out gaze upon the depths of the truth that is manifested, we shall find the historically great within the particular, but in the universal the commonplace, the unhistorically constant, which is, so to speak, the fluid medium of the factual and the correct.

If, between the most distant cultures, a common possession forms the substratum of humanity, it is quite especially surprising and important to note that there are always divergences as well, where we thought we had found an absolute universal—that somewhere something is missing which is otherwise typical of man, and also that the absolutely universal always possesses an abstract character, a uniformity.

That which, by the yardstick of the universal, is a mere particularisation, may be precisely the fulfillment of true historicity. The unity of mankind can take root only in the relationship of these historical particulars to one another, which is not essentially divergence, but rather a positively original content, not the instance of a universal, but a link in the one comprehensive historicity of mankind.

III. PROGRESS

The road leads forward in knowledge and technological ability, one step succeeds the other, that which has been acquired may be passed on in the identical shape and become the property of all. As a result, there passes through the history of individual cultures, and of all cultures, a line of growing acquisitions, which is, however, confined to the impersonal, universally valid knowledge and ability of consciousness in general.

In this domain, world history may be conceived of as a development in an ascending line, with retrogressions and standstills it is true, but on the whole with perpetual augmentation of the possession to which men and peoples make their contribution, and which, by nature accessible to all men, also becomes the possession of all. Historically we see the stages of this advance, and in the present we stand at the highest point. This is only a line in the whole, however. Humanity itself, the ethos of man, his goodness and wisdom, make no progress. Art and poetry are indeed comprehensible to all, but not typical of all; they are bound to peoples and their epochs, each one at a unique and unsurpassable height.

Hence there is progress in knowledge, in technology, in the prerequisites for new human possibilities, but not in the substance of humanity. Progress in substance is refuted by the facts. The peoples which had reached the highest levels perished, succumbing to those inferior to them. Cultures were destroyed by barbarians. The physical annihilation of the highest types of men by the oppressive realities of the mass is a fundamental phenomenon of history. The average that multiples the most, the growth of the thoughtless populace, triumphs without a struggle through mere existence *en masse* over that which is spiritually higher. There is a constant counter-selection of those who are inferior, e.g. in conditions under which cunning and brutality promise lasting advantages. One inclines toward the proposition: Everything exalted perishes, everything inferior endures.

Against such a generalisation, we can point to the recurrence of the great, even if it remains silent for centuries and longer. But how fragile, how dubious and uncertain is this endurance!

These are said to be only setbacks, only contingent ruin. In the long run there is reason to believe in substantial progress. But precisely these contingencies, these destructions are, at any rate in the foreground, the overwhelming basic happening of history.

It is said things need not continue to be as they have been till now. It is up to us to guide the course of events better. But this is the Utopian idea that everything can be fabricated, the principle of 'breeding' applied to the realm of man, where the object can never be known, surveyed and manipulated.

It is said ruin is the consequence of guilt. If we only expiate our sins and prove ourselves in a pure life, things will be different. Indeed, this has been the exhortation since the ancient prophets—but we do not know upon what route, when or how, the good of a world order will follow from the ethically pure life. We may not deny the reality that the ethically good as such is by no means crowned with success—nor is it done for the sake of success. But the ethically good that assumes responsibility for success and the consequences remains the one great chance.

Progress will indeed bring a unity of the knowable, but not the unity of mankind. The unity of universally valid truth which, wherever it is found, remains the same in its unending advance, appears only in science and technology. This universally communicable and transferable truth, which addresses itself to the understanding alone, is not the unity of mankind. This progress brings a unity of the understanding. It links men in the understanding, so that they discuss rationally with one another; but it leaves them capable of annihilating each other with the same weapons of technology. For the understanding only links understanding as a whole, not men. It brings no genuine communication and no solidarity.

IV. UNITY IN SPACE AND TIME

The unity of man springs from life on the common natural soil (unity of the planet), and from existence in the one common time.

In the course of history intercourse developed—with setbacks. The multiplicity of the naturally given, the manifoldness of peoples and countries, existed for a long time in unrelated contiguity. The path of intercourse linked them, caused tribes to amalgamate into peoples, peoples into groups of peoples, countries into continents, and then to fall apart again. It enabled men of different peoples to catch sight of one another and then forget each other again, until the moment of conscious and factual connexion of all to all began, and intercourse became uninterrupted—either in real consummation, or in the rupture of warfare. The history of mankind as perpetual mutual exchange in the unity of intercourse commenced.

Men had long ago taken possession of the surface of the earth, with the exception of the polar regions, deserts and high mountain-chains, in the course of many thousands of years of migration. Mankind was always mobile. Amazing journeys were made at the threshold of history. The Northmen came to Greenland and America, the Polynesians crossed the whole Pacific, the Malays reached Madagascar. The languages of Negro Africa and of America are each so closely related amongst themselves as to indicate continual intercourse within these continents. Inventions, tools, ideas, legends travelled long distances across the earth in primeval historical times, always in short stages, as though passed from one hand to the other. Only Australia, and perhaps America, remained in isolation for a long time; but even they were not absolutely isolated (there are striking parallels between Eastern Asia and Mexico). Isolation does not mean that no man of another country was ever carried to their shores, but that they were never subjected to any perceptible foreign influence.

In the course of history great empires were formed, which, for a while, increased the contact between men within their domains. Then they disintegrated again, the highways of intercourse were interrupted, relations broken off, knowledge of the existence of the others forgotten. There were peoples which, from time to time, shut themselves off from the outer world—such as Egypt, Japan and China; but every wall erected was ultimately broken through again.

During the last five hundred years, the Europeans have drawn the whole earth into their communications net. They have carried their civilisation to all parts of the world and have taken for themselves goods of civilisation which they did not possess. They brought their domestic animals, useful plants and weapons, their manufactures and machines, their customs and their beliefs and all the evils of their world; they fetched potatoes, maize, quinine, cocoa, tobacco, the hammock, etc. It was they who first made the unity of the earth conscious, intercourse systematic, lasting and reliable.

This intercourse between peoples has meant a continual growing together of mankind, the creation of unity through the planet's becoming one to the consciousness, and ultimately to the actions, of men.

There is no sign of a unity of the most ancient history of cultural evolution as radiating out from one point on the earth. As far as empirical vision can see, there is rather a dispersion of men; we see the many endeavours and then the stimulus afforded by contacts between men and cultures, development resulting from the superimposition of various cultures and peoples ensuing upon conquests, and the significance of racial mixture, which either had a levelling effect or brought about exceptional achievements. Always happening is rendered historical by intercourse; it is a thrusting toward unity, not procedure from an originally given unity.

Unity through the one terrestrial soil, through common enclosure in space and time, is nevertheless the most superficial unity, which is certainly not identical with the unity of history. It is common to all reality and not the portion of man alone. The mere co-existence of men on the closed surface of the earth, which they fill, does not of itself constitute the unity of mankind. This unity is made possible by intercourse. It is by no means this intercourse *per se*, however, but only the outcome of that which takes place in this intercourse.

A glance at the globe shows the narrow strip, which is furthermore interrupted at several places (it runs from the Mediterranean region to China), that gave birth to everything spiritual which is valid today. There is no geographical right to historical equality.

V. PARTICULAR UNITIES

In the movement of human affairs there are, to our cognition, many lines which run separately from one another and subsequently meet— or particular lines which, although they recur typically, represent only features of the whole, not the whole itself.

Thus there is the circumscribed sequence of a particular set of cultural phenomena. A few generations cohere in typical stylistic sequences or developments of thought, from their origin to their disintegration.

There are unities of cultures as *de facto* common worlds of life-forms, dispositions, ideas, units of faith, the peoples in their provenance, their language, their destiny—the religions as 'world religions', which disseminate transcendentally procured attitudes to life in ethos, faith and outlook over wide areas—the States as power units which mould everything else.

These unities lack universality. They are individual unities alongside others, cultures alongside cultures. There are many peoples, religions, States. These stand in relation to one another, cultures in silent exchanges, States in warfare and the mutual acceptance of politics, religions in mission and disputation. All of them undergo transformation, are not finally fixed, run into one another.

History shows the great factual unities in their powerfulness, the spheres of culture as, so to speak, subterranean dissemination that forms men without the use of force, the peoples as unconscious, prehistorical movements, the religions as 'world religions', though always within limits, the States as empires.

All these unities are wont to intersect and overlay one another. The coincidence of all unities reached its peak in China after the founding of the United Empire. Culture, religion and the State all coincided. The whole was the one world of man, the one empire, beyond which, to the consciousness of the Chinese, there was nothing except the primitive barbarians on the frontiers, who, as a potential component of the empire, had mentally already been incorporated into it. If the 'Central Empire' is compared with the Roman Empire the difference is considerable. The Roman Empire was a relatively transient phenomenon, although in the sequel the idea of this empire cast a spell that lasted for a thousand years. Beyond its frontiers there were Teutons and Parthians as real forces which were never vanquished. Despite the cosmic-religious unity of paganism, it was unable to permeate its peoples with this unity, as happened in China; its genesis rather caused the simultaneous growth of Christianity, which broke through it.

B. *Unity through meaning and goal*

If the manifold facts which represent a unity, or point to unity, do not suffice to constitute the unity of history, a different starting-point is perhaps possible. Unity is not a fact, but a goal. The unity of history is perhaps produced by men's ability to understand each other in the idea of the One, in the one truth, in the world of the spirit, in which all things are meaningfully related to one another and belong together, however alien to each other they may be at the outset.

Unity springs from the meaning in the direction of which history occurs, a meaning that lends significance to that which, without it, would remain nugatory in dispersion.

This goal may appear as a concealed meaning, which no one intended, but which the observer tries out interpretively, or then apprehends as conscious purpose, as will to unity. The meaning is expressed as the goal of history:

(1) The goal is taken to be *civilisation* and the *humanisation* of man. What this may be, beyond the ordering of existence is, however, by no means clearly determined, but itself historical. As the ordering of existence, however, the goal is legal world order. The path of history leads out of dispersion *via* merely *de facto* contact in peace and war to cohabitation on earth in a real unity achieved through the rule of law. This unity would, through the ordering of existence, give scope to all the potentialities of the human soul and spirit.

(2) The goal is taken to be *liberty* and the consciousness of liberty. Everything that has happened up to now is to be construed as an attempt to attain liberty.

But the process that will reveal to us what liberty is has no end.

The will to a world order of law does not make its immediate goal liberty, but only political liberty, which gives human existence scope for all the possibilities of genuine liberty.

(3) The goal is taken to be the *noble man* and the creation of the spirit, the production of culture in communal conditions; it is taken to be the genius.

The urge is to the most lucid consciousness. The unity of meaning originates from the point at which man becomes most decisively conscious of himself in extreme situations—where he puts the most profound questions—where he finds the creative answers by which his life is guided and which give it its characteristic stamp. This unity in the nobility of humanity does not consist in the diffusion of implements and knowledge, not in the extent of conquests and imperial jurisdiction, not in extreme formations such as killing asceticism or the sort of training imposed on the Janizaries—not in the permanence and stability of institutions and fixations—but in the radiant moments of the most profound lucidity of consciousness, of essential revelations.

This most essential element may then be a minute speck in the stream of history. But it may begin to work like a ferment in the totality of events. Or it may remain ineffectually in memory, ready to take effect, a question put to the future. Or it may find in the world no echo to its unique nobility, vanish without recollection, and exist only for transcendence.

That such peaks appear irreplaceably valuable to us, rests upon the fact that they fall within the province of a unity which we have always presupposed and never really known, a unity without which, as its goal, origin and justification, there would be no history.

(4) The goal is taken to be the *manifestation of Being in man,* the perception of being in its depths, that is, the manifestation of the Godhead.

Such goals are attainable in every present, and indeed are attained—up to a point; they are regained in a perennial process of loss and devaluation. They are realised by every generation in its own way.

This does not mean that the single, overall goal of history is achieved, however. The imaginary goal of the future tends rather to turn our attention back to the present, which must not be let slip.

The unity of history *per se* is not laid bare by any interpretation of meaning. Every formulation, even if it hits the highest target, remains at a goal which is not the Comprehensive, at least not in the sense that all other goals could be derived from one particular concept, so that the unity of the goal would lay open to view the one meaning of history. Hence all supposed goals do indeed become factors within history, if they are desired or if faith is bestowed on them, but they are never anything that covers the whole of history.

Every meaning is present to the consciousness of men as an intended meaning in manifold shape. Within it we humans raise ourselves aloft to the One, without having it at our disposal as a content of knowledge.

At all times, however, the craving to know and believe one meaning as single and all-embracing is satisfied. And if every meaning that is absolutised is bound to come to grief, new generations in their turn immediately seek, through their philosophers, an all-embracing meaning that has governed, and is governing, history, and which, once it has been conceived, can also be assimilated into their own will as an intended meaning and taken as a guide (as in the Christian philosophy of history, as in Hegel, in Comte, etc.).

This unity is brought into view in an interpretive total conception of history.

C. *Unity for the thinking total conception*

To comprehend the unity of history, i.e. to think of universal history as a whole, is the urge of historical knowledge in search of its ultimate meaning.

Philosophical consideration of history has therefore enquired after the unity that holds mankind together. Men settled the globe, but they were scattered and did not know of one another, lived in the most diverse guises and spoke thousands of languages. In earlier times, anyone who thought of universal history, because of the narrowness of his horizon, constructed a unity at the expense of restriction; amongst ourselves, for instance, he restricted himself to the West, in China to the Central Empire. That which lay beyond had no part in it and was regarded as a life of barbarians, primitive peoples, which were certainly an object of ethnological interest, but not of history. Unity consisted in the presupposition of the tendency to cause all the still unknown peoples of the earth to participate, stage by stage, in the one—namely, one's own—culture, to bring them into one's own sphere of order.

If faith presupposed one fundament and one goal, the idea sought to recognise these in real history. Assumptions of a knowledge of unity, either given by divine revelation or intelligible to reason, were attempts at constructing the one history of mankind.

God's passage through history became visible in the West in the succession of His acts running from Creation, *via* expulsion from Paradise, announcement of His will through the prophets, redemption through His appearance in person at the turning-point of the ages, to the end in the anticipated Last Judgement. That which was first thought of by the Jewish prophets, then assumed Christian form through St. Augustine, which was repeated and inflected from Joachim Fiore to Bousset, secularised from Lessing and Herder to Hegel, was always this knowledge of the one whole history, in which everything has its place. A series of fundamental principles of human existence made their appearance which, apprehended in their depths, taught what truly is and happens.

Such a construction, however—magnificently as it has been believed and expressed throughout two millennia—breaks down:

(a) If I know the whole, every human existence has its place in the whole. It is not for itself, but serves a path. It is not immediate to transcendence, but through the medium of a position in time, which narrows it and makes it a part. Every human existence, every period, every people, is mediatised. Against this the original relationship to the Godhead, the infinitude of the Comprehensive, which can be whole at any time, revolts.

(b) In the knowledge of the whole, the greater proportion of human reality, whole peoples, epochs and cultures, fall to one side as of no account. They are no more than chance and incidental products of natural happening.

(c) History is not closed and does not reveal its origin. For this construction, however, it is closed. The beginning and end are invented as an addition in the shape of an alleged revelation. In fact, two mutually exclusive fundamental conceptions of history confront one another.

Either history is visible as a whole, and as the unity of a knowable evolution with a beginning and an end. I myself with my period stand at the particular point, thought of either as the lowest or the highest point yet reached.

Or history is actually, and for my consciousness, unclosed. I hold myself open to the future. It is an attitude of waiting and of seeking the truth, of not yet knowing even that which already is, but which will be fully understandable only from the vantage point of the future. In this basic attitude even the past is unconcluded: it still lives, its decisions are not totally, but only relatively, final; they can be revised. That which was is still capable of re-interpretation. That which seemed to have been decided becomes once more a query. That which has been, has still to reveal to us what it is. It does not lie there as an inert residue. There is more in the past than what has so far been objectively and rationally extracted from it. The thinker himself is still standing in the evolution that is history; he is not at the end, and hence—from his position on a hill with a restricted view, not on the world-mountain from which everything is visible—he knows the directions of possible ways, and yet does not know the origin and goal of the whole.

Hence history may appear to us as a field for experiment, unity vanishes in the infinitude of the possible. The permanent basic attitude is one of questioning. The calm of a great symbol of the whole, of an image of the unity of everything, that erases time and with it past and future, is only a halting-place in time, not the finality of a known truth.

If history is not to disintegrate into the dispersion of the fortuitous, into a coming and going without direction, into the pathlessness of many sham paths, then the idea of the unity of history is inescapable. The only question is the manner in which it is apprehended.

We have drawn up a long list of negations: The unity of history is not to be apprehended by knowledge. It cannot be construed as the unity of man's biological origin. As the unity of the earth's surface and as common enclosure by real time it is a purely external unity. The unity of the all-embracing goal cannot be demonstrated. The idea of a world order of law is directed toward the substrata of human existence, not toward the meaning of history *in toto,* and is itself still a query. Unity cannot be comprehended by reference to the identity of a universally valid truth, for this unity relates only to the understanding. It is not progress toward a goal or in a process that goes on into infinity. Unity does not consist in the most lucid consciousness, nor in the nobility of spiritual creation. It is not contained in a meaning toward which everything happens or ought to happen. Nor is unity to be discerned as the articulated organism of a totality of mankind. The totality of history is not truly present in a visual image either as reality or as meaning.

He who does not fall in with the arrogant assumption of an all-embracing comprehension of history as a unity, will nonetheless see in all these strivings for unity a dash of truth. This becomes fallacious if the particular is carried over onto the whole. It remains true as an indication and a sign.

Every line of development, every typical form, all facts of unity are simplifications within history that becomes fallacious when they are used as a means of seeing through history in its totality. The important thing is to apprehend the manifoldness of these lines, forms, unities, but to remain open to that which lies beyond them, in which these phenomena occur, to remain open to man and to the always present whole of humanity; this humanity embraces everything and bears within itself that which, despite all its magnificence, is never more than one phenomenon amongst others.

There remains the demand constituted by the idea of unity. We are confronted by universal history as a task.

(*a*) At the least, there remains the scanning of all human happening in the whole world. In the alternative between dispersed isolation and essential centralisation, neither of the two extremes is accepted; instead a pertinent, constructive classification of history is sought. Even if every construction of the unity of history will always make abysmal nescience felt in knowledge, the way of classification under the idea of a unity is nevertheless possible.

(*b*) This unity is then supported by the closedness of the planet, which, as space and soil, is entire and susceptible of control; furthermore, by the exactitude of chronology in the one time, even if it is abstract; in addition, by the unity of the root of the human race, which is of one species, a biological fact which points to common derivation.

(*c*) The principal basis for unity is the fact that men meet each other in the one spirit of a universal capacity for understanding. Men find one another in a comprehensive spirit, which, although no one sees it as a whole, nonetheless contains all. Unity finds its most decisive expression in relation to the one God.

(*d*) The idea of unity is concretely present in the consciousness of universal possibilities. The openness with which things are looked at increases the claim that everything can acquire importance for everything, and is of concern to everything through the mere fact of its existence. We live in the consciousness of a space in which nothing is indifferent, which opens up distant vistas as concerning us, and which at the same time indicates the current present as a decision over the road that will be taken. With our eyes on the earliest beginnings, which never go as far back as the origin, and with our eyes on the future, which is always unconcluded, possibilities become known in an incomprehensible whole, so that the unity of the whole is manifested in the decisiveness of the present fulfilment of the task.

(*e*) If a tenable and finished picture of the whole is out of reach, there remain forms in which images of the whole are from time to time disclosed. These forms are:

History is seen in hierarchies of value, in its origins, in its crucial stages. The real is divided up into the essential and the inessential.

History stands under a whole that was called Providence, and was later conceived of as a law. Although the concrete shape it has taken is erroneous, this idea of the whole will remain an extreme notion of that which is not seen, but within which we see, which cannot be planned, but within which planning must be carried out. History as a whole is unique, is specifically historical and not merely natural happening. There remains the idea of an order of the whole, in which everything has its proper place. It is not mere fortuitous multiformity, but all the features of the fortuitous are merged in the one great basic feature of history.

As an interpretation of unity we, for our part, have projected a schema of world history which seems today in the closest accord with openness and unity and empirical reality. Our exposition of world history sought to derive historical unity from the Axial Period, which was common to the whole of mankind.

The word axis was not intended to convey the concealed interior, round which the foreground of phenomena at all times revolves, that element which is itself timeless, but which extends through all ages and is enveloped by the dust-clouds of the solely present. The appellation axis was bestowed rather upon an era around the middle of the last millennium B.C., for which everything that preceded it would appear to have been a preparation, and to which everything subsequent actually, and often in clear consciousness, relates back. The world history of humanity derives its structure from this period. It is not an axis of which we might assert a permanent absoluteness and uniqueness. But it is the axis of the short world history that has taken place up till now, that which, in the consciousness of all men, might represent the basis of the historical unity they recognise in solidarity. This real axis would then be the incarnation of an ideal axis, around which mankind in its movement is drawn together.

Summary

We seek to apprehend the unity of history in images of the whole, which demonstrate the historicity of mankind *per se* in an empirically founded structure—wherein the fundamental fact remains the boundless openness into the future and the short beginning: we are just starting. Into the future in fact, and as the past in interpretation, history is an open, infinite world of relationships of meaning, which, at any rate from time to time, seem to flow into one growing common meaning.

The theme is: not one of those universal categories, not historical laws, but enquiry after the unity of history in its factual, perceptibly given, unique shape, which is not a law, but the historical arcanum itself. This shape we call the structure of history. It must be construed, in its spatial-temporal localisation, as the spiritual reality of humanity.

The interpretive contemplation of history becomes a determination of man's will. Unity becomes his goal. Contemplation of the past is related to this goal. It becomes conscious, for example, as world peace in world order through a legal order aimed at the liberation from want and the bestowal of happiness upon, as nearly as possible, everyone.

This goal relates, however, only to the substratum of existence, which it is possible for all to attain in common. It is true that this unity in the preconditions for all human possibilities would be of immense importance; it is not the final goal, however, but in turn a means.

Unity is sought at a higher level in the totality of the world of human being and creating. With this in view, the unity of past history is derived from the emphasis of that which concerns all men, of that which is essential to all.

What this is, however, can become manifest only in the movement of living together. The demand for boundless communication testifies to the solidarity of all men in potential understanding. But that which is known, fashioned, aimed at does not, in itself, constitute unity, nor does the image of a goal; all these constitute unity only when they enter into the communication of man with man. The ultimate question is then:

Does the unity of mankind consist in unification on the basis of a common faith, in the objectivity of that which is thought and believed in common to be true, in an organisation of the one eternal truth by an authority that spans the earth?

Or is the only unity truly attainable to us humans unity through communication of the historically manifold origins, which are mutually concerned with one another, without becoming identical in the manifestation of idea and symbol—a unity which leaves the One concealed in manifoldness, the One that can remain true only in the will to boundless communication, as an endless task in the interminable testing of human possibilities?

All assertions of absolute alienness, of the permanent impossibility of mutual understanding, remain the expression of resignation in lassitude, of failure before the most profound demand of humanity—the intensification of temporary impossibilities into absolute impossibilities, the extinction of inner readiness.

The unity of history will never be consummated in the accomplished unification of mankind. History lies between origin and goal, the idea of unity is at work in it. Man follows his great highway of history, but never terminates it by realising its final goal. The unity of mankind is, rather, the bourne of history. That is to say: Achieved, consummate unity would be the end of history. History remains movement, under the guidance of unity, accompanied by notions and ideas of unity.

Unity is contained in such notions as these: Mankind stems from one origin, from which it has evolved in infinite division, and strives toward the re-unification of that which has been split up. Complete obscurity surrounds the one origin, however. Wherever we come across man he is already in the dispersion and differentiation of individuals and races; we see several cultural evolutions, manifold beginnings, which must have been preceded by an already human evolution that we do not know. Unity guides us as the notion of an organism which is reaching perfection in the mutuality of the many. All such notions are vague, however.

Notions of unity delude us, if we take them to be more than symbols. Unity as the goal is an unending task; for all unities which become visible to us are particular, are only preconditions for a possible unity; or they are levelling processes, behind which abysmal alienness, repulsion and conflict lie concealed.

It is not possible to formulate a clear and consistent picture of perfect unity, even in the realm of ideas. This unity cannot become real, either as the complete man, or as the right organisation of the world, or as final, penetrating and open mutual understanding and agreement.

The One is rather the infinitely remote point of reference, which is origin and goal at one and the same time; it is the One of transcendence. As such it cannot be, so to speak, taken captive; it cannot become the exclusive possession of an historical faith that could be enforced upon all as truth *per se*.

If universal history as a whole proceeds from the One to the One, it does so in such a way that everything accessible to us lies between these ultimate poles. There is a becoming of unities, an enthusiastic seeking of unity; and then again a passionate smashing of unities.

Thus this deepest unity is elevated to an invisible religion, to the realm of spirits, the secret realm of the manifestation of Being in the concord of souls. Historically, however, there remains movement, which, always between beginning and end, never attains to, nor continuously is, what it really signifies.

PART SIX

Neo-Orthodoxy

Introduction

The development of twentieth-century philosophy, as it has been repeatedly pointed out in this book, presents itself as a revolt against or departure from idealism. Nowhere is this pattern exhibited more strikingly, and yet paradoxically, than in that philosophic discipline that for want of a better name goes under the somewhat questionable title of the philosophy of religion.

In some quarters this century has been marked by an extraordinary renovation in religious thinking. Where some materialists of the nineteenth century looked forward to the following age as one in which religion might perish from the earth, this century on the contrary has seen some new prophetic fervor directed toward preserving and defending the traditional religions. The ancient pieties have been once again proclaimed, and the banners of faith unfurled. There have been new and original attempts to understand the basic phenomena of religion, and not merely from a negative and debunking attitude of anthropology. Theology has once again become intellectually exciting, and certain theologians even fashionable. To be sure, this intellectual phenomenon has not affected the ways of nations or the march of the modern world along the iron paths of secularism and technology. Still, it is a remarkable thing to have occurred at all; and though it may betoken something different from what its proponents feel for it, this religious current of thought must be taken as a clear symptom of the time we live in.

One might have expected a very definite sympathy with idealism from this new religious vein of thought, since the religious aspiration within idealism has always been a strong, perhaps even dominant motive. In the initiator of idealism within modern philosophy, namely Bishop Berkeley, the religious motive is very practical and forthright:

as an official of the Church (as well as a great dialectician) he wants to refute materialism because it increases religious doubts and leads finally to religious skepticism. If Kant would seem to weaken the case of religion because he abolished rational theology and showed that it was impossible to demonstrate the existence of God, yet on the other hand he protects religion as a sphere legitimately accessible to faith; if you cannot prove the existence of God, at least you know that the opponent of religion cannot disprove His existence; God as an object simply lies beyond the realm of the provable or disprovable, and it is simply, in Kant's view, a categorical mistake to invoke the word proof in relation to Him. Hegel, coming after Kant, became a much more aggressive champion of religious thought: his philosophy itself is ultimately a religious vision, though clothed in the conceptual language of reason. (Hegel's earliest writings, it may be worth recalling, were directly theological in nature, Kant's were scientific; that suggests in good part the measure of difference between these two idealistic thinkers.) But it is just in this proclamation of Reason as capable of doing the work of religion entirely, of spinning the whole vision of religion out of its own conceptual storehold, that Hegel comes to grief at the hands of contemporary theologians. Reason, in Hegel, dispenses with the necessities of faith and revelation—at least for those intellectuals who are able to clamber to the heights of the Hegelian philosophy; while the humbler members of mankind can only get their religion out of the crude symbols and images of holy scripture. Nor is there any distinct mode of experience required as a basis for the construction of religious concepts. For Hegel, reason seeking to comprehend itself goes forth on its own momentum to meet the Absolute.

This is precisely the point of Kierkegaard's attack upon Hegel, as we have seen earlier: the Hegelian system would make Christianity, and Christian faith, unnecessary. This system is the vision of the world as it might appear to God, but not to mortal man in his finitude and incompleteness. Faith is not a mode of human experience that can be eventually subsumed under reason; it is a variety of experience (to use the phrase of William James) that is utterly alien and incomprehensible to reason. On this point Kierkegaard has rather carried the day against Hegel among contemporary theologians—the only exception would be among Catholic theologians, who still defend the demonstrative rigor of rational theology, though even among these there have been remarkable inroads of Kierkegaardian or existentialist influence; accordingly, contemporary descriptions of faith as a distinct and unique mode of man's being fall within that general pattern of twentieth-century thinking that we have labeled, following James, as "radical pluralism." Theologians and religious philosophers have been led to examine the varieties of experience that underlie the towering superstructure of theological concepts. In some cases it is almost as if the religious thinker in seeking to renew the old must re-create the experience that lay at its sources, and therefore has to follow the maxim of Husserl: "To the things themselves!"

But is this renewal of religious thought, even granted its limited influence upon a few intellectuals and its total lack of influence on the march of external history, really in any way a sign of our time? To gauge whether or not it is, we have only to invoke two representative figures of this and the preceding century.

If for a moment we step outside philosophy, probably no better index of the difference between the twentieth and the nineteenth century can be had than a comparison of two typical literary men of the two centuries, our contemporary T. S. Eliot and the mid-Victorian Matthew Arnold. The comparison is all the more apt since Eliot himself has consciously cast himself somewhat in the role of a contemporary Arnold. Both poets, both critics, they are also literary men who claim to be spokesmen for their age and so take upon themselves the responsibility of public pronouncement on contemporary issues. It is in this latter, quasi-philosophical role that we are interested here to bring forward the comparison. The differences between Arnold and Eliot as poets, as well as their differences as critics, would illuminate an extraordinary change in the sensibilities of the two centuries. But that is a matter for strictly literary interpretation. We confine ourselves to their pronouncements as public seers—and particularly on the one subject of religion.

Where Arnold suffers all the typical nineteenth-century pains at his loss of faith and argues to replace all religious dogma by poetry, Eliot makes a sensational return to the bosom of the Anglican Church and accepts its dogmas and traditions as the substance of Christianity. Is this return to orthodoxy typical of the twentieth century? Obviously not, if one measures the typical by sheer number; despite all the publicity about a "revival of religion" some years back, the numbers of people who are turning to the churches are but a drop in the bucket compared with the millions of people throughout the world who remain indifferent to religion or are even militantly antireligious. T. S. Eliot is not typical of his time in the sense that there are millions like him. Quite the contrary. But the exceptional man is typical of his time in another sense of the word "typical": he expresses an attitude of mind or spirit that could not be arrived at earlier in history. Eliot, of course, is a profoundly contemporary figure both as poet and critical intelligence—an almost radar-like sensitivity to contemporary life has been one of the most powerful features of his poetry. And his profession of traditional and dogmatic Anglo-Catholicism is contemporary in this same sense— whether or not it be as benighted and reactionary as many critics have made out; for it is an attitude that is fully conscious of itself in difference and opposition to the previous century. In this sense it belongs to the twentieth century as distinctly as Arnold's agnosticism does to the previous century. It is unlikely that Arnold could have imagined anything quite like it. History is full of such abruptly turning corridors.

In any case, however matters stand with these typical poets, the fact is that the twentieth century has seen within philosophy itself an extraordinary rebirth of traditional religious thought. And the movements in question have been contemporary in the sense that they have been very much aware of themselves as different from the attitudes of the period immediately previous. They are thus both new—in the sense that they do in some sense belong to *this* time of ours—and also traditional, in the attempt to keep something alive more or less in a form in which it once had life. Hence our term "neo-Orthodoxy," and the decision of the two editors to include some specimens of this type of thought as a final illustration of that complex and problematic thing that is the philosophy of the twentieth century.

The authors here—Etienne Gilson, Paul Tillich, Martin Buber— represent the three dominant religious traditions of Western civilization: Catholicism, Protestantism, and Judaism. Each of these thinkers has exploited powerfully the resources of his tradition; yet with each the attempt to renew the tradition is so far from being a mere idle repetition of the past that all three of them are a mild scandal to the more rigidly orthodox within their own folds: Gilson's more recent interpretations of the philosophy of St. Thomas Aquinas have been compromised, according to the more hard-shelled Thomists, by existentialist elements; Buber's religion strikes orthodox Jews as much too "Hassidic" and mystical; and Tillich's theology is for a good many Protestant theologians altogether too secular and "psychological." Clearly, these three philosophers are "neo" as well as "orthodox"—and for some tastes altogether too "neo."

Etienne Gilson (1884-   ) is probably the greatest historian of medieval philosophy within this century. In a series of remarkable studies of the philosophers of the Middle Ages—of St. Augustine, of St. Bonaventure, and above all of St. Thomas Aquinas—he has probably done more than any other single scholar for the understanding of this long period in the intellectual history of the West. Indeed, the exhumation of the philosophy of the Middle Ages has been one of the most significant achievements of twentieth-century scholarship. Only a few years back the history of philosophy was taught as something that came to an end in the ancient world with Plotinus, the last of the great Greek Platonists, and began again with the first of the moderns, René Descartes, in the seventeenth century. For a thousand years, it appeared, philosophy had disappeared or else was carried on in so trivial a fashion by the medieval philosophers that their existence need hardly be reported to present-day students. You can still find in use textbooks on the history of philosophy that exhibit this point of view.

Now, this correction of our views on the history of philosophy is not merely a matter of more accurate historical understanding. It is also a matter of philosophical importance. Whatever philosophy may be—and the twentieth century, as the reader must have gathered by this time, hardly leaves us with any unique and final determination of the nature of philosophy—whatever it may be, it is surely no less than what it was from the beginning: an effort toward greater consciousness on the part of man. This effort requires that philosophy must also become conscious of its own history. This should be obvious from our last section. Human understanding is historical, and cannot grasp itself with any degree of completeness apart from history—and this is true of philosophical understanding. The history of philosophy is not an inert sequence of dates and facts, strung out like beads on a rosary, external to the activity of philosophy itself; on the contrary, it is internalized within philosophy itself in the struggle of philosophers who, in elaborating their own thoughts, must assimilate and transform the past. Just to the extent that philosophers saw a hole of a thousand years between the last Greeks and the first moderns, these philosophers were not able to grasp the nature of Western philosophy.

We are therefore indebted to the Neo-Thomists and Neo-Scholastics generally—whatever other philosophic objections we may have to their excessive partisanship—for making better known to us the historical background against which Descartes and modern philosophy have to be understood. No doubt, it is excessive partisanship when Descartes is represented as a total fall from the truth that had already been expressed by St. Thomas four centuries earlier. Yet one part of this verdict is not at variance with the verdict pronounced by other contemporary philosophers of secular persuasion—Whitehead and Heidegger, notably. The step from the Middle Ages into Descartes is a step forward for the mathematical and technical intelligence, but also a step away from Being. Descartes' *Cogito, ergo sum* (I think, therefore I am) leaves us the thinking ego exiled in upon its own certainty. Whatever cogitations it has about nature are purely quantitative or mathematical ones, since matter is understood essentially as *extension* in three dimensions. Thomism had at least preserved a good deal of Aristotelian naturalism, and the mind is still understood as the organic "form" of the body. (The Cartesian mind is mathematical and technical intelligence severed from the life of the body—what an extraordinary prophecy of the cultural explosions of our own day, in Nietzsche, Freud, or D. H. Lawrence!) The question, however, presents itself whether this departure from Being in the historical shift from St. Thomas to Descartes can be accurately described by returning to the concepts of St. Thomas. For the understanding of what happened historically we need new concepts after the fact; Heidegger here has much more to tell us than the Neo-Thomists about what happened historically with Descartes.

Gilson, to be sure, has described Thomism as Christian existentialism.

Indeed, it is to be taken as the real and true existentialism—all the other brands are either fragmentary or contaminated by a one-sided distortion of a basically true insight. The question arises, however, whether this "existentialistic" interpretation of St. Thomas would have arisen without the boom of modern existentialism. Gilson strongly denies that this latter has influenced him to look back and find existentialistic doctrine in St. Thomas. It is a fact, however, that the earlier interpretations of St. Thomas by Gilson do not mention at all a metaphysical revolution (as Gilson sees it, a revolution fundamentally existentialist in character) that Gilson's later interpretations posit as the very core of Thomistic thought. The earlier interpretations date from years long before the popular advent of existentialism. So far as they read anything back into the texts of St. Thomas from a contemporary context it is the then current controversy between realism and idealism, and St. Thomas is extolled primarily as a realist—in the midst of a then current boom of the revival of realism earlier in this century. Of course, there is no reason why an interpreter of a past philosophy should not take his guiding threads from contemporary influence. Gilson, however, denies such influences.

However, this question of possible contemporary borrowing in his interpretation is much less significant than the actual points wherein Gilson locates the "existentialism" of St. Thomas. The first point is St. Thomas's contention that the basic fact about anything is the primary act of being—*actus essendi*—that posits it in existence; and this act of existing is prior to the essence of the thing. This tallies pretty well with the existentialist formula, as laid down by Sartre: "Existence precedes essence." (In Sartre the formula is restricted to human existence: man first exists and proceeds to make himself what he is out of his own freedom and the historical conditions within which that freedom works.) The second basic point in the "existentialism" of St. Thomas is the Thomistic doctrine of the real distinction between essence and existence. This means that within any natural (and therefore contingent) thing the essence of the thing and its act of existing are not identical. There is, as it were, a hiatus or cleft within the thing between its existence and its essence. This is the very mark of its contingency. If there were not this cleft of nonidentity between the essence and the existence of the thing, it would be a Necessary Being like God, who is indeed according to St. Thomas identical with his own very act of Being. Deus est suum esse.

This second point, according to Gilson, is what radically separates Thomism from Aristotelianism, and stamps the former as a fundamentally Christian philosophy. For Aristotle the world was eternal, and the priority of essence over existence reappears in the shape of the doctrine of the fixity of natural forms; hence the Aristotelian universe is fundamentally a closed and static one, where the forms of becoming perpetually repeat themselves in endless cycles. By contrast the Christian St. Thomas holds that the world was created out of nothing by the infinite God, who is, as the Bible puts it, He who is; and this world, as a contingent world, still remains in the hollow of God's hand, and retains the marks of its creation in the very metaphysical core of its being—in the separation between existence and essence. With such a creation, time and becoming are more real than in Aristotle, since they have a real beginning and move toward a real end. Thus this Christian universe is not the closed and static universe of endless self-repetition of the ancient Greek.

So this orthodoxy—or contemporary interpretation of an orthodoxy—returns us in the end to a distinctly contemporary climate of opinion that has certainly heard the names of Bergson, William James, and the existentialists. The dominant tendency here becomes the emphasis upon existence as open rather than closed, contingent rather than determined, creative of new things rather than the fixed repetition of the past. If M. Gilson finds all these matters already understood—and as he repeatedly says, better understood—in a philosophy of the thirteenth century, this should not displease those of us who are willing to find corroboration wherever we can. Some of us, however, will not want to go quite so far as M. Gilson in the conclusion of one of his most recent books where he declares that Thomism is the synthesis of Hegel and Kierkegaard!

Paul Tillich (1886-   ), now Professor of Theology at Harvard University, is probably nowadays the best known of Protestant theologians among the general public, though not perhaps the most popular with fellow theologians. Karl Barth, no doubt, would be a purer and more strict representative of the Protestant tradition, but Barth's writing is almost purely in theology and it is difficult to isolate any purely philosophical passages. Tillich, then, is the best choice here as the philosophical voice of Protestantism, however controversial his theological doctrines may appear to more orthodox divines.

The main philosophical influences upon Tillich are Kant and Heidegger. Tillich starts from the Kantian rejection of Natural or Rational Theology: the existence of God cannot be demonstrated, Kant had argued, and Tillich carries this further (borrowing here from Pascal and Kierkegaard) by saying that the God who would be the object of a proof is not relevant to the needs of religion. Such a proof, or disproof, is simply beside the point. It is on this point too that Tillich declares himself against traditional theism. Traditional theism converts God into an *object*—for the sake of the so-called proofs of the existence of God. But when God is placed as an object among objects, then all the criticisms by scientific skepticism can be invoked as to the justification for positing such an entity at all; and with this the whole discussion moves on a level of objectification that no longer has any living relation with human subjectivity that prays to God. Hence, Tillich calls for a new God "beyond the God of Theism." For this he has been mistakenly accused of atheism. Such is the tidy and mechanical mind of some critics: if a man objects to traditional theism, then of course his doctrine can only be atheism.

The theology of our age, with the exception of Catholicism, has generally followed the Kantian rejection of Natural or Rational Theology. This is the emphasis of Martin Buber too, who has declared that God cannot be measured at all by man-made logic and that the plane on which man confronts God is not that of logical objectivity where science deals with its objects. The position of Catholicism, on the other hand, is that it is an *article of faith* that the existence of God is demonstrable since Scripture (in which the faithful must believe) has said:

> For the invisible things of Him from the creation of the world are clearly seen, being understood from the things that are created. St. Paul, Romans 1:20

But even here it is left open to the believer to reject any particular proof since he is required only to believe that God's existence is demonst*rable,* not demonst*rated.* No Catholic can be excommunicated for rejecting any *particular* proof of God's existence, be it a proof by St. Thomas or any other theologian; but the Catholic would be outside his faith if he were to assert that no valid proof at all would *ever possibly* be produced.

This step forward by contemporary theologians takes us beyond the age of tiresome atheism, beyond the negative criticism of the Enlightenment and the nineteenth century. All that is a stage of the past. Its point was to rescue religion from a world of objects with which religion had no business. Today the philosophy of religion centers around the distinct sphere of faith. Religion has lost its alliance with classical rationalism, which developed over the centuries from the Greeks to the end of the eighteenth century. Perhaps it is one of the signal philosophic facts of our century that Classical Rationalism itself has come to its demise. In any case, religious thinking has never been quite the same since the devastating critique by Kant and the passionate polemic of Kierkegaard for a faith that reason could not grasp.

The influence of Heidegger upon Tillich has to do principally with the Heideggerian interpretation of man as a creature of care or self-concern. As mentioned earlier, apropos of Heidegger, the philosophic force and novelty of this interpretation was that it no longer saw man principally as a percipient consciousness, an epistemological subject, as in Descartes or Hume. Perception and conception are rooted in a deeper stratum of existence. Of course, this view was already present in St. Augustine: the human person who is the subject of St. Augustine's *Confessions* is not the perceiving consciousness that forms the subject of epistemological discussion by philosophers, but the anxious and total personality involved with his own salvation. But the advantage of Heidegger's treatment was that it developed this point of view (in *Being and Time,* 1927) in full and copious detail, and above all with a full consciousness of the modern tradition from Descartes onward that it was setting out to destroy. Hence, it lay ready to hand for Tillich, and he in turn has made good use of it.

Man, then, is a being concerned with his own being. In fact, his very being is to be concerned with his own being. Self-concern involves concern with others and concern with things. Among the various concerns that may make up a human life some are more basic than others. A man may be concerned with making money because he is concerned to enjoy certain pleasures. On the other hand, he may deny himself all the pleasures in life just in order to make money. His is then the religion of Mammon, the demoniacal worship of the Golden Calf. Religion is thus, according to Tillich, the system (the concrete and organized totality) of our ultimate concerns. Or, more accurately, it is the system of *symbols* that express our ultimate concerns. A religion, by this definition, need not be a good thing, for a man's ultimate concerns may be evil; and Tillich does in fact discuss the subject of demoniacal religions.

The objection to Tillich's views has usually centered on his interpreting religion as a system of symbols. For some critics this looks very close to naturalism. Had not George Santayana, the most famous apostle of naturalism in the century, offered many years back in his *Interpretations of Poetry and Religion* a symbolic account of religion just like this? To be sure, Santayana justifies religion as symbolic; but this does not mean at all that his and Tillich's interpretation are identical. For Santayana the religious symbols are known and understood, and where they have value they are symbolic of something entirely human in its meaning. The justification of religion, to the extent that he justifies it at all, is for Santayana principally *aesthetic.* Catholicism pleases him because it is beautiful, and he remains scornful of Protestantism because it is iconoclastic and anti-aesthetic. But for Tillich the symbols of religion still have a connection with *faith.* They are symbolic of realities quite beyond any complete grasp on the part of our ordinary knowledge and understanding, even though these symbols do enter in active and understandable ways into the affairs of human life. Whatever else it may be, at least Tillich's interpretation is not a justification of religion as poetry.

With Martin Buber (1878-   ), Jewish scholar and Jewish seer, this volume comes to an end. This has not been planned exactly as a triumphant organ close—the material simply happened to fall out this way. On the other hand, it is not exactly dying away with a whimper, for Buber is one of the most pungent and powerful minds of the time, as will be particularly known to those who have had direct contact with this extraordinary personality on his recent visits to this country.

However the future may rank him as a thinker, Buber must certainly be judged an exemplary *man* of his time.

Buber is not a "school" or "professional" philosopher. Though his philosophic culture is profound and broad, Buber has dealt with philosophic problems only as they have been incidental to his interpretations of religion. He began his career under the influence of Hasidism, a mystical movement among the Jews in eighteenth-century Poland. His explorations also took him as far afield as Zen Buddhism, a branch of Oriental religion that is now enjoying a great vogue in this country. Gradually, however, Buber's religious views came to cluster around what seemed to him to be the center of Biblical religion: the confrontation of man and God in the situation of I-and-thou. In Genesis the Lord addresses Abraham, "ABRAHAM, WHERE ART THOU?"; and Abraham replies, "Here I am." The uniqueness of the Biblical account, which in this respect has no parallel in the scriptures of any other religion, is the directness, even abruptness, with which God addresses the human person and the latter responds.

I and Thou is probably the book by Buber best known in this country. Its aim is to explore the meaning and scope of the I-Thou relation. When we treat anything merely as an object, it has the status of the third-person neuter pronoun "it." This is true also when we treat a human person as an object, although when we do it we rarely stoop to the accuracy of using "it" and may still in fact address him as "you." The world of neutral objects—the world of technology and science—is the world of the it. Opposed to it is the world of the I-Thou. When we speak to the other in the full depth of his human personality, we no longer think of him as "it" but address him as "thou"; and only in the resonance of saying "thou" are we able truly to say "I." There is no real "I" that exists as a purely private ego.

Here is an answer to solipsism that may lack all the dialectic of the British discussion of the problem of other minds, but it is not altogether certain that it does not go closer to the root of the matter. After all, to argue that there are no good reasons for doubting that other minds than my own exist is to concede too much to the solipsist at the start: namely, that there is an ego that is capable of existing by itself, although it just happens that there are other minds too and we have no reason to doubt that there are. This is all right if one is talking about the ego as an empty epistemological subject; but if one is talking about the human person, then there is no doubt that Buber is right and the person has not attained to the subjectivity of "I" unless somewhere in his experience he has been able to address another person (or being) as "Thou."

For Buber God is the Absolute Thou—the Being to whom man in prayer can be surrendered and open in the full concreteness of his being. The danger of the modern age, as Buber sees it, is that the world of the it has encroached upon the world of the I-Thou. Peoples become the masses, to be manipulated like any other objects if one only has the proper techniques. In this climate of the "it," people are less and less able to say "I" to the other's "thou." Least of all are they capable of saying "I" to the Absolute Thou, God; and so this becomes, in Buber's words, the age of the eclipse of God, when (the image is Buber's) the human apparatus is no longer capable of tuning in on the messages that God is broadcasting.

Perhaps it is well to bring this volume to a close on this great traditional note of the Jewish prophet. Yet Buber is not all prophet; he is also a powerful critic, singularly direct in going to the heart of another thinker's position. His criticisms of Kierkegaard, Marx, Nietzsche, Heidegger and others are among the most incisive ever written on these men. From an intellectual standpoint, these criticisms reveal Buber at his best as a thinker. Yet the criticism is sustained at its center by the basic insight of the prophet: for what Buber objects to in the interpretations of man by modern thinkers is that the relation to God is left out and in the death of this relation man ceases to be man. Modern man, as Buber puts it, is a creature "at the edge"—and indeed sometimes over the edge and into the abyss. The famous death of God about which Nietzsche talked would not, in Buber's view, mark the birth of a new race of mankind but the end of man altogether.

With this last, we are aware, we leave the reader turned toward the future on a very gravely problematical issue. But the characteristic of this century, as has already been indicated in this volume, is that with it human existence has become thoroughly problematical. At least, to close with Buber may raise for the reader the question whether the Hebraic tradition is not as central to Western civilization as the Greek tradition, which gave us science. This is something on which the West may have to make up its mind very shortly.

W.B.

Etienne Gilson

THE SPIRIT OF THOMISM [1]

The texture of Thomism is made from a very small number of principles which continually penetrate one another. Perhaps, when all is said and done, all these principles are various aspects of one central notion, the notion of being. Human thought is satisfied only when it grasps an existence; but our intellection of a being is never limited itself to the sterile apprehension of something given. The apprehended being invites our intellect to explore it; it invites intellectual activity by the very multiplicity of aspects which it reveals. Inasmuch as a being is not distinguished from itself, it is one. In this sense we can say that *being* and *one* are coincident. No essence divides itself without losing at the same time its being and its unity. But since a being is by definition inseparable from itself, it lays the basis of the truth which can be affirmed about it. To say what is true is to say what is, and is to attribute to each thing the very being that it marks. Thus it is the being of a thing which founds its truth; and it is the truth of a thing which underlies the truth of thought.

We think the truth of a thing when we attribute to it the being that it is. It is thus that accord is established between our thought and its object; and it is this accord which provides the basis for what is true in our knowledge just as the intimate accord which subsists between its object and the eternal thought which God has of it establishes the truth of the thing outside our thought. The line of the relationships of truth is therefore only one aspect of the line of the relationships of being.

[1] From: *A Gilson Reader*, Etienne Gilson, edited by Anton C. Pegis, Ch. 16. Copyright © 1957 by Doubleday & Company, Inc., New York. Reprinted by permission.

We find exactly the same thing in the case of the good. Every being in so far as it is knowable is the basis of truth. But in so far as it is defined by a certain quantity of perfection, and consequently in so far as it is, it is desirable and presents itself to us as a good; and hence the movement to take possession of it which arises in us when we find ourselves in its presence. Thus the same being, without the addition of anything from outside, displays before us its unity, its truth, and its goodness. Whatever the relationship of identity which our thought can affirm in any one of the moments of the doctrinal synthesis, whatever the truth we set forth or good we desire, our thought always refers to being in order to establish its accord with itself, in order to assimilate its nature by way of knowledge or to enjoy its perfection through the will.

But Thomism is not a system if by this is meant a global explanation of the world deduced or constructed, in an idealistic manner, from *a priori* principles. The content of the notion whose content can be defined once and for all and set forth in an *a priori* way. There are many ways of being, and these ways must be ascertained. The one most immediately given to us is our own and that of corporeal things among which we pass our life. Each one of us "is," but in an incomplete and deficient manner. In the field of experience directly accessible to us we meet only substantial composites analogous to ourselves, forms engaged in matters by so indissoluble a bond that their very "engagement" defines these beings and that God's creative action, when it puts them into existence, directly produces the compounds of matter and form that constitute their beings. However imperfect such a being may be, it does possess perfection to the extent that it possesses being. We already find in it the transcendental relations of unity, truth, goodness, and beauty which are inseparable from it and which we have defined. But we note at the same time that, for some deep reason which we have still to determine, these relations are not fixed, closed, definite. Everything takes place—and experience verifies this—as though we had to struggle in order to establish these relationships instead of enjoying them peacefully. We are, and we are identical with ourselves, but not completely so. A sort of margin keeps us a little short of our definition. We do not fully realize human essence nor even the complete notion of our individuality. Hence, we are not involved in a simple manner of being, but in a permanent effort to maintain ourselves in being, to conserve ourselves, realize ourselves. It is just the same with all the sensible beings which we find around us. The world is under the constant impulse of forces, it is driven by various movements, it is forever becoming, like man himself ceaselessly passing from one state to another.

This universal becoming is normally expressed in terms of the distinction of potency and act, which extends to all given beings within our experience. These notions add nothing to the notion of being. Act always is being; potency always is possible being. Just as Aristotle had stated the universal extension of this principle without attempting to define it, St. Thomas readily uses it without explanation. It is a sort of postulate, a formula stating as a fact the definite modes of being given to us in experience. Any essence which does not completely realize its definition is act in the measure in which it does realize it, potency in the measure in which it does not, and privation in the measure in which it does not realize it. In so far as it is in act, it is the active principle which will release the motion of realization. It is from the actuality of form that all endeavors of this kind proceed; it is the source of motion, the reason of becoming; it is cause. Once more, it is the being in things which is the ultimate reason of all the natural processes we have been stating. It is being as such which communicates its form as efficient cause, which produces change as a moving cause, and assigns to it a reason for being produced as final cause. We are dealing, then, with beings which are ceaselessly moved by a fundamental need to preserve and complete themselves.

Now we cannot reflect upon an experience like this without noticing that it does not contain the adequate explanation of the facts it places before us. This world of becoming which is in motion in order to find itself, these heavenly spheres continually seeking themselves in the successive points of their orbits, these human souls which capture and assimilate being by their intellect, these substantial forms forever searching out new matter in which to realize themselves, do not contain in themselves the explanation of what they are. If such beings were self-explaining, they would be lacking nothing. Or, inversely, they would have to be lacking nothing before they could be self-explaining. But then they would no longer move in search of themselves; they would repose in the integrity of their own essence at length realized; they would cease to be what they now are.

It is, therefore, outside the world of potency and act, above becoming, and in a being which is totally what it is, that we must look for the sufficient reason of the universe. But this being reached by thought is obviously of a different nature than the being we observe, for if it were not different from the being which experience gives, there would be no advantage in positing it. Thus the world of becoming postulates a principle removed from becoming and placed entirely outside it.

But then a new problem arises. If the being we postulate from experience is radically different from the one given to us in experience, how can we know it through this experience and how will it help us to explain what we experience? Nothing can be deduced or inferred about a being from some other being which does not exist in the same sense as the first one does. Our thought would be quite inadequate to proceed to such a conclusion unless the reality in which we moved formed, by its hierarchical and analogical structure, a sort of ladder leading toward God.

It is precisely because every operation is the realization of an essence, and because every essence is a certain measure of being and perfection, that the universe reveals itself to us as a society made up of superiors and inferiors. The very definition of each essence ranks it immediately in its proper place in this hierarchy. To explain the operation of an individual thing, not only must we have the definition of this individual, but we must also have the definition of the essence which it embodies in a deficient manner. And the species itself is not enough because the individuals which embody the species are ceaselessly striving to realize themselves. Thus it becomes necessary either to renounce trying to account for this operation or else to seek for its explanation at a higher level, in a superior grade of perfection.

From here on, the universe appears essentially a hierarchy and the philosophical problem is to indicate its exact arrangement and to place each class of beings in its proper grade. To do this, one principle of universal value must always be kept in mind: that the greater or less can be appraised and classified only in relation to the maximum, the relative in relation to the absolute. Between God Who is Being, pure and simple, and complete nothingness, there come near God pure intelligences known as angels and near nothingness material forms. Between angels and material nature come human creatures on the borderline between spirits and bodies. Thus the angels reduce the infinite gap separating man from God and man fills in the gap between angels and matter.

Each of these degrees has its own mode of operation since each being operates according as it is in act and as its degree of actuality merges with its degree of perfection. The orderly and arranged hierarchy of beings is thus made complete by the orderly and arranged hierarchy of their operations, and in such a way that the bottom of the higher degree invariably comes into close contact with the top of the lower. Thus the principle of continuity gives precision and determination to the principle of perfection. Actually, both of these principles but express the higher law governing the communication of being. There is no being save the divine being in which all creatures participate; and creatures differ from one another only by reason of their greater or lesser degree of participation in the divine being.[2] Their perfection must, accordingly, be measured by the distance separating them from God. It is in thus differentiating themselves from one another that they arrange themselves into a hierarchy.

If this is true, it is analogy alone which enables our intelligence to arrive at a transcendent God from sensible things. It is analogy, too, which alone permits us to say that the universe has its existence from a transcendental principle and yet is neither confused with it nor added to it. The similarity of the analogue has, of course, to be explained, and

[2] *Summa Theologiae*, I, q. 44, a. 1.

it can be explained only by means of what the analogue imitates: "For beings (*ens*) is not said of many equivocally, but analogically, and thus must be reduced to unity." [3] But at the same time that it possesses enough of its model's being to require it as its cause, it possesses it in such a manner that the being of this cause does not become involved in that of the thing caused. And because the word "being" signifies two different modes of existence which applied to God and to creatures, no problem of addition or subtraction can arise. The being of creatures is only an image, an imitation of the divine being. Even as reflections appear about a flame, increasing, decreasing, and disappearing, without the substance of the flame being effected, so the likenesses freely created by the divine substance owe all their being to this substance. They subsist only through it, yet borrow nothing from its *per se* mode of being, a mode very different from their own. They neither add to it nor subtract from it even in the least degree.

These two principles, analogy and hierarchy, enable us to explain the creature through a transcendent Creator. They also permit us to maintain relations between them and to extend bonds between them which become the constitutive principles of created essences and the laws which serve to explain them. Whatever physics or natural philosophy ultimately shows to be the nature of things, it has necessarily to remain subordinate to a metaphysics of being. If creatures are similitudes in what concerns their basic origin, then it is to be expected that analogy will serve to explain the universe just as it explains creation. To account for the operation of a being, we shall always have to show that its operation is based, beyond its essence, in its act-of-being. And to give account of this essence will always be to show that a definite degree of participation in being, corresponding exactly to what this essence is, ought to have a place in our universe. But why was such a determined similitude required by a universe like ours? It is because the similitudes of any model can be essentially different only if they are more or less perfect. A finite system of images of an infinite being must have all the real degrees of likeness which can appear within the bounds assigned to the system by the free will of the Creator. The metaphysical explanation of a physical phenomenon must always be concerned with putting an essence in its place in a hierarchy.

This sense of hierarchy shows the profound influence of the Pseudo-Dionysius on the thought of St. Thomas. There is no denying this influence; and it explains why some have wished to rank the author of the *Summa Theologiae* among the disciples of Plotinus. Only when we strictly limit its range does such a thesis become acceptable. The Areopagite furnishes the framework of the hierarchy. He firmly implants in thought the need for a hierarchy. He makes it impossible not to consider the universe as a hierarchy. But he left for St. Thomas the task

[3] *Summa Contra Gentiles*, II, chap. 15.

of completing it; and even though Dionysius assigns the various grades in the hierarchy, he does not know the law which governs their arrangement and distribution.

But is it true to say that St. Thomas thought of the content of this universal hierarchy in a neo-Platonic spirit? If we except with numerous reservations the case of pure spirits, it is quite apparent that the answer is no. The God of St. Thomas the Christian is the same as St. Augustine's. That St. Augustine was under neo-Platonic influence does not mean that his God could be confused with the God of Plotinus. Between Plotinian speculation and the theology of the Fathers of the Church there stands Jehovah, the personal God, Who acts by intelligence and will, and Who freely places outside Himself that real universe which His Wisdom chose from an infinity of possible universes. Between this freely created universe and God the Creator there is an impassable abyss and no other continuity than the continuity of order. Properly speaking, the world is an ordered discontinuity. Must we not see that we are here far removed from neo-Platonic philosophy? To make of St. Thomas a Plotinian, or even a neo-Platonizer, is to confuse him with the adversaries he resisted so energetically.

The distance between the two philosophers is no less noticeable when we move from God to man. We said that St. Thomas' God was not the God of Plotinus but the Christian God of Augustine. Neither is St. Thomas' man the man of Plotinus. The opposition is particularly sharp right at the heart of the problem: in the relation between soul and body, and in the doctrine of knowledge which results from this. In Platonism there is the affirming of the extreme independence and almost complete aseity of the soul; this allows for Platonic reminiscence and even for the momentary return to the One through the ecstatic union. But in Thomism there is a most energetic affirming of the physical nature of the soul and vigilant care to close all paths which might lead to a doctrine of direct intuition of the intelligible in order to leave open no other road than that of sense knowledge. Platonism locates mystical knowledge in the natural prolongation of human knowledge; in Thomism, mystical knowledge is added to and coordinated with natural knowledge, but is not a continuation of it. All we know about God is what our reason teaches us about Him after reflecting upon the evidence of the senses. If we want to find a neo-Platonic doctrine of knowledge in the middle ages, we will have to look elsewhere than in St. Thomas.

This becomes clearer when we put aside the consideration of this particular problem and examine directly the Thomistic hierarchy of the universe. We have had a great deal to say about God and His creative power, about the angels and their functions, about man and his operations. We have considered, one after the other, all creatures endowed with intellect, and the First Intelligence itself. What we have seen is that the nature and compass of the many kinds of knowledge it has been given to us to acquire have varied very considerably according to the greater or less perfection of the reality which was its object. One who wishes to extract a clear notion of the spirit of Thomistic philosophy must first examine the ladder of being, and then inspect the values which locate each order of knowledge in its proper degree.

What is knowing? It is apprehending what is. There is no other perfect knowledge. Now it is immediately apparent that all knowledge, properly so called, of the higher degrees in the universal hierarchy is relentlessly refused us. We know that God and pure intelligences exist, but we do not know what they are. There is no doubting, however, that the awareness of a deficiency in our knowledge of God leaves us with a burning desire for higher and more complete knowledge. Nor can it be doubted that, if knowing consists in grasping the essence of the object known, God, angels, and, generally speaking, anything of the purely intelligible order are by definition beyond the grasp of our intellect. This is why, instead of having an intuition of the Divine Essence, we have but a vast number of concepts which, taken together, are a confused sort of imitation of what would have been a true notion of the Divine Essence. When all that we have been able to say about such a subject is put together, the result is a collection of negations or analogies, nothing more.

Where, then, does human knowledge find itself at home? When is it in the presence of its own object? Only at that point where it comes into contact with the sensible. And although it does not here totally penetrate the real, because the individual as such implies or presupposes matter and is therefore beyond expression, still reason is in control of the field in which it is working. In order to describe man—that is, the human composite—to describe the animal and its operations, the heavenly bodies and their powers, mixed bodies or the elements, rational knowledge remains proportioned to the order or rank of the objects it is exploring. Although its content is incomplete, it is nevertheless positive. What is original and truly profound in Thomism is not an attempt either to establish science more solidly or to extend it. St. Thomas places the proper object of the human intellect in the sensible order, but he does not consider the study of this order to be the highest function of the knowing faculty. The proper object of the intellect is the quiddity of the sensible, but its proper function is to make the sensible intelligible.[4] From the particular object on which its light falls it draws something universal. It can do this because this particular object carries the divine image naturally impressed upon it as the mark of its origin. The intellect is, in the proper sense of the term, born and made for the universal. Hence its straining toward that object which is by definition vigorously

---

4 *Sum. Theol.*, II-II, q. 180, a. 5, ad 1; *De Venitate*, q. XIII, a. 3.

636   NEO-ORTHODOXY

inaccessible, the Divine Being. Here reason knows very little, but what little it knows surpasses in dignity and value any other kind of certitude.[5]

All great philosophies, and St. Thomas' is no exception, present a different front according to the particular needs of the age which turns to them. It is hardly surprising, then, that, in a time like ours when so many minds are seeking to re-establish between philosophy and concrete reality bonds which idealism has broken, Thomists of different varieties should be insisting upon the notion of the act-of-being in his philosophy. The fact that they have reached analogous conclusions quite independently of one another makes their convergence still more significant. Restricting ourselves to recent statements, we can find any number of remarks like the following: The proper object of the intelligence is being, "not only *essential* or quidditative but existential." Or again: The entire thought of St. Thomas "seeks existence itself, though not, as in the case with practical philosophy, to produce it, but to know it." [6] Or again: "Thomistic philosophy is an existential philosophy." Mr. Maritain, the author of these statements, explains them at length in a special section of his *A Digression on Existence and Philosophy*.

When Maritain speaks in this way about St. Thomas, he is trying to make us understand that all human knowledge, including the metaphysician's, begins from sense knowledge and ultimately returns to it "not in order to know their essence. It (i.e., metaphysics) does so to know how they exist, for this too metaphysics should know, to attain their mode of existence, and then to conceive by analogy the existence of that which exists immaterially, which is purely spiritual." [7]

This is a lesson of the greatest importance. The only trouble is that the various statements of it are so compact that they tend to obscure its full significance. To insist on the existential character of Thomism in the above sense is to resist the very natural tendency of the human mind to remain on the level of abstraction. The very art of teaching fosters this tendency. How is anyone to teach without explaining, simplifying, abstracting? We tend to keep both ourselves and others on this level of conceptual abstraction which is so satisfying to the mind. First we disentangle essences from concrete reality; then we hold back the moment when we must again blend these essences into the unity of the concrete. We are afraid that we may fall back into the confusion from which we set out and which it is the very object of analysis to remove. Some hold back this moment so long that they never allow it to arrive. In this case, philosophy is reduced to making cuts into the real, following the

---

[5] *Summa Contra Gentiles,* I, chap. 5, ad *Apparet.*
[6] Jacques Maritain, *A Preface to Metaphysics* (*Seven Lessons on Being*) (London: Sheed and Ward, 1943), pp. 21, 24. The lectures published in this volume date from 1932 to 1933.
[7] *Op. cit.,* p. 23.

cleavage plane of essences, as if knowing from what essences the real is composed were the same as knowing existing reality. This reality is only directly apprehended by us in and through sensible knowledge, and this is why our judgments attain their object only when, directly or indirectly, they are resolved into it: "In other words the *res sensibilis visibilis,* the visible object of sense, is the touchstone of every judgment, *ex qua debemus de aliis judicare,* by which we must judge of everything else, because it is the touchstone of existence." [8]

Lest the metaphysician forget this principle, or rather, lest he be unaware of the point of view which it imposes on him, he should immerse himself in existence, enter ever more deeply into it "by means of as keen a sensitive (or aesthetic) perception as possible, and also by his experience of suffering and of existential conflicts, in order that, away up in the third heaven of the natural intelligence, he may devour the intelligible substance of things." After this comes the almost inevitable remark: "Need we add that the professor who is only a professor, who is withdrawn from existence, who has become insensible to this third degree of abstraction, is the direct opposite of the true metaphysician? Thomistic metaphysic is called *scholastic,* from the name of its most bitter trial. Scholarly pedagogy is its particular enemy. It must ceaselessly combat and subdue the professorial adversary attacking from within." [9]

It could hardly be put better. But just let us see what happens when we neglect to push judgments beyond abstract essences to the actually existing concrete. St. Thomas has noted that the properties of the essence are not the same when it is taken abstractly in itself as when taken in the state of concrete actualization in a really existing being. In fact he explains himself so explicitly on this point that we might as well let him speak for himself.

"Whatever be the object considered in the abstract, we can truly say that it contains no foreign element; that is, nothing outside and beyond its essence. It is in this way that we speak of *humanity* and *whiteness* and everything else of this kind. The reason for this is that *humanity* is then designated as that by which something is a man, and *whiteness* as that by which something is white. Now, formally speaking, a thing is a man only by something pertaining to the formal reason of man. Similarly, a thing is only formally white by what pertains to the formal reason of whiteness. This is why abstractions like these can include nothing foreign to themselves. It is quite different in the case of something signified concretely. Indeed, *man* signifies something possessing humanity, and white, something that has whiteness. Now the fact that man has humanity or whiteness does not prevent him from having something else which does not depend on the formal reason of humanity or whiteness. It is enough that it be not opposed to it. This is why *man* and

8 *Ibid.*
9 *Op. cit.,* p. 24.

white can have something more than humanity and whiteness. More-over, it is for this reason that *whiteness* and *humanity* may be called parts of something, but are not predicated of concrete beings them-selves, because a part is never predicated of the whole of which it is a part." [10]

If we apply these observations to philosophy, we shall see how, in the approach to problems, perspectives vary according to whether we avoid or face them. The philosopher begins with the experience com-mon to everyone. And he ought in the end to return to this same common experience in so far as it is this which he set out to explain. The only way to succeed is to begin with an analysis, pushed as far as possible, of the various elements included in the factual data which go to make up this experience. Here we have as first task the breaking up of the concrete into its intelligible elements. Whatever we find out has to be separated into its parts and each part isolated from the others. This can be done only by means of a distinct concept for each element. A necessary condition in thus distinguishing any concept is that it contain everything its definition includes, and nothing else. This is why every abstract essence is distinguished from the others as its concept is from theirs, and is only distinguished from them in that it excludes them. *Humanity* is that by which a man is a man, and it is that exclusively. So far is *humanity* from including *whiteness*, that there are men who are not white. Inversely, *whiteness* is that by which what is white is white. This does not include *humanity*. There can be an incredible number of white beings none of them men. Thus our inquiry into the real leads us to break down the confusion of the concrete into an enormous number of intelligible essences each quite distinct in so far as it cannot be reduced to the others.

Does philosophy consist in these abstract essences taken in the state of abstraction in which we are right now considering them? To say Yes is to become involved in a philosophy of the quiddity. We mean by this not simply a philosophy that calls upon quiddities, for this necessity is co-essential to all human knowledge, but a philosophy whose notion of the real reduces it to the essence, or quiddity. History shows us many such philosophies. Indeed their very classifications are innumerable, but there is no need to go into them here. This attitude concerns us primarily in that it expresses a natural tendency of the reason to think by "clear and distinct ideas," and consequently to reject as obscure and confused whatever does not allow itself to be included within the limits of purely quidditative notions. From this point of view, the "simple natures" on which Descartes worked are no different from the essences of the tree of Porphyry which he denounced as sterile.

Let us go farther. Whatever method we invoke, and even if we begin by admitting that the concept cannot be the ultimate object of philos-

[10] *In Boet. de Hebdomadibus,* chap. II; *Opuscula Omnia,* ed. P. Mandonnet (Paris: P. Lethielleux, 1927), vol. I, pp. 173-174.

ophy, we end up in actual fact with a philosophy of the quiddities whenever we fail to carry research beyond the level of abstract notions. A simple glance at the history of the various philosophies leads to this same conclusion. Restricting ourselves to Thomistic philosophy, we have to choose between locating its ultimate object in the grasping of the essences out of which the concrete real is made up, in which case our highest mode of knowing is a sort of intellectual intuition of pure essences, or assigning to Thomistic philosophy as its ultimate term rational knowledge of the concrete real through the essences engaged in the metaphysical texture of that concrete real.

Whatever we may think, there can be no doubting that the thought of St. Thomas, in first intention, turned toward knowledge of the existing concrete given in sensible experience and of the first causes of this existing concrete whether they be sensible or not. The whole philosophy we have been studying, from metaphysics to moral philosophy, bears testimony of this. This is why it is and remains philosophy in the proper sense and not, in the widely spread pejorative sense of the term, a "scholasticism." Every philosophy engenders its own scholastic presentation, its own school-doctrine, its own scholasticism. But the terms "philosophy" and "scholasticism" designate specifically distinct facts. Every philosophy worthy of the name starts out from the real and returns thereto. Every scholasticism starts from a philosophy and returns thereto. Philosophy degenerates into scholasticism the moment when, instead of taking the existing concrete as object of its reflections in order to study it deeply, penetrate it, throw more and more light upon it, it applies itself rather to the statements which it is supposed to explain, as if these statements themselves and not what they shed light on were the reality itself.

To fall into this error is to become quite incapable of understanding even the history of philosophy. Because understanding a philosophy is not merely reading what it says in one place in terms of what it says in another; it is reading it at each moment in terms of what it is actually speaking about. An error like this is far more harmful to philosophy itself than to the history of philosophy. St. Thomas' teaching has degenerated into scholasticism whenever and wherever it has been cut off from the real, the only object on which its illuminating rays can properly be focused. This is not a reason for believing that Thomism is a scholasticism, for its object is not Thomism but the world, man, and God, attained as existing beings in their very existence. It is therefore true that in this first sense the philosophy of St. Thomas is existential in the fullest sense of the word.

Beyond this first sense, there is another far more radical one which commands our attention even more imperatively. In this case, however, the very expression "existential philosophy," which is so inviting in itself, lends itself to so many misunderstandings that we stand in dread of the birth and spread of new "scholastic" controversies if, that is,

certain necessary precautions are not taken. It is a rather modern expression; and although it has arisen out of problems as old as Western
thought, it can hardly be applied to the doctrine of St. Thomas without
giving the impression of striving to rejuvenate it from without by fit-
ting it up in modern dress. To attempt something like this is hardly
wise. It even has the effect of aligning Thomism with philosophies
which in certain fundamental points are its direct contrary. To speak of
"existential philosophy" today brings immediately to mind such names
as Kierkegaard, Heidegger, Jaspers, and so on. In these we find divergent tendencies. No Thomism conscious of what it really is itself could
under any circumstances fully align itself with any of them. To do so
would only lay it open to the charge of seeking artificial rejuvenation,
of postponing its threatening dissolution by laying claim to a title generally conceded to recent philosophies still full of vitality. The whole
undertaking would be undignified and profitless to all parties concerned and could only lead to misunderstandings which it would take
generations to remove.

The first and most serious of these misunderstandings would be to
give the impression that Thomism was *one more* existential philosophy; whereas what really ought to be the issue at stake is whether or
not these philosophies to which Thomism is being likened have really
any right to be called existential philosophies at all. Assuredly these
are philosophies very much concerned with existence. But they really
only deal with it as an object of a possible phenomenology of human
existence, as though the primacy of existence signified chiefly that primacy of ethics which Kierkegaard so strongly insisted upon. If we look
here for a philosophy that passes beyond the phenomenological and
establishes the act-of-being as the keystone of metaphysics, we shall
look in vain. But this is just what St. Thomas has done. As philosophy
of the act-of-being, Thomism is not *another* existential philosophy, it
is the only one. All those phenomenologies which are on the hunt for an
ontology seem unconsciously to be moving in its direction as though
driven on by the natural desire of their own justification.

What characterizes Thomism is the decision to locate actual existence in the heart of the real as an act of transcending any kind of
quidditative concept and, at the same time, avoiding the double error
of remaining dumb before its transcendence or of denaturing it in objectifying it. The only means of speaking about the act-of-being is to
grasp it in a concept, and the concept which directly expresses it is the
concept of being. Being is *that which is;* that is, *that which has the act-
of-being.* It is quite impossible to come to the act-of-being by an intellectual intuition which grasps it directly, and grasps nothing more.
To think is to conceive. But the proper object of a concept is always
an essence, or something presenting itself to thought as an essence; in
brief, an object. The act-of-being, however, is an act. It can be grasped
only by or in the essence whose act it is. A pure *est* is unthinkable; but

an *id quod est* can be thought. But every *id quod est* is first a being. And because there is no concept anterior to this, being is the first principle of knowledge. It is so in itself; it is so in the philosophy of St. Thomas. Such a philosophy has every claim to be called a "philosophy of being."

If it is true that even the possibility of philosophy is tied up with the use of the quidditative concept, it is also true that the name which correctly designates a philosophy is drawn from the concept its first principle is based on. This cannot be the act-of-being because, taken in itself, the act-of-being is not the object of a quidditative concept. It must, then, inevitably be being. To call Thomism an existential philosophy does not call into question the legitimacy of its traditional title, but only confirms it. Since existence can be conceived only in the concept of being, Thomism is always a philosophy of being, even though called existential.

It seems proper to make this point because the abstract notion of being is, by its very definition, ambivalent. In a "that which is" (*id quod est*), or a "having being" (*esse habens*), we can spontaneously emphasize either the *id quod* and the *habens* or the *esse* and the *est*. Not only can we do this, but we actually do so, and usually it is the "that which" (*id quod*) and the "having" (*habens*) which we emphasize because they place before us the "thing" which exists; that is, being as the object of the quidditative concept.

This natural tendency to abstract and to confine ourselves to the abstract concept is so strong that it has been responsible for the appearance of several forms of Thomism in which *esse*—that is, the very act-of-being—seems to have no effective role to play. By yielding to this natural tendency, we abstract from *esse* and make Thomism a philosophy of the *id quod*. In order to rectify this situation, it is just as well to qualify Thomism as an "existential philosophy." To recall in this way the full meaning of *ens* in St. Thomas' language is to guard against impoverishing both *ens* itself and the philosophy whose first principle it is. It is to forget that the concept signified by *ens* implies direct reference to existence: *nam ens dicitur quasi esse habens*.[11]

It might be argued that a new expression like this is superfluous, because everyone is quite aware of what it is meant to express. This may be so. But it is not enough that everyone know it. Everyone must think it as well, and it is perhaps harder to do this than might be suspected. The history of the distinction between essence and existence and the endless controversies to which the same distinction is giving rise in our own day show that there is a very real difficulty. The very controversy itself is revealing. It shows how easy it is to substitute the abstract concept of existence for the concrete notion of the act-of-being, to "essentialize" the act-of-being, to make an act into the object

[11] *In XII Metaphysicorum,* lectio 1, ed. Cathala, no. 2419.

of a simple concept. The temptation to do this is so strong that scholars began to do it in the first generation after St. Thomas. So far as we can tell from research done up to the present, Giles of Rome is the starting point of the controversies over essence and existence. Now it has often been noted that this resolute defender of the distinction spontaneously expressed himself as though essence were one thing, existence another. Whether he consciously went so far as to reify the act-of-being has not been adequately demonstrated. But for our purposes it is quite enough merely to observe that his language betrays a marked tendency to conceive of *esse* as though it were a thing, and consequently to conceive the distinction between essence and existence as between two things. Indeed, he actually writes: "Existence and essence are two things." [12] Many other professed Thomists since his time have expressed themselves in identical terms. But little is to be gained by making this distinction if existence itself is taken as an essence. To call Thomism an "existential philosophy" serves to focus attention on this very important point.

But we have still to come to the chief justification of the expression "existential" as applied to Thomistic philosophy. It is not enough to say of all being that its concept connotes its *esse,* and that this *esse* must be taken as an act. It must also be said that this *esse* is the act of the same being whose concept connotes it. In every *esse habens* the *esse* is the act of the *habens* which possesses it, and the effect of this act upon what receives it is precisely this—to make a being of it.

If we accept this thesis in all its force and with all its ontological implications we come immediately to that well-known Thomistic position: *nomen ens imponitur ab ipso esse.*[13] So we might as well say that the act-of-being is the very core of being since being draws everything, even its name, from the act-of-being. What characterizes Thomistic ontology thus understood is not so much the distinction between essence and existence as the primacy of the act-of-being, not over and above being, but within it. To say that Thomistic philosophy is "existential" is to stress more forcibly than usual that a philosophy of being thus conceived is first of all a philosophy of the act-of-being.

There would be no advantage in making a great to-do about the act-of-being to the point of forgetting about the reality of the essence or even in allowing oneself to belittle its importance. Essences are the intelligible stuff of the world. Hence ever since Socrates, Plato, and Aristotle, philosophy has been one long hunt for essences. But the great question is to know whether we will bring home the game dead or

---

[12] Giles of Rome, *Theoremata de Esse et Essentia,* ed. E. Hocedez (Louvain, 1930), p. 127, line 12. On the interpretation of this expression, see the Introduction to this work, pp. 54-56. As Father Hocedez puts it, the dinstinction *inter rem et rem,* taken literally, amounts to making the distinction between essence and existence a distinction between essence and essence (p.55).

[13] *In IV Metaph.,* lect. 2, ed. Cathala, no. 558.

alive. An essence is dead when it is deposited in the understanding as a quiddity, without preserving its contact with the act-of-being. It is certainly a lot easier to handle dead essences. Reason surrounds them from all sides through the definitions she can give them. The mind knows what each of them contains, is assured that none of them either is or can be anything other than it is, and is secure against surprise from any quarter. One can, without fear, deduce *a priori* the properties of essences and even calculate beforehand all their possible combinations.

But a philosophy of the act-of-being cannot be satisfied by such methods. It wants to know which, among all the possible combinations of these essences, has actually been realized. This will very probably lead it to assert that many real combinations of essences are the very ones which would have been regarded as rather unlikely or perhaps even judged *a priori* to be impossible. No doubt living essences find in their own acts of existing a fertility and invention quite beyond the powers of the bare definitions of their concepts. Neither essence nor existence has any meaning apart from the other. Taken separately, they are but two abstractions. The only finite reality which the understanding can fruitfully explore is concrete being itself, the original, unique, and, in the case of man, unpredictable and free actualization of an inexhaustible essence by its own act-of-being.

It is rather difficult to find in St. Thomas a single concrete problem whose solution is not ultimately based on this principle. He is primarily a theologian; and it is in constructing his theology with such striking technical originality that he best proves his fertility of mind. Wherever his philosophy touches his theology there is to be seen that new light with which the act-of-being illumines all it touches. Sometimes, when St. Thomas brings up problems and notions not central to his real interests, he allows them to stand like hardened essences in the margin, as it were, of his work. He neither takes the time to rejuvenate them by bringing them into contact with the act-of-being, nor appears to feel the need for doing so. But had he undertaken to do something like this, his philosophy would still remain with its face turned to the future. It will always be thus because the principle to which he makes his appeal is the fertile energy of an act rather than the fixed expression of a concept. A universe like this will never stop surrendering its secret unless someday it ceases to be.

This is because it is an ordered plurality of real essences perfected by their acts-of-being. Such must perforce be the case, since this universe is made up of beings, and since a being is "something having an act-of-being." Each being has its own proper act-of-being, distinct from that of every other: *habet enim res unaquaeque in seipsa esse proprium ab omnibus aliis rebus distinctum.*[14] Let us go further: it is by this act-of-being which it has that it is a being, because it is by it that it is—

---

[14] *Summa Contra Gentiles,* I, chap. 14, ad *Est autem.*

unumquodque est per suum esse.[15] And if we can say, as it is often said, that a being's acting proceeds from its act-of-being—*operatio sequitur esse*—it is not merely in the sense of "like being like operation," but also and especially because the acting of a being is only the unfolding in time of the first act-of-being which makes it to be. It is this way that we get a notion of the efficient cause which is in agreement with the immediate certitudes of common sense and confers on them that metaphysical profundity which they lack by nature. There are many who feel that the efficient cause extends right to the very existence of its effect. And it is here precisely that they find complete justification: *causa importat influxum quemdam in esse causati.*[16]

God is the only being to which this formula, which is valid for others, cannot as such be applied. Of Him it cannot be said that He is *by* His act-of-being, He is His act-of-being. Since we can only think in terms of being, and since we can only grasp a being as an essence, we have to say that God has an essence. But we must hasten to add that what in Him serves as an essence is His act-of-being: *In Deo non est aliud essentia vel quidditas quam suum esse.*[17] The act-of-being is the act of acts; it is the primary energy of a being and from it all operations proceed (*operatio sequitur esse*). Since God is very *Esse,* the operation belonging to Him and only to Him is the producing of acts-of-being. To produce an act-of-being is what we call creating. Creating is, therefore, action proper to God: *Ergo creatio est propria Dei actio.*[18] And as it is as Act-of-Being that He alone has the power to create, the act-of-being is His proper effect: *esse est ejus proprius effectus.*[19]

The linking of these fundamental notions is rigidly necessary. As God is by essence the Act-of-Being itself, the created act-of-being must be His proper effect: *Cum Deus sit ipsum esse per suam essentiam, oportet quod esse creatum sit proprius effectus ejus.*[20] Once this conclusion has been reached, it becomes in its turn the principle of a long line of consequences, for every effect resembles its cause, and that by which the effect is most profoundly indebted to its cause is that by which it resembles it most. If therefore being is created, its primary resemblance to God lies in its own act-of-being: *omne ens, in quantum habet esse, est Ei simile.*[21]

From this we see right away that it is the act-of-being in each being that is most intimate, most profound and metaphysically primary. Hence the necessity, in an ontology which does not stop at the level of abstract essence, of pushing right to the existential root of every being

---

[15] *Op. cit.,* I, chap. 22, ad *Item, unumquodque;* cf. *op. cit.,* II, chap. 53.

[16] *In IV Metaph.,* lect. 1, ed. Cathala, no. 751. On the doctrine, see J. de Finance, *Etre et agir dans la philosophie de saint Thomas* (Paris: G. Beauchesne, 1945).

[17] *Summa Contra Gentiles,* I, chap. 21, ad *Ex his autem.*

[18] *Ibid.,* ad *Adhuc, effectus.*

[19] *Op. cit.,* II, chap. 22, ad *Item, omnis virtus.*

[20] *Sum. Theol.,* I, q. 8, a. 1.

[21] *Summa Contra Gentiles,* II, chap. 22, ad *Nullo autem;* cf. II, chap. 53.

in order to arrive at the very principle of its unity: *unumquodque secundum idem habet esse et individuationem.*[22]

Such is, in a particular way, the solution of the problem of the metaphysical structure of the human being. Where the essence of the body and the essence of the soul are taken separately, there can be no return to that concrete unity which a man is. The unity of a man is first of all the unity of his soul, which is really only the unity of his own *esse*. It is the same act-of-being which has issued forth from the divine *Esse,* which passes through the soul, which animates the body, and which penetrates even the tiniest cells of that body. When all is said and done, this is why, although the soul is a substance, its union with the body is not accidental: "It does not follow that the body is united with it accidentally because the selfsame act-of-being that belongs to the soul is conferred on the body." [23]

Thus that knowing being, man, is bound to God by its deepest ontological root, and has to look no farther for the entrance to the paths which will lead it to the knowledge of its cause. If it pursues its metaphysical analysis far enough, any being whatsoever will place it in the presence of God. God is in everything as its cause. His action affects it in its very act-of-being. Hence it is at the heart of what it is that God is actually present: *Oportet quod Deus sit in omnibus rebus, et intime.*[24] To prove God is to reclimb by reason from any finite act-of-being whatsoever, to the pure Act-of-Being which causes it. Here the knowledge of man reaches its ultimate terminus. When God has been established as the supreme Act-of-Being, philosophy ends and mystical theology begins. More simply put, reason asserts that what it knows depends in its very root upon the God it does not know: *cum Deo quasi ignoto conjungimur.*[25] To understand St. Thomas in this way is not at all to de-essentialize his philosophy. It is rather to restore real essence to it, to re-establish it in its full right. Essence is far more than the quiddity which satisfies reason; it is that by which, and in which, being has existence: *quidditatis nomen sumitur ex hoc quod diffinitionem significat; sed essentia dicitur secundum quod per eam et in ea ens habet esse.*[26] There is nothing further to be said. But it is worth repeating, because the human mind is so constituted that anyone is quite capable of forgetting it.

It has been rightly insisted that we must distinguish whatever separates *problem* from *mystery,* and upon the need for the metaphysician to pass beyond the first plane into the second. But neither is to be sacrificed for the sake of the other. When philosophy abandons the problem in order to immerse itself in the mystery, it ceases to be philosophy and becomes mysticism. Whether we like it or not, problems are the very

[22] *Quaest. Disp. de Anima,* a. 1, ad 2.
[23] *Ibid.,* ad 2.
[24] *Sum. Theol.,* I, q. 8, a. 1.
[25] *Summa Contra Gentiles,* III, chap. 49.
[26] *De Ente et Essentia,* chap. I.

stuff out of which philosophy is fashioned. To think is to know by concepts. Yet as soon as we begin to interpret the real in terms of quidditative concepts we are involved in the order of problems. We are here face to face with the inescapable, and even those who tend most strongly to escape from it must perforce recognize it. "What cannot be problematized cannot be examined nor objectified, and this by definition." [27] If philosophizing is a kind of examining of the real, philosophy can deal with the real only to the extent that the real can be problematized. The philosopher can get to God only by way of the problem of His existence, which the problem of His nature follows hard upon. He is then confronted with the problem of God's action and of God's government in the world. There are as many problems as there are mysteries, and they are met not only when philosophy talks about God. Man's science is alive with mysteries, as knowledge and liberty so eloquently testify.

Nor does mystery dwell only in the world of matter. Reason has for centuries been challenged by such obscure facts as efficient causality and the presence of quality. To give up the problematizing of mysteries would be to give up philosophizing. This is not the way to seek the solution of the crisis confronting philosophy today. But if we must not abandon problems, neither ought we to abandon mystery. The real danger begins where problems are confronted by the mystery and pretend to be self-sufficient and to lay claim to an autonomy that they do not actually possess. The moment a philosophy makes this mistake it is victimized by its own combinations of abstract concepts and enters a game that will never end. In fact it enters the realm of the antinomies of pure reason. Kant was not wrong when he said that escape from the antinomies was impossible. We need only add that the philosophic reason has every invitation not to enter, because such a reason ought not to be a discussion of pure problems or a flight from mystery; it ought to be a perpetually renewed effort to treat every problem as though it were bound up in a mystery or to problematize mystery by examining it with the help of concepts.

There is, to be sure, a mystery that can be called the object *par excellence* of philosophy, since metaphysics presupposes it; namely, the act-of-being. The philosophy of St. Thomas locates this mystery in the heart of the real and so insures itself against the risk, so fatal to metaphysical thought, of growing sterile in the very purity of abstraction. To a certain point, Aristotle had already walked in this way. His reformation had been to give philosophy an object that was, not the ideal essence conceived by thought, but real being as it is and as it behaves. With Aristotle, *ousia,* reality, is no longer the Idea, it is substance that merits the title. In order to measure the scope of this revolution, we have only to compare the solutions to the problem of the

[27] Gabriel Marcel, *Etre et avoir* (Paris: Aubier, 1935), p. 183.

first principle of all things proposed by Aristotle and Plato. When Plato takes up the problem, he sets out from an analysis of the real which disengages the intelligible element from it and then proceeds back from one intelligible condition to another until he comes to the first. It is the Good in itself; an Idea, that is, an hypostasized abstraction. Aristotle sets out from the concrete substance given in sensible experience; that is, he sets out from the existent. Then, contrary to Plato, he begins by bringing into evidence the active principle of its being and of its operations. Then he proceeds back from one ontological condition to another until he comes to the first condition. It is Pure Act that thus becomes the highest reality because it alone fully deserves the name of being—that on which everything else depends because everything else imitates it in an eternally recommenced effort to imitate in time its immovable actuality.

The distinctive work of St. Thomas was to push into the interior of being itself. He pushed back as far as the secret principle that establishes, not the actuality of being as substance, but the actuality of being as being. To the age-old question (even Aristotle referred to it as old), What is being? St. Thomas replied: It is that which has the act of existing. An ontology such as this loses nothing of the intelligible reality accessible to man under the form of concepts. Like that of Aristotle, it never grows tired of analyzing, classifying, defining, but it always remembers that, in what is most intimate within it, the real object it is struggling to define is beyond definition. It is not an abstraction; it is not even a thing; it is not even merely the formal act which makes it to be such-and-such a thing; it is the act that posits it as a real being in existence, by actualizing the very form that makes it intelligible.

A philosophy like this is at grips with the secret energy that causes its object. It finds in the meaning of its limitation the principle of its very fertility. It will never believe that it has come to the end of its inquiry because its end is beyond what it can enclose within the limits of a concept. In the case of Thomism, we are not dealing with a philosophy that turns its back on existence and consequently cannot see it. Rather we have to do with a philosophy that faces existence and never stops looking at it. Of course, we cannot see existence, but we know it is there and we can at least posit it, by an act of judgment, as the hidden root of what we can see and attempt to define. This is also why Thomistic ontology refuses to be limited to what the human mind knew about being in the thirteenth century. It even refuses to allow itself to be halted by what we know about it in the twentieth. It invites us to look beyond present-day science toward that primitive energy from which both knowing subject and object known arise.

If all beings "are" in virtue of their own act-of-being, each one of them breaks through the enclosing frame of its own definition. Better, perhaps, it has no proper definition: *individuum est ineffabile.* Yes, the individual is ineffable, but because it is too big rather than because it is too little, St. Thomas' universe is peopled with living essences sprung from a source as secret and rich as their very life. His world, by a filiation more profound than so many superficial dissimilarities might indicate, projects into Pascal's world rather than into Descartes'. In Pascal's world, the imagination is more likely to grow weary of producing concepts than nature to tire of providing them. There "all things hide a mystery; all things are veils hiding God." [28] Is not this what St. Thomas had already said with a simplicity no less striking than Pascal's: God is in all things, and that intimately —*Deus est in omnibus rebus, et intime?* For of such a universe two things can be said at the same time. Everything in it possesses its own act-of-being, distinct from that of all others. Yet, deep within each of them there lies hidden the same Act-of-Being, which is God.

If we want to recapture the true meaning of Thomism we have to go beyond the tightly woven fabric of its philosophical doctrines into its soul or spirit. What lies back of the ideas is a deep religious life, the interior warmth of a soul in search of God. There have in the recent past been prolonged and subtle disputes as to whether, according to St. Thomas, men experience a natural desire for their supernatural end. Theologians must ultimately decide such questions. They have to reach some kind of agreement about expressions and formulas which concern God's transcendence and still do not allow man to be separated from Him. The historian can at least say that St. Thomas leaves questions only partially settled, like the projecting stones of an unfinished wall awaiting the hand of a second builder. The very gaps in St. Thomas' work suggest that nature awaits the finishing touches of grace.

At the basis of this philosophy, as at the basis of all Christian philosophy, there is a deep awareness of wretchedness and need for a comforter who can be only God: "Natural reason tells man that he is subject to a higher being because of the defects he discerns in himself, defects for which he requires help and direction from some higher being. Whatever this being may be, it is commonly spoken of as God." [29] This is the natural feeling which grace excites in the Christian soul and which the perfection of charity brings to fulfillment when this soul is the soul of a saint. The burning desire of God which in a John of the Cross overflows into lyric poems is here transcribed into the language of pure ideas. Their impersonal formulation must not make us forget that they are nourished on the desire for God and that their end is the satisfaction of this desire.

There is no point in seeking, as some appear to do, an interior life underlying Thomism which is specifically and essentially different from Thomism itself. We ought not to think that the learned arrange-

[28] Pascal, *Pensées et opuscules,* ed. L. Brunschvicg (ninth ed., Paris: Librairie Hachette, 1920), p. 215.
[29] St. Thomas Aquinas, *Sum. Theol.,* II-II, q. 85, a. 1.

ment of the *Summa Theologiae* and the unbroken advance of reason constructing stone by stone this mighty edifice was for St. Thomas but the fruit of a superficial activity beneath which there moved deeper, richer, and more religious thinking. The interior life of St. Thomas, in so far as the hidden stirrings of so powerful a personality can be revealed, seems to have been just what it should have been to be expressed in such a doctrine. Nothing could be more desirable, nothing more indicative of an ardent will than his demonstrations fashioned from clearly defined ideas, presented in perfectly precise statements, and placed in a carefully balanced arrangement. Only a complete giving of himself can explain his mastery of expression and organization of philosophic ideas. Thus his *Summa Theologiae,* with its abstract clarity, its impersonal transparency, crystallizes before our very eyes and for all eternity his interior life. If we would recapture the deep and intense spirit of this interior life, there is nothing more useful than to reassemble for ourselves, but in terms of the order he gave them, the various elements that go to make up his remarkable *Summa*. We should study its internal structure and strive to arouse in ourselves the conviction of its necessity. Only that will to understand, shared between ourselves and St. Thomas the philosopher, will serve to make us see that this tremendous work is but the outward glow of an invisible fire, and that there is to be found behind the order of its ideas that powerful impulse which gathered them together.

Only thus does Thomism appear in all its beauty. It is a philosophy which creates excitement by means of pure ideas, and does so by sheer faith in the value of proofs and denials based on reason. This will become more evident to those who are disturbed by the very real difficulties encountered in the beginning, if they consider what St. Thomas' spirituality really was. If it were true that his philosophy were inspired by one spirit, his spirituality by another, the difference would become apparent by comparing his manner of thinking with his manner of praying. But a study of the prayers of St. Thomas which have been preserved, and which are so satisfying that the Church has placed them in the Roman breviary, shows that they are not characterized by the note of rapture or emotion or spiritual relish common enough in many forms of prayer. St. Thomas' fervor is completely expressed in the loving petitioning of God for what He should be asked for, and in becoming manner. His phrases tend to be rather rigid because the rhythms are so balanced and regular. But his fervor is genuine, deep, and readily recognizable and reflects the careful rhythms of his thought: "I pray Thee, that this holy Communion may be to me, not guilt for punishment, but a saving intercession for pardon. Let it be to me an armor of faith and a shield of good-will. Let it be to me a casting out of vices; a driving away of all evil desires and fleshly lusts; an increase of charity, patience, humility, obedience, and all virtues; a firm defense against the plots of all my enemies, both seen and unseen; a perfect quieting of all motions of sin, both in my flesh and in my spirit; a firm cleaving unto Thee, the only and true God, and a happy ending of my life." [30] Spirituality like this is more eager for light than for taste. The rhythm of his phrases, the pleasing sonority of his Latin words never modifies the perfect order of his ideas. But the discriminating taste can always perceive, beneath the balanced cadence of his expression, a religious emotion that is almost poetic.

Indeed, because he serves reason so lovingly, St. Thomas actually becomes a poet, and, if we believe a disinterested judge, the greatest Latin poet of the middle ages. Now it is remarkable that the lofty beauty of the works attributed to this poet of the Eucharist depend almost entirely on the aptness and concentration of his expressions. Poems like the *Oro te devote* and *Ecce panis angelorum* can almost be called little theological treatises and they have supplied generations of faithful Christians with inspiration and devotion. Perhaps the most distinctive of all his poems is the *Pange lingua* which inspired Rémy de Gourmont to say, in words matching, almost, the flawless beauty of the style he was attempting to describe: "The inspiration of St. Thomas is fired by an unwavering genius, a genius at once strong, sure, confident, and exact. What he wants to say, he speaks out boldly, and in words so resounding that doubt grows fearful and takes to flight." [31]

> *Pange lingua gloriosi corporis mysterium*
> *Sanguinisque pretiosi quem in mundi pretium*
> *Fructus ventris generosi Rex effudit gentium.*
>
> *Nobis datus, nobis natus ex intacta Virgine*
> *Et in mundo conversatus, sparso verbi semine*
> *Sui moras incolatus miro clausit ordine.*

And so we pass from St. Thomas' philosophy to his prayer, and from his prayer to his poetry without becoming aware of any change of context. And indeed there is no change! His philosophy is as rich in beauty as his poetry is laden with thought. Of both *Summa Theologiae* and *Pange lingua* we can say that his is an unwavering genius, strong, sure, confident, and exact. What he wants to say, he speaks out boldly and with a firmness of thought that doubt itself grows fearful and takes to flight.

Nowhere else, perhaps, does so demanding a reason respond to the call of so religious a heart. St. Thomas considered man as marvelously

[30] It is interesting to compare this prayer with the prayer attributed to St. Bonaventure which immediately follows it in the breviary. The contrast is striking.
[31] R. de Gourmont, *Le latin mystique* (Paris: Les Editions Crès, 1922), pp. 273-274, 275. All texts dealing with the spirituality of St. Thomas are brought together by Father Sertillanges in his *Prières de saint Thomas d' Aquin* (Paris: Art Catholique, 1920).

equipped for the knowledge of phenomena; but he did not think that the most adequate human knowledge was the most useful and the most beautiful to which man could aspire. He locates man's reason among sensible things as in its proper domain; but in equipping it for the exploration and conquest of this kingdom, he invites it to prefer another which is not merely the kingdom of man but that of the children of God. Such is the thought of St. Thomas. If we grant that a philosophy is not to be defined in terms of the elements it borrows but in terms of the spirit that quickens it, we shall see in Thomism neither Plotinianism nor Aristotelianism but, above all, Christianity. It is a philosophy that set out to express in rational language the total destiny of the Christian man. But, while constantly reminding him that here below he travels the paths of exile along which there is no light and no horizon, yet it has never ceased to guide his steps toward those distant peaks from which can be seen, far off in the mists, the borders of the Promised Land.

Paul Tillich

COURAGE AND
INDIVIDUALIZATION[1]

EXISTENTIALIST FORMS OF THE COURAGE TO BE AS ONESELF

1. *The Existential attitude and Existentialism*

Late romanticism, Bohemianism, and romantic naturalism had prepared the way for present-day Existentialism the most radical form
of the courage to be as oneself. In spite of the large amount of literature
which has appeared recently about Existentialism it is necessary for
our purpose to deal with it from the point of view of its ontological
character and its relation to the courage to be.

We must first of all distinguish the existential attitude from philosophical or artistic Existentialism. The existential attitude is one of involve-
ment in contrast to a merely theoretical or detached attitude. "Existential" in this sense can be defined as participating in a situation, especially
a cognitive situation, with the whole of one's existence. This includes
temporal, spatial, historical, psychological, sociological, biological conditions. And it includes the finite freedom which reacts to these conditions and changes them. An existential knowledge is a knowledge in
which these elements, and therefore the whole existence of him who
knows, participate. This seems to contradict the necessary objectivity
of the cognitive act and the demand for detachment in it. But knowledge depends on its object. There are realms of reality or—more ex-

actly—of abstraction from reality in which the most complete detachment is the adequate cognitive approach. Everything which can be expressed in terms of quantitative measurement has this character. But it is most inadequate to apply the same approach to reality in its infinite concreteness. A self which has become a matter of calculation and management has ceased to be a self. It has become a thing. You must participate in a self in order to know what it is. But by participating you change it. In all existential knowledge both subject and object are transformed by the very act of knowing. Existential knowledge is based on an encounter in which a new meaning is created and recognized. The knowledge of another person, the knowledge of history, the knowledge of a spiritual creation, religious knowledge—all have existential character. This does not exclude theoretical objectivity on the basis of detachment. But it restricts detachment to one element within the embracing act of cognitive participation. You may have a precise detached knowledge of another person, his psychological type and his calculable reactions, but in knowing this you do not know the person, his centered self, his knowledge of himself. Only in participating in his self, in performing an existential break-through into the center of his being, will you know him in the situation of your break-through to him. This is the first meaning of "existential," namely existential as the attitude of participating with one's own existence in some other existence.

The other meaning of "existential" designates a content and not an attitude. It points to a special form of philosophy: to Existentialism. We have to deal with it because it is the expression of the most radical form of the courage to be as oneself. But before going into it we must show why both an attitude and a content are described with words which are derived from the same word, "existence." The existential attitude and the Existentialist content have in common an interpretation of the human situation which conflicts with a nonexistential interpretation. The latter asserts that man is able to transcend, in knowledge and life, the finitude, the estrangement, and the ambiguities of human existence. Hegel's system is the classical expression of essentialism. When Kierkegaard broke away from Hegel's system of essences he did two things: he proclaimed an existential attitude and he instigated a philosophy of existence. He realized that the knowledge of that which concerns us infinitely is possible only in an attitude of infinite concern, in an existential attitude. At the same time he developed a doctrine of man which describes the estrangement of man from his essential nature in terms of anxiety and despair. Man in the existential situation of finitude and estrangement can reach truth only in an existential attitude. "Man does not sit on the throne of God," participating in his essential knowledge of everything that is. Man has no place of pure objectivity above finitude and estrangement. His cognitive function is as existentially conditioned as his whole being. This is the connection of the two meanings of "existential."

The Existentialist point of view

Turning now to Existentialism not as an attitude but as a content, we can distinguish three meanings: Existentialism as a *point of view,* as *protest,* and as *expression.* The Existentialist point of view is present in most theology and in much philosophy, art, and literature. But it remains a point of view, sometimes without being recognized as such. After some isolated forerunners had appeared Existentialism as protest became a conscious movement with the second third of the 19th century, and as such has largely determined the destiny of the 20th century. Existentialism as expression is the character of the philosophy, art, and literature of the period of the World Wars and all-pervading anxiety of doubt and meaninglessness. It is the expression of our own situation.

A few examples of the Existentialist point of view may be given. Most characteristic, and at the same time most decisive for the whole development of all forms of Existentialism, is Plato. Following the Orphic descriptions of the human predicament he teaches the separation of the human soul from its "home" in the realm of pure essences. Man is estranged from what he essentially is. His existence in a transitory world contradicts his essential participation in the eternal world of ideas. This is expressed in mythological terms, because existence resists conceptualization. Only the realm of essences admits of structural analysis. Wherever Plato uses a myth he describes the transition from one's essential being to one's existential estrangement, and the return from the latter to the former. The Platonic distinction between the essential and the existential realms is fundamental for all later developments. It lies in the background even of present-day Existentialism.

Other examples of the Existentialist point of view are the classical Christian doctrines of the fall, sin, and salvation. Their structure is analogous to the Platonic distinctions. As in Plato, the essential nature of man and his world is good. It is good in Christian thought because it is a divine creation. But man's essential or created goodness has been lost. The fall and sin have corrupted not only his ethical but also his cognitive qualities. He is subjected to the conflicts of existence and his reason is not exempted from them. But as in Plato a transhistorical memory has never been lost even in the most estranged forms of human existence, so in Christianity the essential structure of man and his world is preserved by the sustaining and directing creativity of God, which makes not only some goodness but also some truth possible. Only because this is so is man able to realize the conflicts of his existential predicament and to expect a restitution of his essential status.

Platonism as well as classical Christian theology have the Existentialist point of view. It determines their understanding of the human situation. But neither of them is Existentialist in the technical sense of the term. The Existentialist point of view is effective within the frame of their Essentialist ontology. This is true not only of Plato but also of Augustine, although his theology contains more profound insights into the negativities of the human predicament than that of anyone else in early Christianity, and although he had to defend his doctrine of man against the Essentialist moralism of Pelagius.

Continuing the Augustinian analysis of man's predicament, we note that monastic and mystical self-scrutiny brought to light an immense amount of the material of depth psychology, which entered theology in its chapters on man's creatureliness, sin, and sanctification. It also appeared in the medieval understanding of the demonic, and it was used by the confessors, especially in the monasteries. Much of the material which is discussed today by depth psychology and contemporary Existentialism was not unknown to the religious "analysts" of the Middle Ages. It was still known to the Reformers, notably to Luther, whose dialectical descriptions of the ambiguities of goodness, of demonic despair and of the necessity for Divine forgiveness have deep roots in the medieval search for the human soul in its relation to God.

The greatest poetic expression of the Existentialist point of view in the Middle Ages is Dante's *Divina Comedia*. It remains, like the religious depth psychology of the monastics, within the framework of scholastic ontology. But within these limits it enters the deepest places of human self-destruction and despair as well as the highest places of courage and salvation, and gives in poetic symbols an all-embracing existential doctrine of man. Some Renaissance artists have anticipated recent Existentialist art in their drawings and paintings. The demonic subjects to which were attracted men like Bosch, Breughel, Grünewald, the Spaniards and south Italians, the late Gothic masters of mass scenes, and many others are expressions of an Existentialist understanding of the human situation (see for example Breughel's Tower of Babel pictures). But in none of them was the medieval tradition completely broken. It was still an Existentialist point of view and not yet Existentialism.

In connection with the rise of modern individualism I have mentioned the nominalistic splitting of universals into individual things. There is a side in nominalism which anticipates motifs of recent Existentialism. This is, for example, its irrationalism, rooted in the breakdown of the philosophy of essences under the attacks of Duns Scotus and Ockham. The emphasis on the contingency of everything that exists makes both the will of God and the being of man equally contingent. It gives to man the feeling of a definite lack of ultimate necessity, with respect not only to himself but also to his world. And it gives him a corresponding anxiety. Another motif of recent Existentialism anticipated by nominalism is the escape into authority, which is a consequence of the dissolution of universals and the inability of the isolated individual to develop the courage to be as oneself. Therefore the nominalists built the bridge to an ecclesiastical authoritarianism which surpassed everything in the early and later Middle Ages and produced modern Catholic collectivism. But even so, nominalism was not Existentialism, although it was one of the most important forerunners of the Existentialist courage to be as oneself. It did not take this step, because even nominalism did not intend to break away from the medieval tradition.

What is the courage to be, in a situation where the Existentialist point of view has not yet burst the Essentialist frame? Generally speaking, it is the courage to be as a part. But this answer is not sufficient. Where there is an Existentialist point of view there is the problem of the human situation experienced by the individual. In the conclusion of the *Gorgias* Plato brings the individuals before the judge of the underworld, Rhadamanthus, who decides on their personal righteousness or injustice. In classical Christianity the eternal judgment concerns the individual; in Augustine the universality of original sin does not change the dualism in the eternal destiny of the individual; monastic and mystical self-scrutiny concerns the individual self; Dante puts the individual, according to his special character, into the different sections of reality; the painters of the demonic produce the feeling that the individual is lonely in the world as it is; nominalism isolates the individual consciously. Nevertheless, the courage to be in all these cases is not the courage to be as oneself. In each case it is an embracing whole from which the courage to be is derived: the heavenly realm, the Kingdom of God, divine grace, the providential structure of reality, the authority of the Church. Yet it is not a return to the unbroken courage to be as a part. It is much more a going ahead or above to a source of courage which transcends both the courage to be a part and the courage to be as oneself.

The loss of the Existentialist point of view

The Existentialist revolt of the 19th century is a reaction against the loss of the Existentialist point of view since the beginning of modern times. While the first part of the Renaissance as represented by Nicholas of Cusa, the academy of Florence, and early Renaissance painting was still determined by the Augustinian tradition, the later Renaissance broke away from it and created a new scientific essentialism. In Descartes the anti-Existential bias is most conspicuous. The existence of man and his world is put into "brackets"—as Husserl, who derives his "phenomenological" method from Descartes, has formulated it. Man becomes pure consciousness, a naked epistemological subject; the world (including man's psychosomatic being) becomes an object of scientific inquiry and technical management. Man in his existential predicament disappears. It was, therefore, quite adequate when recent philosophical Existentialism showed that behind the *sum* (I am) in Descartes' *Cogito ergo sum* lies the problem of the nature of this *sum* which is more than mere *cogitatio* (consciousness)—namely existence in time and space and under the conditions of finitude and estrangement.

Protestantism in its rejection of ontology seemed to re-emphasize the Existentialist point of view. And indeed the Protestant reduction of the dogma to the confrontation of human sin and divine forgiveness, and the presuppositions and implications of this confrontation, served the Existentialist point of view—but with a decisive limitation: the abundance of Existentialist material discovered in connection with the monastic self-scrutiny of the Middle Ages was lost, not in the Reformers themselves but in their followers, whose emphasis was on the doctrines of justification and predestination. The Protestant theologians stressed the unconditional character of the divine judgment and the free character of God's forgiveness. They were suspicious of an analysis of human existence, they were not interested in the relativities and ambiguities of the human condition. On the contrary: they believed that such considerations would weaken the absolute No and Yes which characterizes the divine-human relationship. But the consequence of this nonexistential teaching of the Protestant theologians was that the doctrinal concepts of the biblical message were preached as objective truth without any attempt to mediate the message to man in his psychosomatic and psychosocial existence. (It was only under pressure of the social movements of the late 19th century and the psychological movements of the 20th century that Protestantism became more open to the existential problems of the contemporary situation.) In Calvinism and sectarianism man became more and more transformed into an abstract moral subject, as in Descartes he was considered an epistemological subject. And when in the 18th century the content of Protestant ethics became adjusted to the demands of the rising industrial society which called for a reasonable management of oneself and one's world, anti-Existentialist philosophy and anti-Existentialist theology merged. The rational subject, moral and scientific, replaced the existential subject, his conflicts and despairs.

One of the leaders of this development, the teacher of ethical autonomy, Immanuel Kant, reserved two places in his philosophy for the Existentialist point of view, one in his doctrine of the distance between finite man and ultimate reality and the other in his doctrine of the perversion of man's rationality by radical evil. But for these Existentialist notions he was attacked by many of his admirers, including the greatest of them, Goethe and Hegel. Both these critics were predominantly anti-Existentialist. In Hegel's attempt to interpret all reality in terms of a system of essences whose more or less adequate expression is the existing world the Essentialist trend of modern philosophy reached its climax. Existence was resolved into essence. The world is reasonable as it is. Existence is a necessary expression of essence. History is the manifestation of essential being under the conditions of existence. Its course can be understood and justified. A courage which conquers the negativities of the individual life is possible for those who participate in the universal process in which the absolute mind actualizes itself. The anxieties of fate, guilt, and doubt are overcome by means of an elevation through the different degrees of meanings toward the highest, the philosophical intuition of the universal process itself. Hegel tries to unite the courage to be as a part (especially of a nation) with the courage to be as oneself (especially as a thinker) in a courage which transcends both and has a mystical background.

It is, however, misleading to neglect the Existentialist elements in Hegel. They are much stronger than is usually recognized. First of all Hegel is conscious of the ontology of nonbeing. Negation is the dynamic power of his system, driving the absolute idea (the essential realm) toward existence and driving existence back toward the absolute idea (which in the process actualizes itself as the absolute mind or spirit). Hegel knows of the mystery and anxiety of nonbeing; but he takes it into the self-affirmation of being. A second Existentialist element in Hegel is his doctrine that within existence nothing great is achieved without passion and interest. This formula of his introduction to the *Philosophy of History* shows that Hegel was aware of the insights of the romantics and the philosophers of life into the nonrational levels of human nature. The third element, which like the two others deeply influenced Hegel's Existentialist enemies, was the realistic valuation of the predicament of the individual within the process of history. History, he says, in the same introduction, is not a place where the individual can reach happiness. This implies either that the individual must elevate himself above the universal process to the situation of the intuiting philosopher or that the existential problem of the individual is not solved. And this was the basis for the Existentialist protest against Hegel and the world which is mirrored in his philosophy.

Existentialism as revolt

The revolt against Hegel's Essentialist philosophy was accomplished with the help of Existentialist elements present, though subdued, in Hegel himself. The first to lead the Existentialist attack was Hegel's former friend Schelling, on whom Hegel had been dependent in earlier years. In his old age Schelling presented his so-called "Positive Philosophie," most of the concepts of which were used by the revolutionary Existentialists of the 19th century. He called Essentialism "negative philosophy" because it abstracts from real existence, and he called Positive Philosophie the thought of the individual who experiences and thinks, and decides within his historical situation. He was the first to use the term "existence" in contradicting philosophical Essentialism. Although his philosophy was rejected because of the Christian myth which he reinterpreted philosophically in Existentialist terms, he influenced many people, notably Sören Kierkegaard.

Schopenhauer used the voluntarist tradition for his anti-Essentialist thinking. He rediscovered characteristics of the human soul and of man's existential predicament which had been covered by the Essentialist tendency of modern thought. At the same time Feuerbach emphasized the material conditions of human existence, and derived religious faith from the desire of man to overcome finitude in a transcendent world. Max Stirner wrote a book in which the courage to be as oneself was expressed in terms of a practical solipsism that destroyed any communication between man and man. Marx belonged to the Existentialist revolt, insofar as he contrasted the actual existence of man under the system of early capitalism with Hegel's Essentialist description of man's reconciliation with himself in the present world. Most important of all the Existentialists was Nietzsche, who in his description of European nihilism presented the picture of a world in which human existence has fallen into utter meaninglessness. Philosophers of life and pragmatists tried to derive the split between subject and object from something which precedes both of them—"life"—and to interpret the objectified world as a self-negation of the creative life (Dilthey, Bergson, Simmel, James). One of the greatest scholars of the 19th century, Max Weber, described the tragic self-destruction of life once technical reason has come into control. At the end of the century all this was still protest. The situation itself was not visibly changed.

Since the last decades of the 19th century revolt against the objectified world has determined the character of art and literature. While the great French impressionists, in spite of their emphasis on subjectivity, did not transcend the split between subjectivity and objectivity but treated the subject itself as a scientific object, the situation changed with Cézanne, Van Gogh, and Munch. From this time on, the question of existence appeared in the disturbing forms of artistic expressionism. The Existentialist revolt, in all its phases, produced a tremendous amount of psychological material. Existentialist revolutionaries like Baudelaire and Rimbaud in poetry, Flaubert and Dostoievsky in the novel, Ibsen and Strindberg in the theater are full of discoveries in the deserts and jungles of the human soul. Their insights were confirmed and methodologically organized by depth psychology, which started at the end of the century. When with July 31, 1914, the 19th century came to an end, the Existentialist revolt ceased to be revolt. It became the mirror of an experienced reality.

It was the threat of an infinite loss, namely the loss of their individual persons, which drove the revolutionary Existentialists of the 19th century to their attack. They realized that a process was going on in which people were transformed into things, into pieces of reality which pure science can calculate and technical science can control. The idealistic wing of bourgeois thinking made of the person a vessel in which universals find a more or less adequate place. The naturalistic wing of bourgeois thinking made of the person an empty field into which sense impressions enter and prevail according to the degree of their intensity. In both cases the individual self is an empty space and the bearer of something which is not himself, something strange by which the self is estranged from itself. Idealism and naturalism are alike in their attitude to the existing person; both of them eliminate his infinite significance and make him a space through which something else passes. Both philosophies are expressions of a society which was devised for the liberation of man but which fell under the bondage of objects it itself had created. The safety which is guaranteed by well-functioning mechanisms for the technical control of nature, by the refined psychological control of the person, by the rapidly increasing organizational control of society—this safety is bought at a high price: man, for whom all this was invented as a means, becomes a means himself in the service of means. This is the background of Pascal's attack on the rule of mathematical rationality in the 17th century; it is the background of the romantics' attack on the rule of moral rationality in the late 18th century; it is the background of Kierkegaard's attack on the rule of depersonalizing logic in Hegel's thought. It is the background of Marx's fight against economic dehumanization, of Nietzsche's struggle for creativity, of Bergson's fight against the spatial realm of dead objects. It is the background of the desire of most of the philosophers of life to save life from the destructive power of self-objectivation. They struggled for the preservation of the person, for the self-affirmation of the self, in a situation in which the self was more and more lost in its world. They tried to indicate a way for the courage to be as oneself under conditions which annihilate the self and replace it by the thing.

EXISTENTIALISM TODAY AND THE COURAGE OF DESPAIR

Courage and despair

Existentialism as it appeared in the 20th century represents the most vivid and threatening meaning of "existential." In it the whole development comes to a point beyond which it cannot go. It has become a reality in all the countries of the Western world. It is expressed in all the realms of man's spiritual creativity, it penetrates all educated classes. It is not the invention of a Bohemian philosopher or of a neurotic novelist; it is not a sensational exaggeration made for the sake of profit and fame; it is not a morbid play with negativities. Elements of all these have entered it, but it itself is something else. It is the expression of the anxiety of meaninglessness and of the attempt to take this anxiety into the courage to be as oneself.

Recent Existentialism must be considered from these two points of view. It is not simply individualism of the rationalistic or romantic or naturalistic type. In distinction to these three preparatory movements it has experienced the universal breakdown of meaning. Twentieth-century man has lost a meaningful world and a self which lives in meanings out of a spiritual center. The man-created world of objects has drawn into itself him who created it and who now loses his subjectivity in it. He has sacrificed himself to his own productions. But man still is aware of what he has lost or is continuously losing. He is still man enough to experience his dehumanization as despair. He does not know a way out but he tries to save his humanity by expressing the situation as without an "exit." He reacts with the courage of despair, the courage to take his despair upon himself and to resist the radical threat of nonbeing by the courage to be as oneself. Every analyst of present-day Existentialist philosophy, art, and literature can show their ambiguous structure: the meaninglessness which drives to despair, a passionate denunciation of this situation, and the successful or unsuccessful attempt to take the anxiety of meaninglessness into the courage to be as oneself.

It is not astonishing that those who are unshaken in their courage to be as a part, either in its collectivist or in its conformist form, are disturbed by the expressions of the Existentialist courage of despair. They are unable to understand what is happening in our period. They are unable to distinguish the genuine from the neurotic anxiety in Existentialism. They attack as a morbid longing for negativity what in reality is courageous acceptance of the negative. They call decay what is actually the creative expression of decay. They reject as meaningless the meaningful attempt to reveal the meaninglessness of our situation. It is not the ordinary difficulty of understanding those who break new ways in thinking and artistic expression which produces the widespread resistance to recent Existentialism but the desire to protect a self-limiting courage to be as a part. Somehow one feels that this is not a true safety; one has to suppress inclinations to accept the Existentialist visions, one even enjoys them if they appear in the theater or in novels, but one refuses to take them seriously, that is as revelations of one's own existential meaninglessness and hidden despair. The violent reactions against modern art in collectivist (Nazi, Communist) as well as conformist (American democratic) groups show that they feel seriously threatened by it. But one does not feel spiritually threatened by something which is not an element of oneself. And since it is a symptom of the neurotic character to resist nonbeing by reducing being, the Existentialist could reply to the frequent reproach that he is neurotic by showing the neurotic defense mechanisms of the anti-Existentialist desire for traditional safety.

There should be no question of what Christian theology has to do in this situation. It should decide for truth against safety, even if the safety is consecrated and supported by the churches. Certainly there is a Christian conformism, from the beginning of the Church on, and there is a Christian collectivism—or at least semicollectivism, in several periods of Church history. But this should not induce Christian theologians to identify Christian courage with the courage to be as a part. They should realize that the courage to be as oneself is the necessary corrective to the courage to be as a part—even if they rightly assume that neither of these forms of the courage to be gives the final solution.

The courage of despair in contemporary art and literature

The courage of despair, the experience of meaninglessness, and the self-affirmation in spite of them are manifest in the Existentialists of the 20th century. Meaninglessness is the problem of all of them. The anxiety of doubt and meaninglessness is, as we have seen, the anxiety of our period. The anxiety of fate and death and the anxiety of guilt and condemnation are implied but they are not decisive. When Heidegger speaks about the anticipation of one's own death it is not the question of immortality which concerns him but the question of what the anticipation of death means for the human situation. When Kierkegaard deals with the problem of guilt it is not the theological question of sin and forgiveness that moves him but the question of what the possibility of personal existence is in the light of personal guilt. The problem of meaning troubles recent Existentialists even when they speak of finitude and guilt.

The decisive event which underlies the search for meaning and the despair of it in the 20th century is the loss of God in the 19th century. Fuerbach explained God away in terms of the infinite desire of the human heart; Marx explained him away in terms of an ideological attempt to rise above the given reality; Nietzsche as a weakening of the will to live. The result is the pronouncement "God is dead," and with him the whole system of values and meanings in which one lived. This is felt both as a loss and as a liberation. It drives one either to nihilism or to the courage which takes nonbeing into itself. There is probably nobody who has influenced modern Existentialism as much as Nietzsche and there is probably nobody who has presented the will to be oneself more consistently and more absurdly. In him the feeling of meaninglessness became despairing and self-destructive.

On this basis Existentialism, that is the great art, literature, and philosophy of the 20th century, reveal the courage to face things as they are and to express the anxiety of meaninglessness. It is creative courage which appears in the creative expressions of despair. Sartre calls one of his most powerful plays *No Exit,* a classical formula for the situation of despair. But he himself has an exit: he can *say* "no exit," thus taking the situation of meaninglessness upon himself. T. S. Eliot called his first great poem "The Wasteland." He described the decomposition of civilization, the lack of conviction and direction, the poverty and hysteria of the modern consciousness (as one of his critics has analyzed it). But it is the beautifully cultivated garden of a great poem which describes the meaninglessness of the Wasteland and expresses the courage of despair.

In Kafka's novels *The Castle* and *The Trial* the unapproachable remoteness of the source of meaning and the obscurity of the source of justice and mercy are expressed in language which is pure and classical. The courage to take upon oneself the loneliness of such creativity and the horror of such visions is an outstanding expression of the courage to be as oneself. Man is separated from the sources of courage—but not completely: he is still able to face and to accept his own separation. In Auden's the *Age of Anxiety* the courage to take upon oneself the anxiety in a world which has lost the meaning is as obvious as the profound experience of this loss: the two poles which are united in the phrase "courage of despair" receive equal emphasis. In Sartre's *The Age of Reason* the hero faces a situation in which his passionate desire to be himself drives him to the rejection of every human commitment. He refuses to accept anything which could limit his freedom. Nothing has ultimate meaning for him, neither love nor friendship nor politics. The only immovable point is the unlimited freedom to change, to preserve freedom without content. He represents one of the most extreme forms of the courage to be as oneself, the courage to be a self which is free from any bond and which pays the price of complete emptiness. In the invention of such a figure Sartre proves his courage of despair. From the opposite side, the same problem is faced in the novel *The Stranger* by Camus, who stands on the boundary line of Existentialism, but who sees the problem of meaninglessness as sharply as the Existentialists. His hero is a man without subjectivity. He is not extraordinary in any respect. He acts as any ordinary official in a small position would act. He is a stranger because he nowhere achieves an existential relation to himself or to his world. Whatever happens to him has no reality and meaning to him: a love which is not a real love, a trial which is not a real trial, an execution which has no justification in reality. There is neither guilt nor forgiveness, neither despair nor courage in him. He is described not as a person but as a psychological process which is completely conditioned, whether he works or loves or kills or eats or sleeps. He is an object among objects, without meaning for himself and therefore unable to find meaning in his world. He represents that destiny of absolute objectivation against which all Existentialists fight. He represents it in the most radical way, without reconciliation. The courage to create this figure equals the courage with which Kafka has created the figure of Mr. K.

A glimpse at the theater confirms this picture. The theater, especially in the United States, is full of images of meaninglessness and despair. In some plays nothing else is shown (as in Arthur Miller's *Death of a Salesman*); in others the negativity is less unconditional (as in Tennessee Williams' *A Streetcar Named Desire*). But it seldom becomes positivity: even comparatively positive solutions are undermined by doubt and by awareness of the ambiguity of all solutions. It is astonishing that these plays are attended by large crowds in a country whose prevailing courage is the courage to be as a part in a system of democratic conformity. What does this mean for the situation of America and with it of mankind as a whole? One can easily play down the importance of this phenomenon. One can point to the unquestionable fact that even the largest crowds of theatergoers are an infinitely small percentage of the American population. One can dismiss the significance of the attraction the Existentialist theater has for many by calling it an imported fashion, doomed to disappear very soon. This is possibly but not necessarily so. It may be that the comparatively few (few even if one adds to them all the cynics and despairing ones in our institutions of higher learning) are a vanguard which precedes a great change in the spiritual and social-psychological situation. It may be that the limits of the courage to be as a part have become visible to more people than the increasing conformity shows. If this is the meaning of the appeal that Existentialism has on the stage, one should observe it carefully and prevent it from becoming the forerunner of collectivist forms of the courage to be as a part—a threat which history has abundantly proved to exist.

The combination of the experience of meaninglessness and of the courage to be as oneself is the key to the development of visual art since the turn of the century. In expressionism and surrealism the surface structures of reality are disrupted. The categories which constitute ordinary experience have lost their power. The category of substance is lost: solid objects are twisted like ropes; the causal interdependence of things is disregarded: things appear in a complete contingency; temporal sequences are without significance, it does not matter whether an event has happened before or after another event; the spatial dimensions are reduced or dissolved into a horrifying infinity. The organic structures of life are cut into pieces which are arbitrarily (from the biological, not the artistic, point of view) recomposed: limbs are dispersed, colors are separated from their natural carriers. The psychological process (this refers to literature more than to art) is reversed: one lives from the future to the past, and this without rhythm or any kind of meaningful organization. The world of anxiety is a world in which the categories, the structures of reality, have lost their validity. Everybody would be dizzy if causality suddenly ceased to be valid. In Existentialist art (as I like to call it) causality has lost its validity.

Modern art has been attacked as a forerunner of totalitarian systems. The answer that all totalitarian systems have started their careers by attacking modern art is insufficient, for one could say that the totalitarian systems fought modern art just because they tried to resist the meaninglessness expressed in it. The real answer lies deeper. Modern art is not propaganda but revelation. It shows that the reality of our existence is as it is. It does not cover up the reality in which we are living. The question therefore is this: Is the revelation of a situation propaganda for it? If this were the case all art would have to become dishonest beautification. The art propagated by both totalitarianism and democratic conformism is dishonest beautification. It is an idealized naturalism which is preferred because it removes every danger of art becoming critical and revolutionary. The creators of modern art have been able to see the meaninglessness of our existence; they participated in its despair. At the same time they have had the courage to face it and to express it in their pictures and sculptures. They had the courage to be as themselves.

The courage of despair in contemporary philosophy

Existential philosophy gives the theoretical formulation of what we have found as the courage of despair in art and literature. Heidegger in *Sein und Zeit* (which has its independent philosophical standing whatever Heidegger may say about it in criticism and retraction) describes the courage of despair in philosophically exact terms. He carefully elaborates the concepts of nonbeing, finitude, anxiety, care, having to die, guilt, conscience, self, participation, and so on. After this he analyses a phenomenon which he calls "resolve." The German word for it, *Entschlossenheit,* points to the symbol of unlocking what anxiety, subjection to conformity, and self-seclusion have locked. Once it is unlocked, one can act, but not according to norms given by anybody or anything. Nobody can give directions for the actions of the "resolute" individual—no God, no conventions, no laws of reason, no norms or principles. *We* must be ourselves, *we* must decide where to go. Our conscience is the call to ourselves. It does not tell anything concrete, it is neither the voice of God nor the awareness of eternal principles. It calls us to ourselves out of the behavior of the average man, out of daily talk, the daily routine, out of the adjustment which is the main principle of the conformist courage to be as a part. But if we follow this call we become inescapably guilty, not through moral weakness but through our existential situation. Having the courage to be as ourselves we become guilty, and we are asked to take this existential guilt upon ourselves. Meaninglessness in all its aspects can be faced only by those who resolutely take the anxiety of finitude and guilt upon themselves. There is no norm, no criterion for what is right and wrong. Resoluteness makes right what shall be right. One of Heidegger's historical functions was to carry through the Existentialist analysis of the courage to be as oneself more fully than anyone else and, historically speaking, more destructively.

Sartre draws consequences from the earlier Heidegger which the later Heidegger did not accept. But it remains doubtful whether Sartre was historically right in drawing these consequences. It was easier for Sartre to draw them than for Heidegger, for in the background of Heidegger's ontology lies the mystical concept of being which is without significance for Sartre. Sartre carried through the consequences of Heidegger's Existentialist analyses without mystical restrictions. This is the reason he has become the symbol of present-day Existentialism, a position which is deserved not so much by the originality of his basic concepts as by the radicalism, consistency, and psychological adequacy with which he has carried them through. I refer above all to his proposition that "the essence of man is his existence." This sentence is like a flash of light which illuminates the whole Existentialist scene. One could call it the most despairing and the most courageous sentence in all Existentialist literature. What it says is that there is no essential nature of man, except in the one point that he can make of himself what he wants. Man creates what he is. Nothing is given to him to determine his creativity. The essence of his being—the "should-be," "the ought-to-be,"—is not something which he finds; he makes it. Man is what he makes of himself. And the courage to be as oneself is the courage to make of oneself what one wants to be.

There are Existentialists of a less radical point of view. Karl Jaspers recommends a new conformity in terms of an all-embracing "philosophical faith"; others speak of a *philosophia perennis;* while Gabriel Marcel moves from an Existentialist radicalism to a position based on the semicollectivism of medieval thought. Existentialism in philosophy is represented more by Heidegger and Sartre than by anybody else.

The courage of despair in the non-creative Existentialist attitude

I have dealt in the last sections with people whose creative courage enables them to express existential despair. Not many people are creative. But there is a noncreative Existentialist attitude called cynicism. A cynic today is not the same person the Greeks meant by the term. For the Greeks the cynic was a critic of contemporary culture on the basis of reason and natural law; he was a revolutionary rationalist, a follower of Socrates. Modern cynics are not ready to follow anybody. They have no belief in reason, no criterion of truth, no set of values, no answer to the question of meaning. They try to undermine every norm put before them. Their courage is expressed not creatively but in their form of life. They courageously reject any solution which would deprive them of their freedom of rejecting whatever they want to reject. The cynics are lonely although they need company in order to show their loneliness. They are empty of both preliminary meanings and an ultimate meaning, and therefore easy victims of neurotic anxiety. Much compulsive self-affirmation and much fanatical self-surrender are expressions of the noncreative courage to be as oneself.

The limits of the courage to be as oneself

This leads to the question of the limits of the courage to be as oneself in its creative as well as its uncreative forms. Courage is self-affirmation "in spite of," and the courage to be as oneself is self-affirmation of the self as itself. But one must ask: What is this self that affirms itself? Radical Existentialism answers: What it makes of itself. This is all it can say, because anything more would restrict the absolute freedom of the self. The self, cut off from participation in its world, is an empty shell, a mere possibility. It must act because it lives, but it must redo every action because acting involves him who acts in that upon which he acts. It gives content and for this reason it restricts his freedom to make of himself what he wants. In classical theology, both Catholic and Protestant, only God has this prerogative: He is *ā sē* (from himself) or absolute freedom. Nothing is in him which is not by him. Existentialism, on the basis of the message that God is dead, gives man the divine "a-se-ity." Nothing shall be in man which is not by man. But man is finite, he is given to himself as what he is. He has received his being and with it the structure of his being, including the structure of finite freedom. And finite freedom is not aseity. Man can affirm himself only if he affirms not an empty shell, a mere possibility, but the structure of being in which he finds himself before action and nonaction. Finite freedom has a definite structure, and if the self tries to trespass on this structure it ends in the loss of itself. The nonparticipating hero in Sartre's *The Age of Reason* is caught in a net of contingencies, coming partly from the subconscious levels of his own self, partly from the environment from which he cannot withdraw. The assuredly empty self is filled with contents which enslave it just because it does not know or accept them as contents. This is true too of the cynic, as was said before. He cannot escape the forces of his self which may drive him into complete loss of the freedom that he wants to preserve.

This dialectical self-destruction of the radical forms of the courage to be as oneself has happened on a world-wide scale in the totalitarian reaction of the 20th century against the revolutionary Existentialism of the 19th century. The Existentialist protest against dehumanization and objectivation, together with its courage to be as oneself, have turned into the most elaborate and oppressive forms of collectivism that have appeared in history. It is the great tragedy of our time that Marxism, which had been conceived as a movement for the liberation of everyone, has been transformed into a system of enslavement of everyone, even of those who enslave the others. It is hard to imagine the immensity of this tragedy in terms of psychological destruction, especially within the intelligentsia. The courage to be was undermined in innumerable people because it was the courage to be in the sense of the revolutionary movements of the 19th century. When it broke down, these people turned either to the neocollectivist system, in a fanatic-neurotic reaction against the cause of their tragic disappointment, or to a cynical-neurotic indifference to all systems and every content.

It is obvious that similar observations can be made on the transformation of the Nietzschean type of the courage to be as oneself into the Fascist-Nazi forms of neocollectivism. The totalitarian machines which these movements produced embodied almost everything against which the courage to be as oneself stands. They used all possible means in order to make such courage impossible. Although, in distinction to communism, this system fell down, its aftermath is confusion, indifference, cynicism. And this is the soil on which the longing for authority and for a new collectivism grows.

The last two chapters, that on the courage to be as a part and that on the courage to be as oneself, have shown that the former, if carried through radically, leads to the loss of the self in collectivism and the latter to the loss of the world in Existentialism. This brings us to the question of our last chapter: Is there a courage to be which unites both forms by transcending them?

COURAGE AND
TRANSCENDENCE[1]

[The courage to accept acceptance]

Courage is the self-affirmation of being in spite of the fact of nonbeing. It is the act of the individual self in taking the anxiety of nonbeing upon itself by affirming itself either as part of an embracing whole or in its individual selfhood. Courage always includes a risk, it is always

[1] From: *The Courage To Be,* Paul Tillich. Copyright © 1952 by Yale University Press, New Haven. Reprinted by permission.

threatened by nonbeing, whether the risk of losing oneself and becoming a thing within the whole of things or of losing one's world in an empty self-relatedness. Courage needs the power of being, a power transcending the nonbeing which is experienced in the anxiety of fate and death, which is present in the anxiety of emptiness and meaninglessness, which is effective in the anxiety of guilt and condemnation. The courage which takes this threefold anxiety into itself must be rooted in a power of being that is greater than the power of oneself and the power of one's world. Neither self-affirmation as a part nor self-affirmation as oneself is beyond the manifold threat of nonbeing. Those who are mentioned as representatives of these forms of courage try to transcend themselves and the world in which they participate in order to find the power of being-itself and a courage to be which is beyond the threat of nonbeing. There are no exceptions to this rule; and this means that every courage to be has an open or hidden religious root. For religion is the state of being grasped by the power of being-itself. In some cases the religious root is carefully covered, in others it is passionately denied; in some it is deeply hidden and in others superficially. But it is never completely absent. For everything that is participates in being-itself, and everybody has some awareness of this participation, especially in the moments in which he experiences the threat of nonbeing. This leads us to a final consideration, the double question: How is the courage to be rooted in being-itself, and how must we understand being-itself in the light of the courage to be? The first question deals with the ground of being as source of the courage to be, the second with courage to be as key to the ground of being.

THE POWER OF BEING AS SOURCE OF THE COURAGE TO BE

The mystical experience and the courage to be

Since the relation of man to the ground of his being must be expressed in symbols taken from the structure of being, the polarity of participation and individualization determines the special character of this relation as it determines the special character of the courage to be. If participation is dominant, the relation to being-itself has a mystical character, if individualization prevails the relation to being-itself has a personal character, if both poles are accepted and transcended the relation to being-itself has the character of faith.

In mysticism the individual self strives for a participation in the ground of being which approaches identification. Our question is not whether this goal can ever be reached by a finite being but whether and how mysticism can be the source of the courage to be. We have referred to the mystical background of Spinoza's system, to his way of deriving the self-affirmation of man from the self-affirmation of the divine sub-

stance in which he participates. In a similar way all mystics draw their
power of self-affirmation from the experience of the power of being-
itself with which they are united. But one may ask, can courage be
united with mysticism in any way? It seems that in India, for example,
courage is considered the virtue of the *kshatriya* (knight), to be found
below the levels of the Brahman or the ascetic saint. Mystical identification transcends the aristocratic virtue of courageous self-sacrifice. It
is self-surrender in a higher, more complete, and more radical form.
It is the perfect form of self-affirmation. But if this is so, it is courage in
the larger though not in the narrower sense of the word. The ascetic
and ecstatic mystic affirms his own essential being over against the
elements of nonbeing which are present in the finite world, the realm of
Maya. It takes tremendous courage to resist the lure of appearances.
The power of being which is manifest in such courage is so great that
the gods tremble in fear of it. The mystic seeks to penetrate the ground
of being, the all-present and all-pervasive power of the Brahman. In
doing so he affirms his essential self which is identical with the power
of the Brahman, while all those who affirm themselves in the bondage
of Maya affirm what is not their true self, be they animals, men, or gods.
This elevates the mystic's self-affirmation above the courage as a
special virtue possessed by the aristocratic-soldiery. But he is not
above courage altogether. That which from the point of view of the
finite world appears as self-negation is from the point of view of ultimate being the most perfect self-affirmation, the most radical form of
courage.

In the strength of this courage the mystic conquers the anxiety of
fate and death. Since being in time and space and under the categories
of finitude is ultimately unreal, the vicissitudes arising from it and the
final nonbeing ending it are equally unreal. Nonbeing is no threat because finite being is, in the last analysis, nonbeing. Death is the negation of that which is negative and the affirmation of that which is positive. In the same way the anxiety of doubt and meaninglessness is
taken into the mystical courage to be. Doubt is directed toward everything that is and that, according to its Maya character, is doubtful.
Doubt dissolves the veil of Maya, it undermines the defense of mere
opinions against ultimate reality. And this manifestation is not exposed
to doubt because it is the presupposition of every act of doubt. Without
a consciousness of truth itself doubt of truth would be impossible. The
anxiety of meaninglessness is conquered where the ultimate meaning is
not something definite but the abyss of every definite meaning. The
mystic experiences step after step the lack of meaning in the different
levels of reality which he enters, works through, and leaves. As long
as he walks ahead on this road the anxieties of guilt and condemnation
are also conquered. They are not absent. Guilt can be acquired on
every level, partly through a failure to fulfill its intrinsic demands,
partly through a failure to proceed beyond the level. But as long as

the certainty of final fulfillment is given, the anxiety of guilt does not become anxiety of condemnation. There is automatic punishment according to the law of karma, but there is no condemnation in Asiatic mysticism.

The mystical courage to be lasts as long as the mystical situation. Its limit is the state of emptiness of being and meaning, with its horror and despair, which the mystics have described. In these moments the courage to be is reduced to the acceptance of even this state as a way to prepare through darkness for light, through emptiness for abundance. As long as the absence of the power of being is felt as despair, it is the power of being which makes itself felt through despair. To experience this and to endure it is the courage to be of the mystic in the state of emptiness. Although mysticism in its extreme positive and extreme negative aspects is a comparatively rare event, the basic attitude, the striving for union with ultimate reality, and the corresponding courage to take the nonbeing which is implied in finitude upon oneself are a way of life which is accepted by and has shaped large sections of mankind.

But mysticism is more than a special form of the relation to the ground of being. It is an element of every form of this relation. Since everything that is participates in the power of being, the element of identity on which mysticism is based cannot be absent in any religious experience. There is no self-affirmation of a finite being, and there is no courage to be in which the ground of being and its power of conquering nonbeing is not effective. And the experience of the presence of this power is the mystical element even in the person-to-person encounter with God.

The divine-human encounter and the courage to be

The pole of individualization expresses itself in the religious experience as a personal encounter with God. And the courage derived from it is the courage of confidence in the personal reality which is manifest in the religious experience. In contradistinction to the mystical union one can call this relation a personal communion with the source of courage. Although the two types are in contrast they do not exclude each other. For they are united by the polar interdependence of individualization and participation. The courage of confidence has often, especially in Protestantism, been identified with the courage of faith. But this is not adequate, because confidence is only one element in faith. Faith embraces both mystical participation and personal confidence. Most parts of the Bible describe the religious encounter in strongly personalist terms. Biblicism, notably that of the Reformers, follows this emphasis. Luther directed his attack against the objective, quantitative, and impersonal elements in the Roman system. He fought for an immediate person-to-person relationship between God and man. In him the courage of confidence reached its highest point in the history of Christian thought. Every work of Luther, especially in his earlier years, is filled with such courage. Again and again he uses the word *trotz*, "in spite of." In spite of all the negativities which he had experienced, in spite of the anxiety which dominated that period, he derived the power of self-affirmation from his unshakable confidence in God and from the personal encounter with him. According to the expressions of anxiety in his period, the negativity his courage had to conquer were symbolized in the figures of death and the devil. It has rightly been said that Albrecht Dürer's engraving, "Knight, Death, and the Devil," is a classic expression of the spirit of the Lutheran Reformation and—it might be added—of Luther's courage of confidence, of his form of the courage to be. A knight in full armor is riding through a valley, accompanied by the figure of death on one side, the devil on the other. Fearlessly, concentrated, confident he looks ahead. He is alone but he is not lonely. In his solitude he participates in the power which gives him the courage to affirm himself in spite of the presence of the negativities of existence. His courage is certainly not the courage to be as a part. The Reformation broke away from the semicollectivism of the Middle Ages. Luther's courage of confidence is personal confidence, derived from a person-to-person encounter with God. Neither popes nor councils could give him this confidence. Therefore he had to reject them just because they relied on a doctrine which blocked off the courage of confidence. They sanctioned a system in which the anxiety of death and guilt never was completely conquered. There were many assurances but no certainty, many supports for the courage of confidence but no unquestionable foundation. The collective offered different ways of resisting anxiety but no way in which the individual could take his anxiety upon himself. He never was certain; he never could affirm his being with unconditional confidence. For he never could encounter the unconditional directly with his total being, in an immediate personal relation. There was, except in mysticism, always mediation through the Church, an indirect and partial meeting between God and the soul. When the Reformation removed the mediation and opened up a direct, total, and personal approach to God, a new nonmystical courage to be was possible. It is manifest in the heroic representatives of fighting Protestantism, in the Calvinist as well as in the Lutheran Reformation, and in Calvinism even more conspicuously. It is not the heroism of risking martyrdom, of resisting the authorities, of transforming the structure of Church and society, but it is the courage of confidence which makes these men heroic and which is the basis of the other expressions of their courage. One could say—and liberal Protestantism often has said—that the courage of the Reformers is the beginning of the individualistic type of the courage to be as oneself.

But such an interpretation confuses a possible historical effect with the matter itself. In the courage of the Reformers the courage to be as oneself is both affirmed and transcended. In comparison with the mystical form of courageous self-affirmation the Protestant courage of confidence affirms the individual self as an individual self in its encounter with God as person. This radically distinguishes the personalism of the Reformation from all the later forms of individualism and Existentialism. The courage of the Reformers is not the courage to be oneself—as it is not the courage to be as a part. It transcends and unites both of them. For the courage of confidence is not rooted in confidence about oneself. The Reformation pronounces the opposite: one can become confident about one's existence only after ceasing to base one's confidence on oneself. On the other hand the courage of confidence is in no way based on anything finite besides onself, not even on the Church. It is based on God and solely on God, who is experienced in a unique and personal encounter. The courage of the Reformation transcends both the courage to be as a part and the courage to be as oneself. It is threatened neither by the loss of oneself nor by the loss of one's world.

Guilt and the courage to accept acceptance

In the center of the Protestant courage of confidence stands the courage to accept acceptance in spite of the consciousness of guilt. Luther, and in fact the whole period, experienced the anxiety of guilt and condemnation as the main form of their anxiety. The courage to affirm oneself in spite of this anxiety is the courage which we have called the courage of confidence. It is rooted in the personal, total, and immediate certainty of divine forgiveness. There is belief in forgiveness in all forms of man's courage to be, even in neocollectivism. But there is no interpretation of human existence in which it is so predominant as in genuine Protestantism. And there is no movement in history in which it is equally profound and equally paradoxical. In the Lutheran formula that "he who is unjust is just" (in the view of the divine forgiveness) or in the more modern phrasing that "he who is unacceptable is accepted" the victory over the anxiety of guilt and condemnation is sharply expressed. One could say that the courage to be is the courage to accept oneself as accepted in spite of being unacceptable. One does not need to remind the theologians of the fact that this is the genuine meaning of the Pauline-Lutheran doctrine of "justification by faith" (a doctrine which in its original phrasing has become incomprehensible even for students of theology). But one must remind theologians and ministers that in the fight against the anxiety of guilt by psychotherapy the idea of acceptance has received the attention and gained the significance which in the Reformation period was to be seen in phrases like "forgiveness of sins" or "justification through faith." Accepting acceptance though being unacceptable is the basis for the courage of confidence.

Decisive for this self-affirmation is its being independent of any moral, intellectual, or religious precondition: it is not the good or the wise or the pious who are entitled to the courage to accept acceptance but those who are lacking in all these qualities and are aware of being unacceptable. This, however, does not mean acceptance by oneself as oneself. It is not a justification of one's accidental individuality. It is not the Existentialist courage to be as oneself. It is the paradoxical act in which one is accepted by that which infinitely transcends one's individual self. It is in the experience of the Reformers the acceptance of the unacceptable sinner into judging and transforming communion with God.

The courage to be in this respect is the courage to accept the forgiveness of sins, not as an abstract assertion but as the fundamental experience in the encounter with God. Self-affirmation in spite of the anxiety of guilt and condemnation presupposes participation in something which transcends the self. In the communion of healing, for example the psychoanalytic situation, the patient participates in the healing power of the helper by whom he is accepted although he feels himself unacceptable. The healer, in this relationship, does not stand for himself as an individual but represents the objective power of acceptance and self-affirmation. This objective power works through the healer in the patient. Of course, it must be embodied in a person who can realize guilt, who can judge, and who can accept in spite of the judgment. Acceptance by something which is less than personal could never overcome personal self-rejection. A wall to which I confess cannot forgive me. No self-acceptance is possible if one is not accepted in a person-to-person relation. But even if one is personally accepted it needs a self-transcending courage to accept this acceptance, it needs the courage of confidence. For being accepted does not mean that guilt is denied. The healing helper who tried to convince his patient that he was not really guilty would do him a great disservice. He would prevent him from taking his guilt into his self-affirmation. He may help him to transform displaced, neurotic guilt feelings into genuine ones which are, so to speak, put on the right place, but he cannot tell him that there is no guilt in him. He accepts the patient into his communion without condemning anything and without covering up anything.

Here, however, is the point where the religious "acceptance as being accepted" transcends medical healing. Religion asks for the ultimate source of the power which heals by accepting the unacceptable, it asks for God. The acceptance by God, his forgiving or justifying act, is the only and ultimate source of a courage to be which is able to take the anxiety of guilt and condemnation into itself. For the ultimate power of self-affirmation can only be the power of being-itself. Everything less than this, one's own or anybody else's finite power of being, cannot overcome the radical, infinite threat of nonbeing which is experienced in the despair of self-condemnation. This is why the courage of confidence, as it is expressed in a man like Luther, emphasizes unceasingly exclusive trust in God and rejects any other foundation for his courage to be, not only as insufficient but as driving him into more guilt and deeper anxiety. The immense liberation brought to the people of the 16th century by the message of the Reformers and the creation of their indomitable courage to accept acceptance was due to the *sola fide* doctrine, namely to the message that the courage of confidence is conditioned not by anything finite but solely by that which is unconditional itself and which we experience as unconditional in a person-to-person encounter.

Fate and the courage to accept acceptance

As the symbolic figures of death and the devil show, the anxiety of this period was not restricted to the anxiety of guilt. It was also an anxiety of death and fate. The astrological ideas of the later ancient world had been revived by the Renaissance and had influenced even those humanists who joined the Reformation. We have already referred to the Neo-Stoic courage, expressed in some Renaissance pictures, where man directs the vessel of his life although it is driven by the winds of fate. Luther faced the anxiety of fate on another level. He experienced the connection between the anxiety of guilt and the anxiety of fate. It is the uneasy conscience which produces innumerable irrational fears in daily life. The rustling of a dry leaf horrifies him who is plagued by guilt. Therefore conquest of the anxiety of guilt is also conquest of the anxiety of fate. The courage of confidence takes the anxiety of fate as well as the anxiety of guilt into itself. It says "in spite of" to both of them. This is the genuine meaning of the doctrine of providence. Providence is not a theory about some activities of God; it is the religious symbol of the courage of confidence with respect to fate and death. For the courage of confidence says "in spite of" even to death.

Like Paul, Luther was well aware of the connection of the anxiety of guilt with the anxiety of death. In Stoicism and Neo-Stoicism the essential self is not threatened by death, because it belongs to being-itself and transcends nonbeing. Socrates, who in the power of his essential self conquered the anxiety of death, has become the symbol for the courage to take death upon oneself. This is the true meaning of Plato's so-called doctrine of immortality of the soul. In discussing this doctrine we should neglect the arguments for immortality, even those in Plato's *Phaedon,* and concentrate on the image of the dying Socrates. All the arguments, skeptically treated by Plato himself, are attempts to interpret the courage of Socrates, the courage to take one's death into one's self-affirmation. Socrates is certain that the self which the executioners will destroy is not the self which affirms itself in his courage to be. He does not say much about the relation of the two selves, and he could not because they are not numerically two, but one in two aspects. But he makes it clear that the courage to die is the test of the courage to be. A self-affirmation which omits taking the affirmation of one's death into itself tries to escape the test of courage, the facing of nonbeing in the most radical way.

The popular belief in immortality which in the Western world has largely replaced the Christian symbol of resurrection is a mixture of courage and escape. It tries to maintain one's self-affirmation even in the face of one's having to die. But it does this by continuing one's finitude, that is one's having to die, infinitely, so that the actual death never will occur. This, however, is an illusion and, logically speaking, a contradiction in terms. It makes endless what, by definition, must come to an end. The "immortality of the soul" is a poor symbol for the courage to be in the face of one's having to die.

The courage of Socrates (in Plato's picture) was based not on a doctrine of the immortality of the soul but on the affirmation of himself in his essential, indestructible being. He knows that he belongs to two orders of reality and that the one order is transtemporal. It was the courage of Socrates which more than any philosophical reflection revealed to the ancient world that everyone belongs to two orders.

But there was one presupposition in the Socratic (Stoic and Neo-Stoic) courage to take death upon oneself, namely the ability of every individual to participate in both orders, the temporal and the eternal. This presupposition is not accepted by Christianity. According to Christianity we are estranged from our essential being. We are not free to realize our essential being, we are bound to contradict it. Therefore death can be accepted only through a state of confidence in which death has ceased to be the "wages of sin." This, however, is the state of being accepted in spite of being unacceptable. Here is the point in which the ancient world was transformed by Christianity and in which Luther's courage to face death was rooted. It is the being accepted into communion with God that underlies this courage, not a questionable theory of immortality. The encounter with God in Luther is not merely the basis for the courage to take upon oneself sin and condemnation, it is also the basis for taking upon oneself fate and death. For encountering God means encountering transcendent security and transcendent eternity. He who participates in God participates in eternity. But in order to participate in him you must be accepted by him and you must have accepted his acceptance of you.

Luther had experiences which he describes as attacks of utter despair (*Anfechtung*), as the frightful threat of a complete meaninglessness. He felt these moments as satanic attacks in which everything was menaced: his Christian faith, the confidence in his work, the Reformation, the forgiveness of sins. Everything broke down in the extreme moments of this despair, nothing was left of the courage to be. Luther in these moments, and in the descriptions he gives of them, anticipated the descriptions of them by modern Existentialism. But for him this was not the last word. The last word was the first commandment, the statement that God is God. It reminded him of the unconditional element in human experience of which one can be aware even in the abyss of meaninglessness. And this awareness saved him.

It should not be forgotten that the great adversary of Luther, Thomas Münzer, the Anabaptist and religious socialist, describes similar experiences. He speaks of the ultimate situation in which everything finite reveals its finitude, in which the finite has come to its end, in which anxiety grips the heart and all previous meanings fall apart, and in which just for this reason the Divine Spirit can make itself felt and can turn the whole situation into a courage to be whose expression is revolutionary action. While Luther represents ecclesiastical Protestantism, Münzer represents evangelical radicalism. Both men have shaped history, and actually Münzer's views had even more influence in America than Luther's. Both men experienced the anxiety of meaninglessness and described it in terms which had been created by Christian mystics. But in doing so they transcended the courage of confidence which is based on a personal encounter with God. They had to receive elements from the courage to be which is based on mystical union. This leads to a last question: whether the two types of the courage to accept acceptance can be united in view of the all-pervasive presence of the anxiety of doubt and meaninglessness in our own period.

Absolute faith and the courage to be

We have avoided the concept of faith in our description of the courage to be which is based on mystical union with the ground of being as well as in our description of the courage to be which is based on the personal encounter with God. This is partly because the concept of faith has lost its genuine meaning and has received the connotation of "belief in something unbelievable." But this is not the only reason for the use of terms other than faith. The decisive reason is that I do not think either mystical union or personal encounter fulfills the idea of faith. Certainly there is faith in the elevation of the soul above the finite to the infinite, leading to its union with the ground of being. But more than this is included in the concept of faith. And there is faith in the personal encounter with the personal God. But more than this is included in the concept of faith. Faith is the state of being grasped by the power of being-itself. The courage to be is an expression of faith and what "faith" means must be understood through the courage to be. We have defined courage as the self-affirmation of being in spite of nonbeing. The power of this self-affirmation is the power of being which is effective in every act of courage. Faith is the experience of this power.

But it is an experience which has a paradoxical character, the character of accepting acceptance. Being-itself transcends every finite being infinitely; God in the divine-human encounter transcends man unconditionally. Faith bridges this infinite gap by accepting the fact that in spite of it the power of being is present, that he who is separated is accepted. Faith accepts "in spite of"; and out of the "in spite of" of faith the "in spite of" of courage is born. Faith is not a theoretical affirmation of something uncertain, it is the existential acceptance of something transcending ordinary experience. Faith is not an opinion but a state. It is the state of being grasped by the power of being which transcends everything that is and in which everything that is participates. He who is grasped by this power is able to affirm himself because he knows that he is affirmed by the power of being-itself. In this point mystical experience and personal encounter are identical. In both of them faith is the basis of the courage to be.

This is decisive for a period in which, as in our own, the anxiety of doubt and meaninglessness is dominant. Certainly the anxiety of fate and death is not lacking in our time. The anxiety of fate has increased with the degree to which the schizophrenic split of our world has removed the last remnants of former security. And the anxiety of guilt and condemnation is not lacking either. It is surprising how much anxiety of guilt comes to the surface in psychoanalysis and personal counseling. The centuries of puritan and bourgeois repression of vital strivings have produced almost as many guilt feelings as the preaching of hell and purgatory in the Middle Ages.

But in spite of these restricting considerations one must say that the anxiety which determines our period is the anxiety of doubt and meaninglessness. One is afraid of having lost or of having to lose the meaning of one's existence. The expression of this situation is the Existentialism of today.

Which courage is able to take nonbeing into itself in the form of doubt and meaninglessness? This is the most important and most disturbing question in the quest for the courage to be. For the anxiety of meaninglessness undermines what is still unshaken in the anxiety of fate and death and of guilt and condemnation. In the anxiety of guilt and condemnation doubt has not yet undermined the certainty of an ultimate responsibility. We are threatened but we are not destroyed. If, however, doubt and meaninglessness prevail one experiences an abyss in which the meaning of life and the truth of ultimate responsibility disappear. Both the Stoic who conquers the anxiety of fate with the Socratic courage of wisdom and the Christian who conquers the anxiety of guilt with the Protestant courage of accepting forgiveness are in a different situation. Even in the despair of having to die and the despair of self-condemnation meaning is affirmed and certitude preserved.

But in the despair of doubt and meaninglessness both are swallowed by nonbeing.

The question then is this: Is there a courage which can conquer the anxiety of meaninglessness and doubt? Or in other words, can the faith which accepts acceptance resist the power of nonbeing in its most radical form? Can faith resist meaninglessness? Is there a kind of faith which can exist together with doubt and meaninglessness? These questions lead to the last aspect of the problem discussed in these lectures and the one most relevant to our time: How is the courage to be possible if all the ways to create it are barred by the experience of their ultimate insufficiency? If life is as meaningless as death, if guilt is as questionable as perfection, if being is no more meaningful than nonbeing, on what can one base the courage to be?

There is an inclination in some Existentialists to answer these questions by a leap from doubt to dogmatic certitude, from meaninglessness to a set of symbols in which the meaning of a special ecclesiastical or political group is embodied. This leap can be interpreted in different ways. It may be the expression of a desire for safety; it may be as arbitrary as, according to Existentialist principles, every decision is; it may be the feeling that the Christian message is the answer to the questions raised by an analysis of human existence; it may be a genuine conversion, independent of the theoretical situation. In any case it is not a solution of the problem of radical doubt. It gives the courage to be to those who are converted but it does not answer the question as to how such a courage is possible in itself. The answer must accept, as its precondition, the state of meaninglessness. It is not an answer if it demands the removal of this state; for that is just what cannot be done. He who is in the grip of doubt and meaninglessness cannot liberate himself from this grip; but he asks for an answer which is valid within and not outside the situation of his despair. He asks for the ultimate foundation of what we have called the "courage of despair." There is only one possible answer, if one does not try to escape the question: namely that the acceptance of despair is in itself faith and on the boundary line of the courage to be. In this situation the meaning of life is reduced to despair about the meaning of life. But as long as this despair is an act of life it is positive in its negativity. Cynically speaking, one could say that it is true to life to be cynical about it. Religiously speaking, one would say that one accepts oneself as accepted in spite of one's despair about the meaning of this acceptance. The paradox of every radical negativity, as long as it is an active negativity, is that it must affirm itself in order to be able to negate itself. No actual negation can be without an implicit affirmation. The hidden pleasure produced by despair witnesses to the paradoxical character of self-negation. The negative lives from the positive it negates.

The faith which makes the courage of despair possible is the acceptance of the power of being, even in the grip of nonbeing. Even in the despair about meaning being affirms itself through us. The act of accepting meaninglessness is in itself a meaningful act. It is an act of faith. We have seen that he who has the courage to affirm his being in spite of fate and guilt has not removed them. He remains threatened and hit by them. But he accepts his acceptance by the power of being-itself in which he participates and which gives him the courage to take the anxieties of fate and guilt upon himself. The same is true of doubt and meaninglessness. The faith which creates the courage to take them into itself has no special content. It is simply faith, undirected, absolute. It is undefinable, since everything defined is dissolved by doubt and meaninglessness. Nevertheless, even absolute faith is not an eruption of subjective emotions or a mood without objective foundation.

An analysis of the nature of absolute faith reveals the following elements in it. The first is the experience of the power of being which is present even in face of the most radical manifestation of nonbeing. If one says that in this experience vitality resists despair one must add that vitality in man is proportional to intentionality. The vitality that can stand the abyss of meaninglessness is aware of a hidden meaning within the destruction of meaning. The second element in absolute faith is the dependence of the experience of nonbeing on the experience of being and the dependence of the experience of meaninglessness on the experience of meaning. Even in the state of despair one has enough being to make despair possible. There is a third element in absolute faith, the acceptance of being accepted. Of course, in the state of despair there is nobody and nothing that accepts. But there is the power of acceptance itself which is experienced. Meaninglessness, as long as it is experienced, includes an experience of the "power of acceptance." To accept this power of acceptance consciously is the religious answer of absolute faith, of a faith which has been deprived by doubt of any concrete content, which nevertheless is faith and the source of the most paradoxical manifestation of the courage to be.

This faith transcends both the mystical experience and the divine-human encounter. The mystical experience seems to be nearer to absolute faith but it is not. Absolute faith includes an element of skepticism which one cannot find in the mystical experience. Certainly mysticism also transcends all specific contents, but not because it doubts them or has found them meaningless; rather it deems them to be preliminary. Mysticism uses the specific contents as grades, stepping on them after having used them. The experience of meaninglessness, however, denies them (and everything that goes with them) without having used them. The experience of meaninglessness is more radical than mysticism. Therefore it transcends the mystical experience.

Absolute faith also transcends the divine-human encounter. In this encounter the subject-object scheme is valid: a definite subject (man) meets a definite object (God). One can reverse this statement and say that a definite subject (God) meets a definite object (man). But in both cases the attack of doubt undercuts the subject-object structure. The theologians who speak so strongly and with such self-certainty about the divine-human encounter should be aware of a situation in which this encounter is prevented by radical doubt and nothing is left but absolute faith. The acceptance of such a situation as religiously valid has, however, the consequence that the concrete contents of ordinary faith must be subjected to criticism and transformation. The courage to be in its radical form is a key to an idea of God which transcends both mysticism and the person-to-person encounter.

THE COURAGE TO BE AS THE KEY TO BEING-ITSELF

Nonbeing opening up being

The courage to be in all its forms has, by itself, revelatory character. It shows the nature of being, it shows that the self-affirmation of being is an affirmation that overcomes negation. In a metaphorical state-ment (and every assertion about being-itself is either metaphorical or symbolic) one could say that being includes nonbeing but nonbeing does not prevail against it. "Including" is a spatial metaphor which indicates that being embraces itself and that which is opposed to it, nonbeing. Nonbeing belongs to being, it cannot be separated from it. We could not even think "being" without a double negation: being must be thought as the negation of the negation of being. This is why we describe being best by the metaphor "power of being." Power is the possibility a being has to actualize itself against the resistance of other beings. If we speak of the power of being-itself we indicate that being affirms itself against nonbeing. In our discussion of courage and life we have mentioned the dynamic understanding of reality by the philosophers of life. Such an understanding is possible only if one ac-cepts the view that nonbeing belongs to being, that being could not be the ground of life without nonbeing. The self-affirmation of being without nonbeing would not even be self-affirmation but an immova-ble self-identity. Nothing would be manifest, nothing expressed, noth-ing revealed. But nonbeing drives being out of its seclusion, it forces it to affirm itself dynamically. Philosophy has dealt with the dynamic self-affirmation of being-itself wherever it spoke dialectically, notably in Neoplatonism, Hegel, and the philosophers of life and process. Theology has done the same whenever it took the idea of the living God seriously, most obviously in the trinitarian symbolization of the in-ner life of God. Spinoza, in spite of his static definition of substance (which is his name for the ultimate power of being), unites philosophi-cal and mystical tendencies when he speaks of the love and knowledge with which God loves and knows himself through the love and knowledge of finite beings. Nonbeing (that in God which makes his self-affirmation dynamic) opens up the divine self-seclusion and reveals him as power and love. Nonbeing makes God a living God. Without the No he has to overcome in himself and in his creature, the divine Yes to himself would be lifeless. There would be no revelation of the ground of being, there would be no life.

But where there is nonbeing there is finitude and anxiety. If we say that nonbeing belongs to being-itself, we say that finitude and anxiety belong to being-itself. Wherever philosophers or theologians have spoken of the divine blessedness they have implicitly (and sometimes explicitly) spoken of the anxiety of finitude which is eternally taken into the blessedness of the divine infinity. The infinite embraces itself and the finite, the Yes includes itself and the No which it takes into itself, blessedness comprises itself and the anxiety of which it is the conquest. All this is implied if one says that being includes nonbeing and that through nonbeing it reveals itself. It is a highly symbolic language which must be used at this point. But its symbolic character does not diminish its truth; on the contrary, it is a condition of its truth. To speak unsymbolically about being-itself is untrue.

The divine self-affirmation is the power that makes the self-affirmation of the finite being, the courage to be, possible. Only because being-itself has the character of self-affirmation in spite of nonbeing is courage possible. Courage participates in the self-affirmation of being-itself, it participates in the power of being which prevails against nonbeing. He who receives this power in an act of mystical or personal or absolute faith is aware of the source of his courage to be.

Man is not necessarily aware of this source. In situations of cynicism and indifference he is not aware of it. But it works in him as long as he maintains the courage to take his anxiety upon himself. In the act of the courage to be the power of being is effective in us, whether we recognise it or not. Every act of courage is a manifestation of the ground of being, however questionable the content of the act may be. The content may hide or distort true being, the courage in it reveals true being. Not arguments but the courage to be reveals the true nature of being-itself. By affirming our being we participate in the self-affirmation of being-itself. There are no valid arguments for the "existence" of God, but there are acts of courage in which we affirm the power of being, whether we know it or not. If we know it, we accept acceptance consciously. If we do not know it, we nevertheless accept it and participate in it. And in our acceptance of that which we do not know the power of being is manifest to us. Courage has revealing power, the courage to be is the key to being-itself.

Theism transcended

The courage to take meaninglessness into itself presupposes a relation to the ground of being which we have called "absolute faith." It is without a *special* content, yet it is not without content. The content of absolute faith is the "God above God." Absolute faith and its consequence, the courage that takes the radical doubt, the doubt about God, into itself, transcends the theistic idea of God.

Theism can mean the unspecified affirmation of God. Theism in this sense does not say what it means if it uses the name of God. Because of the traditional and psychological connotations of the word God such an empty theism can produce a reverent mood if it speaks of God. Politicians, dictators, and other people who wish to use rhetoric to make an impression on their audience like to use the word God in this sense. It produces the feeling in their listeners that the speaker is serious and morally trustworthy. This is especially successful if they can brand their foes as atheistic. On a higher level people without a definite religious commitment like to call themselves theistic, not for special purposes but because they cannot stand a world without God, whatever this God may be. They need some of the connotations of the word God and they are afraid of what they call atheism. On the highest level of this kind of theism the name of God is used as a poetic or practical symbol, expressing a profound emotional state or the highest ethical idea. It is a theism which stands on the boundary line between the second type of theism and what we call "theism transcended." But it is still too indefinite to cross this boundary line. The atheistic negation of this whole type of theism is as vague as the theism itself. It may produce an irreverent mood and angry reaction of those who take their theistic affirmation seriously. It may even be felt as justified against the rhetorical-political abuse of the name God, but it is ultimately as irrelevant as the theism which it negates. It cannot reach the state of despair any more than the theism against which it fights can reach the state of faith.

Theism can have another meaning, quite contrary to the first one: it can be the name of what we have called the divine-human encounter. In this case it points to those elements in the Jewish-Christian tradition which emphasize the person-to-person relationship with God. Theism in this sense emphasizes the personalistic passages in the Bible and the Protestant creeds, the personalistic image of God, the word as the tool of creation and revelation, the ethical and social character of the kingdom of God, the personal nature of human faith and divine forgiveness, the historical vision of the universe, the idea of a divine purpose, the infinite distance between creator and creature, the absolute separation between God and the world, the conflict between holy God and sinful man, the person-to-person character of prayer and practical devotion. Theism in this sense is the nonmystical side of biblical religion and historical Christianity. Atheism from the point of view of this theism is the human attempt to escape the divine-human encounter. It is an existential—not a theoretical—problem.

Theism has a third meaning, a strictly theological one. Theological theism is, like every theology, dependent on the religious substance which it conceptualizes. It is dependent on theism in the first sense insofar as it tries to prove the necessity of affirming God in some way; it usually develops the so-called arguments for the "existence" of God. But it is more dependent on theism in the second sense insofar as it tries to establish a doctrine of God which transforms the person-to-person encounter with God into a doctrine about two persons who may or may not meet but who have a reality independent of each other.

Now theism in the first sense must be transcended because it is irrelevant, and theism in the second sense must be transcended because it is one-sided. But theism in the third sense must be transcended because it is wrong. It is bad theology. This can be shown by a more penetrating analysis. The God of theological theism is a being beside others and as such a part of the whole of reality. He certainly is considered its most important part, but as a part and therefore as subjected to the structure of the whole. He is supposed to be beyond the ontological elements and categories which constitute reality. But every statement subjects him to them. He is seen as a self which has a world, as an ego which is related to a thou, as a cause which is separated from its effect, as having a definite space and an endless time. He is a being, not being-itself. As such he is bound to the subject-object structure of reality, he is an object for us as subjects. At the same time we are objects for him as a subject. And this is decisive for the necessity of transcending theological theism. For God as a subject makes me into an object which is nothing more than an object. He deprives me of my subjectivity because he is all-powerful and all-knowing. I revolt and try to make *him* into an object, but the revolt fails and becomes desperate. God appears as the invincible tyrant, the being in contrast with whom all other beings are without freedom and subjectivity. He is equated with the recent tyrants who with the help of terror try to transform everything into a mere object, a thing among things, a cog in the machine they control. He becomes the model of everything against which Existentialism revolted. This is the God Nietzsche said had to be killed because nobody can tolerate being made into a mere object of absolute knowledge and absolute control. This is the deepest root of atheism. It is an atheism which is justified as the reaction against theological theism and its disturbing implications. It is also the deepest root of the Existentialist despair and the widespread anxiety of meaninglessness in our period.

Theism in all its forms is transcended in the experience we have called absolute faith. It is the accepting of the acceptance without somebody or something that accepts. It is the power of being-itself that accepts and gives the courage to be. This is the highest point to which our analysis has brought us. It cannot be described in the way the God of all forms of theism can be described. It cannot be described in mystical terms either. It transcends both mysticism and personal encounter, as it transcends both the courage to be as a part and the courage to be as oneself.

The God above God and the courage to be

The ultimate source of the courage to be is the "God above God"; this is the result of our demand to transcend theism. Only if the God of theism is transcended can the anxiety of doubt and meaninglessness be taken into the courage to be. The God above God is the object of all mystical longing, but mysticism also must be transcended in order to reach him. Mysticism does not take seriously the concrete and the doubt concerning the concrete. It plunges directly into the ground of being and meaning, and leaves the concrete, the world of finite values and meanings, behind. Therefore it does not solve the problem of meaninglessness. In terms of the present religious situation this means that Eastern mysticism is not the solution of the problems of Western Existentialism, although many people attempt this solution. The God above the God of theism is not the devaluation of the meanings which doubt has thrown into the abyss of meaninglessness; he is their potential restitution. Nevertheless absolute faith agrees with the faith implied in mysticism in that both transcend the theistic objectivation of a God who is a being. For mysticism such a God is not more real than any finite being, for the courage to be such a God has disappeared in the abyss of meaninglessness with every other value and meaning.

The God above the God of theism is present, although hidden, in every divine-human encounter. Biblical religion as well as Protestant theology are aware of the paradoxical character of this encounter. They are aware that if God encounters man God is neither object nor subject and is therefore above the scheme into which theism has forced him. They are aware that personalism with respect to God is balanced by a transpersonal presence of the divine. They are aware that forgiveness can be accepted only if the power of acceptance is effective in man—biblically speaking, if the power of grace is effective in man. They are aware of the paradoxical character of every prayer, of speaking to somebody to whom you cannot speak because he is not "somebody," of asking somebody of whom you cannot ask anything because he gives or gives not before you ask, of saying "thou" to somebody who is nearer to the I than the I is to itself. Each of these paradoxes drives the religious consciousness toward a God above the God of theism.

The courage to be which is rooted in the experience of the God above the God of theism unites and transcends the courage to be as a part and the courage to be as oneself. It avoids both the loss of oneself by participation and the loss of one's world by individualization. The acceptance of the God above the God of theism makes us a part of that which is not also a part but is the ground of the whole. Therefore our self is not lost in a larger whole, which submerges it in the life of a limited group. If the self participates in the power of being-itself it receives itself back. For the power of being acts through the power of the individual selves. It does not swallow them as every limited whole, every collectivism, and every conformism does. This is why the Church, which stands for the power of being-itself or for the God who transcends the God of the religions, claims to be the mediator of the courage to be. A church which is based on the authority of the God of theism cannot make such a claim. It inescapably develops into a collectivist or semi-collectivist system itself.

But a church which raises itself in its message and its devotion to the God above the God of theism without sacrificing its concrete symbols can mediate a courage which takes doubt and meaninglessness into itself. It is the Church under the Cross which alone can do this, the Church which preaches the Crucified who cried to God who remained his God after the God of confidence had left him in the darkness of doubt and meaninglessness. To be as a part in such a church is to receive a courage to be in which one cannot lose one's self and in which one receives one's world.

Absolute faith, or the state of being grasped by the God beyond God, is not a state which appears beside other states of the mind. It never is something separated and definite, an event which could be isolated and described. It is always a movement in, with, and under other states of the mind. It is the situation on the boundary of man's possibilities. It *is* this boundary. Therefore it is both the courage of despair and the courage in and above every courage. It is not a place where one can live, it is without the safety of words and concepts, it is without a name, a church, a cult, a theology. But it is moving in the depth of all of them. It is the power of being, in which they participate and of which they are fragmentary expressions.

One can become aware of it in the anxiety of fate and death when the traditional symbols, which enable men to stand the vicissitudes of fate and the horror of death have lost their power. When "providence" has become a superstition and "immortality" something imaginary that which once was the power in these symbols can still be present and create the courage to be in spite of the experience of a chaotic world and a finite existence. The Stoic courage returns but not as the faith in universal reason. It returns as the absolute faith which says Yes to being without seeing anything concrete which could conquer the non-being in fate and death.

And one can become aware of the God above the God of theism in the anxiety of guilt and condemnation when the traditional symbols that enable men to withstand the anxiety of guilt and condemnation have lost their power. When "divine judgment" is interpreted as a psychological complex and forgiveness as a remnant of the "father-image," what once was the power in those symbols can still be present and create the courage to be in spite of the experience of an infinite gap between what we are and what we ought to be. The Lutheran courage returns but not supported by the faith in a judging and forgiving God. It returns in terms of the absolute faith which says Yes although there is no special power that conquers guilt. The courage to take the anxiety of meaninglessness upon oneself is the boundary line up to which the courage to be can go. Beyond it is mere non-being. Within it all forms of courage are re-established in the power of the God above the God of theism. *The courage to be is rooted in the God who appears when God has disappeared in the anxiety of doubt.*

Martin Buber

Ne connaîtrons-nous jamais l'homme?—ROUSSEAU

WHAT IS MAN?[1]

SECTION ONE: THE PROGRESS OF THE QUESTION

I: *Kant's questions*

1.

Rabbi Bunam von Przysucha, one of the last great teachers of Hasidism, is said to have once addressed his pupils thus: "I wanted to write a book called *Adam,* which would be about the whole man. But then I decided not to write it."

In these naive-sounding words of a genuine sage the whole story of human thought about man is expressed. From time immemorial man has known that he is the subject most deserving of his own study, but he has also fought shy of treating this subject as a whole, that is, in accordance with its total character. Sometimes he takes a run at it, but the difficulty of this concern with his own being soon overpowers and exhausts him, and in silent resignation he withdraws—either to consider all things in heaven and earth save man, or to divide man into departments which can be treated singly, in a less problematic, less powerful and less binding way.

The philosopher Malebranche, the most significant of the French philosophers who continued the Cartesian investigations, writes in the foreword to his chief work *De la recherche de la vérité* (1674): "Of all

[1] From: *Between Man and Man,* Martin Buber, Ch. 5. The Macmillan Company, New York, and Routledge & Kegan Paul, Ltd., London. Reprinted by permission.

human knowledge the knowledge of man is the most deserving of his study. Yet this knowledge is not the most cultivated or the most developed which we possess. The generality of men neglect it completely. And even among those who busy themselves with this knowledge there are very few who dedicate themselves to it—and still fewer who successfully dedicate themselves to it." He himself certainly raises in his book such genuinely anthropological questions as how far the life of the nerves which lead to the lungs, the stomach, and the liver, influences the origin of errors; but he too established no doctrine of the being of man.

2.

The most forcible statement of the task set to philosophical anthropology was made by Kant. In the *Handbook* to his lectures on logic, which he expressly acknowledged—though he himself did not publish it and though it does not reproduce his underlying notes authentically—he distinguishes between a philosophy in the scholastic sense and a philosophy in the universal sense (*in sensu cosmico*). He describes the latter as "the knowledge of the ultimate aims of human reason" or as the "knowledge of the highest maxim of the use of our reason." The field of philosophy in this cosmopolitan significance may, according to Kant, be marked off into the following questions. "1. What can I know? 2. What ought I to do? 3. What may I hope? 4. What is man? Metaphysics answers the first question, ethics the second, religion the third and anthropology the fourth." And Kant adds: "Fundamentally all this could be reckoned as anthropology, since the first three questions are related to the last." This formulation repeats the three questions of which Kant says, in the section of his *Critique of Pure Reason* entitled *Of the ideal of the supreme good,* that every interest of the reason, the speculative as well as the practical, is united in them. In distinction from the *Critique of Pure Reason* he here traces these questions back to a fourth question, that about the being of man, and assigns it to a discipline called anthropology, by which—since he is discussing the fundamental questions of human philosophizing—only philosophical anthropology can be understood. This, then, would be the fundamental philosophical science.

But it is remarkable that Kant's own anthropology, both what he himself published and his copious lectures on man, which only appeared long after his death, absolutely fails to achieve what he demands of a philosophical anthropology. In its express purpose as well as in its entire content it offers something different—an abundance of valuable observations for the knowledge of man, for example, on egoism, on honesty and lies, on fancy, on fortune-telling, on dreams, on mental diseases, on wit, and so on. But the question, what man is, is simply not raised, and not one of the problems which are implicitly set us at the same time by this question—such as man's special place in the cosmos, his connexion with destiny, his relation to the world of things, his understanding of his fellow-men, his existence as a being that knows it must die, his attitude in all the ordinary and extraordinary encounters with the mystery with which his life is shot through, and so on—not one of these problems is seriously touched upon. The *wholeness* of man does not enter into this anthropology. It is as if Kant in his actual philosophizing had had qualms about setting the question which he formulated as the fundamental one.

A modern philosopher, Martin Heidegger, who has dealt (in his *Kant and the Problem of Metaphysics,* 1929) with this strange contradiction, explains it by the *indefiniteness* of the question, what man is. The way of asking the question about man, he says, has itself become questionable. In Kant's first three questions it is man's *finitude* which is under discussion: "What *can* I know?" involves an inability, and thus a limitation; "What *ought* I to do?" includes the realization that something has not yet been accomplished, and thus a limitation; and "What *may* I hope?" means that the questioner is given one expectation and denied another, and thus it means a limitation. The fourth question is the question about "finitude in man", and is no longer an anthropological question at all, for it is the question about the essence of existence itself. As the basis of metaphysics anthropology is replaced by "fundamental ontology".

Whatever this finding represents, it is no longer Kant. Heidegger has shifted the emphasis of Kant's three questions. Kant does not ask: "What *can* I know?" but "What *can* I *know?*" The essential point here is not that there is something I can do and thus something else that I cannot do; nor is it that there is something I know and thus something else that I do not know; but it is that I *can know* something, and that I can then ask what that is that I can know. It is not my finitude that is under discussion here, but my real participation in knowing what there is to know. And in the same way "What ought I to do?" means that there *is* something I ought to do, and thus that I am not separated from "right" doing, but precisely by being able to *come to know* my "ought" may find the way to the doing. Finally, "What may I hope?" does not assert, as Heidegger thinks, that a "may" is made questionable here, and that in the expectation a want of what may not be expected is revealed; but it asserts, first, that there is something for me to hope (for obviously Kant does not mean that the answer to the third question is "Nothing"), secondly, that I am permitted to hope it, and thirdly, that precisely because I am permitted I can learn what it is that I may hope. That is what *Kant* says. And thus in Kant the meaning of the fourth question, to which the first three can be reduced is, what sort of a being is it which is able to know, and ought to do, and may hope? And the fact that the first three questions can be reduced to this question means that the knowledge of the essence of this being will make plain to me *what*, as such a being, it can know, *what*, as such a being, it ought to do, and *what*, as such a being, it may hope. This also means that indissolubly connected with the finitude which is given by the ability to know *only* this, there is a participation in infinity, which is given by the ability to know at all. The meaning is therefore that when we recognize man's finitude we must *at the same time* recognize his participation in infinity, not as two juxtaposed qualities but as the twofold nature of the processes in which alone man's existence becomes recognizable. The finite has its effect on him and the infinite has its effect on him; he shares in finitude and he shares in infinity.

Certainly Kant in his anthropology has neither answered nor undertaken to answer the question which he put to anthropology—What is man? He lectured on another anthropology than the one he asked for— I should say, in terms of the history of philosophy, an earlier anthropology, one that was still bound up with the uncritical "science of man" of the 17th and 18th centuries. But in formulating the task which he set to the philosophical anthropology he asked for, he has left a legacy.

3.

It is certainly doubtful to me as well whether such a discipline will suffice to provide a foundation for philosophy, or, as Heidegger formulates it, a foundation for metaphysics. For it is true, indeed, that I continually learn what I can know, what I ought to do, and what I may hope. It is further true that philosophy contributes to this learning of mine: to the first question by telling me, in logic and epistemology, what being able to know means, and in cosmology and the philosophy of history and so on, what there is to know; to the second question by telling me, in psychology, how the "ought to do" is carried out psychically, and in ethics, the doctrine of the State, æsthetics and so on, what there is to do; and to the third question by telling me, at least in the philosophy of religion, how the "may hope" is displayed in actual faith and the history of faith—whereas it can certainly not tell me what there is to hope, since religion itself and its conceptual elaboration in theology, whose task this is, do not belong to philosophy. All this is agreed. But philosophy succeeds in rendering me such help in its individual disciplines precisely through each of these disciplines *not* reflecting, and not being able to reflect, on the wholeness of man. Either a philosophical discipline shuts out man in his complex wholeness and considers him only as a bit of nature, as cosmology does; or (as all the other disciplines do) it tears off its own special sphere from the wholeness of man, delimits it from the other spheres, establishes its own basic principles and develops its own methods. In addition it has to remain open and accessible, first to the ideas of metaphysics itself as the doctrine of being, of what is and of existence, secondly to the findings of the philosophical branch disciplines, and thirdly to the discoveries of philosophical anthropology. But least of all may it make itself dependent on the latter; for in every one of those disciplines the possibility of its achieving anything in thought rests precisely on its objectification, on what may be termed its "de-humanization," and even a discipline like the philosophy of history, which is so concerned with the actual man, must, in order to be able to comprehend man *as a historical being,* renounce consideration of the whole man—of which the kind of man who is living outside history in the unchanging rhythm of nature is an essential part. What the philosophical disciplines are able to contribute to answering Kant's first three questions, even if it is only by clarifying them, or teaching me to recognize the problems they contain, they are able to do only by *not* waiting for the answer to the fourth question.

Nor can philosophical anthropology itself set itself the task of establishing a foundation either for metaphysics or for the individual philosophical sciences. If it attempted to answer the question *What is man?* in such a general way that answers to the other questions could be derived from it, it would miss the very reality of its own subject. For it would reach, instead of the subject's genuine wholeness, which can become visible only by the contemplation of all its manifold nature, a false unity which has no reality. A legitimate philosophical anthropology must know that there is not merely a human species but also peoples, not merely a human soul but also types and characters, not merely a human life but also stages in life; only from the systematic comprehension of these and of all other differences, from the recognition of the dynamic that exerts power within every particular reality and between them, and from the constantly new proof of the one in the many, can it come to see the wholeness of man. For that very reason it cannot grasp man in that absoluteness which, though it does not speak out from Kant's fourth question, yet very easily presents itself when an answer is attempted—the answer which Kant, as I have said, avoided giving. Even as it must again and again distinguish within the human race in order to arrive at a solid comprehension, so it must put man in all seriousness into nature, it must compare him with other things, other living creatures, other bearers of consciousness, in order to define his special place reliably for him. Only by this double way of distinction and comparison does it reach the whole, real man who, whatever his people or type or age, knows, what no being on earth but he can know, that he goes the narrow way from birth towards death, tests out what none but he can, a wrestling with destiny, rebellion and reconciliation, and at times even experiences in his own blood, when he is joined by choice to another human being, what goes on secretly in others.

Philosophical anthropology is not intent on reducing philosophical problems to human existence and establishing the philosophical disciplines so to speak from below instead of from above. It is solely intent on knowing man himself. This sets it a task that is absolutely different from all other tasks of thought. For in philosophical anthropology man himself is given to man in the most precise sense as a subject. Here, where the subject is man in his wholeness, the investigator cannot content himself, as in anthropology as an individual science, with considering man as another part of nature and with ignoring the fact that he, the investigator, is himself a man and experiences his humanity in his inner experience in a way that he simply cannot experience any part of nature—not only in a quite different perspective but also in a quite different dimension of being, in a dimension in which he experiences only this one part of all the parts of nature. Philosophical knowledge of man is essentially man's self-reflection (*Selbstbesinnung*), and man can reflect about himself only when the cognizing person, that is, the philosopher pursuing anthropology, first of all reflects about himself as a person. The principle of individuation, the fundamental fact of the infinite variety of human persons, of whom this one is only one person, of this constitution and no other, does not relativize anthropological knowledge; on the contrary, it gives it its kernel and its skeleton. In order to become genuine philosophical anthropology, everything that is discovered about historical and modern man, about men and women, Indians and Chinese, tramps and emperors, the weak-minded and the genius, must be built up and crystallized round what the philosopher discovers by reflecting about himself. That is a quite different matter from what, say, the psychologist undertakes when he completes and clarifies by reference to his own self in self-observation, self-analysis and experiment, what he knows from literature and observation. For with him it is a matter of individual, objectivized processes and phenomena, of something that is separated from connexion with the whole real person. But the philosophical anthropologist must stake nothing less than his real wholeness, his concrete self. And more; it is not enough for him to stake his self as an *object* of knowledge. He can know the *wholeness* of the person and through it the wholeness of *man* only when he does not leave his *subjectivity* out and does not remain an untouched observer. He must enter, completely and in reality, into the act of self-reflection, in order to become aware of human wholeness. In other words, he must carry out this act of entry into that unique dimension as an act of his *life,* without any prepared philosophical security; that is, he must expose himself to all that can meet you when you are really living. Here you do not attain to knowledge by remaining on the shore and watching the foaming waves, you must make the venture and cast yourself in, you must swim, alert and with all your force, even if a moment comes when you think you are losing consciousness: in this way, and in no other, do you reach anthropological insight. So long as you "have" yourself, have yourself as an object, your experience of man is only as of a thing among things, the wholeness which is to be grasped is not yet "there"; only when you *are,* and nothing else but that, is the wholeness there, and able to be grasped. You perceive only as much as the reality of the "being there" incidentally yields to you; but you do perceive that, and the nucleus of the crystallization develops itself.

An example may clarify more precisely the relation between the psychologist and the anthropologist. If both of them investigate, say, the phenomenon of anger, the psychologist will try to grasp what the angry man feels, what his motives and the impulses of his will are, but the anthropologist will also try to grasp what he is doing. In respect of this phenomenon self-observation, being by nature disposed to weaken the spontaneity and unruliness of anger, will be especially difficult for both of them. The psychologist will try to meet this difficulty by a specific division of consciousness, which enables him to remain outside with the observing part of his being and yet let his passion run its course as undisturbed as possible. Of course this passion can then not avoid becoming similar to that of the actor, that is, though it can still be heightened in comparison with an unobserved passion, its course will be different: there will be a release which is willed and which takes the place of the elemental outbreak, there will be a vehemence which will be more emphasized, more deliberate, more dramatic. The anthropologist can have nothing to do with a division of consciousness, since he has to do with the unbroken wholeness of events, and especially with the unbroken natural connexion between feelings and actions; and this connexion is most powerfully influenced in self-observation, since the pure spontaneity of the action is bound to suffer essentially. It remains for the anthropologist only to resign any attempt to stay outside his observing self, and thus when he is overcome by anger not to disturb it in its course by becoming a spectator of it, but to let it rage to its conclusion without trying to gain a perspective. He will be able to register in the act of recollection what he felt and did then; for him memory takes the place of psychological self-experience. But as great writers in their dealings with other men do not deliberately register their peculiarities and, so to speak, make invisible notes, but deal with them in a natural and uninhibited way, and leave the harvest to the hour of harvest, so it is the memory of the competent anthropologist which has, with reference to himself as to others, the concentrating power which preserves what is essential. In the moment of life he has nothing else in his mind but just to live what is to be lived, he is there with his whole being, undivided, and for that very reason there grows in his thought and recollection the knowledge of human wholeness.

II: *From Aristotle to Kant*

1.

The man who feels himself solitary is the most readily disposed and most readily fitted for the self-reflection of which I am speaking; that is, the man who by nature or destiny or both is alone with himself and his problematic, and who succeeds, in this blank solitude, in meeting himself, in discovering man in his own self, and the human problematic in his own. The times of spiritual history in which anthropological thought has so far found its depth of experience have been those very times in which a feeling of strict and inescapable solitude took possession of man; and it was the most solitary men in whom the thought became fruitful. In the ice of solitude man becomes most inexorably a question to himself, and just because the question pitilessly summons and draws into play his most secret life he becomes an experience to himself.

In the history of the human spirit I distinguish between epochs of habitation and epochs of homelessness. In the former, man lives in the world as in a house, as in a home. In the latter, man lives in the world as in an open field and at times does not even have four pegs with which to set up a tent. In the former epochs anthropological thought exists only as a part of cosmological thought. In the latter, anthropological thought gains depth and, with it, independence. I will give a few examples of both, which offer a glance at a few chapters of the *prehistory* of philosophical anthropology.

Bernhard Græthuysen (a pupil of my teacher Wilhelm Dilthey, the founder of the history of philosophical anthropology) rightly said of Aristotle, in a work called *Philosophical Anthropology* (1931), that with him man ceases to be problematic, with him man speaks of himself always as it were in the third person, is only a "case" for himself, he attains to consciousness of self only as "he," not as "I." The special dimension, in which man knows himself as he can know himself alone, remains unentered, and for that reason man's special place in the cosmos remains undiscovered. Man is comprehended only in the world, the world is not comprehended in him. The tendency of the Greeks to understand the world as a self-contained space, in which man too has his fixed place, was perfected in Aristotle's geocentric spherical system. The hegemony of the visual sense over the other senses, which appears among the Greeks for the first time, as a tremendous new factor in the history of the human spirit, the very hegemony which enabled them to live a life derived from *images* and to base a culture on the forming of images, holds good in their philosophy as well. A visual image of the universe (*Weltbild*) arises which is formed from visual sense-impressions and objectified as only the visual sense is able to objectify, and the experiences of the other senses are as it were ret-rospectively recorded in this picture. Even Plato's world of ideas is a visual world, a world of forms that are seen. But it is not before Aris-totle that the visual image of the universe is realized in unsurpassa-ble clarity as a universe of *things,* and now man is a thing among these things of the universe, an objectively comprehensible species beside other species—no longer a sojourner in a foreign land like the Pla-tonic man, but given his own dwelling-place in the house of the world, not, indeed, in one of the highest storeys, but not in one of the lower, either, rather in the respectable middle. The presupposition for a phil-osophical anthropology in the sense of Kant's fourth question is lacking here.

2.

The first to pose the genuine anthropological question anew, and in the first person—more than seven centuries after Aristotle—was Augustine. The solitude out of which he asked the question can only be under-stood when one realizes that that round and unified world of Aristotle had long since collapsed. It collapsed because the soul of man, di-vided against itself, could no longer grasp as truth anything but a world which was divided against itself. In place of the sphere which had collapsed there now arose two autonomous and mutually hostile king-doms, the kingdom of light and the kingdom of darkness. We meet them again in almost every system of that widespread and manifold spiritual movement of gnosis, which at that time seized the embar-rassed heirs of the great oriental and antique cultures, split the god-head and emptied value from creation; and in the most consistent of these systems, in Manichæism, there is even, consistently, a double earth. Here man can no longer be a thing among things, and he can have no fixed place in the world. Since he consists of soul and body he is divided between the two kingdoms, he is simultaneously the scene and the prize of the struggle. In each man the original man who fell is manifested; in each man the problematic of being is stated in terms of life. Augustine emerged from the school of Manichæism. Homeless in the world, solitary between the higher and the lower powers, he re-mains homeless and solitary even after he found salvation in Christian-ity as a redemption that had *already taken place.* So he asks Kant's question in the first person, and not, indeed, as with Kant, as an ob-jectivized problem, which the hearers of his logic lectures could certainly not understand as a question directed to themselves; but he takes up the question of the psalmist again in real address, with an-other sense and in another tone: *What is man that thou art mindful of* him? He asks for information from one who can give it: *quid ergo sum, Deus meus? quæ natura mea?* He does not mean only himself; the word *natura* says clearly that in his person he means man, that man whom he calls the *grande profundum,* the great mystery. And he even draws that same anthropological conclusion which we have heard in Malebranche; he does it in his famous accusation of men, that they marvel at mountains, at the waves of the sea and the course of the stars, but "relinquish" themselves without being astonished at themselves. This wonder of man at himself, which Augustine demands as a result of his own self-experience, is something quite different from the wonder with which Aristotle in his metaphysic makes all philosophizing begin. The Aristotelian man wonders at man among the rest, but only as a part of a quite astonishing world. The Augustinian man wonders at that in man which cannot be understood as a part of the world, as a thing among things; and where that former wondering has already passed into methodical philosophizing, the Augustinian wondering manifests itself in its true depth and uncanniness. It is not philosophy, but it affects all future philosophy.

In the post-augustinian west it is not the contemplation of nature, as with the Greeks, but faith which builds a new house in the cosmos for the solitary soul. The Christian cosmos arises; and this was so real for every mediæval Christian that all who read the *Divina Commedia* made in spirit the journey to the nethermost spiral of hell and stepped up over Lucifer's back, through purgatory, to the heaven of the Trinity, not as an expedition into lands as yet unknown, but as a crossing of regions already fully mapped. Once again there is a self-enclosed universe, once again a house in which man is allowed to dwell. This universe is still more finite than that of Aristotle, for here finite time too is taken into the image in all seriousness—the finite time of the Bible, which here appears, however, transformed into a Christian form. The pattern of this image of the universe is a cross, whose vertical beam is finite space from heaven to hell, leading right across the heart of the human being, and whose cross-beam is finite time from the creation of the world to the end of days; which makes time's centre, the death of Christ, fall coveringly and redemptively on the centre of space, the heart of the poor sinner. The mediæval image of the universe is built round this pattern. In it Dante painted life, the life of man and spirits, but the conceptual framework was set up for him by Thomas Aquinas. As of Aristotle, so too it is true of Aquinas, though he was a theologian, and therefore in duty bound to know about the real man who says "I" and is addressed as "Thou", that man speaks here "as it were always in the third person." In Aquinas's world-system man is indeed a separate species of a quite special kind, because in him the human soul, the lowest of the spirits, is substantially united with the human body, the highest of physical things, so that man appears as it were as "the horizon and the dividing line of spiritual and physical nature". But Aquinas knows no special problem and no special problematic of human life, such as Augustine experienced and expressed with trembling heart.

The anthropological question has here come to rest again; in man, housed and unproblematic, no impulse stirs to questioning self-confrontation, or it is soon appeased.

3.

In the late middle ages there already emerged a new earnestness about man as man. The finite world still hedged man safely in; *hunc mundum haud aliud esse, quam amplissimam quandam hominis domum,* says Carolus Bovillus as late as the sixteenth century. But the same Bovillus cries to man: *homo es, sistere in homine,* and thus takes up the motif that had been expressed by the great Cusa before him: *homo non vult esse nisi homo.* This by itself certainly does not imply that man by his nature steps out of and forth from the world. For Cusa there is not a thing which would not prefer its own being to all being and its own way of being to all other ways of being; all that is wishes in eternity to be nothing but itself, but to be this one thing always more perfectly in the way proper to its nature; it is precisely from this that the harmony of the universe grows, for every being contains everything in a special "contraction."

But with man there is also thought, the reason which measures and values. He has in himself all created things, like God; but God has them in himself as the archetypes, man has them in himself as relations and values. Cusa compares God to the coining master of the mint, and man to the money-changer with his scale of values. God can create all, we can know all; we can know all because we too carry all in ourselves potentially. And soon after Cusa, Pico della Mirandola draws from this proud self-assurance the anthropological conclusion, which again reminds us of the words of Malebranche: *nos autem peculiare aliquid in homine quaerimus, unde et dignitas ei propria et imago divinae substantiae cum nulla sibi creatura communis comperiatur.* Here the theme of anthropology already clearly appears. But it appears without that setting of the problematic which is indispensable for the genuine establishment of anthropology—the deadly earnestness of the question about man. Man steps forth here in such autonomy and such consciousness of power that the real question does not step up to him. These thinkers of the Renaissance affirm that man can know, but the Kantian question, *what* he can know, is still quite foreign to them: he can know all. It is true that the last in the series of these thinkers, Bovillus, excepts God: the human spirit cannot reach God, but Bovillus lets the whole universe be known by man, who has been created outside it as its spectator, in fact, as its eye. So securely are these pioneers of a new era still housed in a secure universe. Cusa, it is true, speaks of the spatial and temporal infinity of the universe, and thus deprives the earth of its central position, and destroys in thought the mediaeval pattern. But this infinity is only one that is thought, it is not yet beheld and lived. Man is not yet solitary again, he has still to learn again to ask the solitary man's question.

But at the same time as Bovillus was extolling the universe as man's *amplissima domus,* all the walls of the house were in fact already crumbling beneath the blows of Copernicus, the unlimited was pressing in from every side, and man was standing in a universe which in actual fact could no longer be experienced as a house. Man was no longer secure, but though at first he had a heroic enthusiasm for the grandeur of this universe, as with Bruno, then a mathematical enthusiasm for its harmony, as with Kepler, yet finally, more than a century after the death of Copernicus and the publication of his work, the new reality of man proved itself to be more powerful than the new reality of the universe. Pascal, a great scientist, a mathematician and a physicist, young and destined to die early, experienced beneath the starry heavens not merely, as Kant did, their majesty, but still more powerfully their uncanniness: *le silence éternel de ces espaces infinis m'effraie.* With a clarity that has not since then been surpassed he discerns the twin infinities, that of the infinitely great and that of the infinitely small, and so comes to know man's limitation, his inadequacy, the casualness of his existence: *combien de royaumes nous ignorent!* The enthusiasm of Bruno and Kepler which as it were skipped man is here replaced by a terribly clear, melancholy yet believing sobriety. It is the sobriety of the man who has become more deeply solitary than ever before, and with a sober pathos he frames the anthropological question afresh: *qu'est ce qu'un homme dans l'infini?* Cusa's sovereignty, in which man boasted that he carried all things in himself and thus that he could know all things, is opposed here by the insight of the solitary man, who endures being exposed as a human being to infinity: *Connaissons donc notre portée: nous sommes quelque chose, et ne sommes pas tout; ce que nous avons d'être nous dérobe la connaissance des premiers principes, qui naissent du néant; et le peu que nous avons d'être nous cache la vue de l'infini.* But, in this renewal of anthropological thought, from the very fact that self-reflection is carried out with such clarity, there is yielded man's special place in the cosmos. *L'homme n'est qu'un roseau, le plus faible de la nature: mais c'est un roseau pensant. Il ne faut pas que l'univers entier s'arme pour l'écraser: une vapeur, une goutte d'eau, suffit pour le tuer. Mais, quand l'univers l'écraserait, l'homme serait encore plus noble que ce qui le tue, parce qu'il sait qu'il meurt et l'avantage que l'univers a sur lui. L'univers n'en sait rien.* This is not the stoic attitude over again; it is the new attitude of the person who has become homeless in infinity, for here everything depends on the knowledge that man's grandeur is born of his misery, that he is different from all things just because even as he passes away he can be a child of the spirit. Man is the being who knows his situation in the universe and is able, so long as he is in his senses, to continue this knowledge. What is decisive is not that this creature of all dares to step up to the universe and know it—however amazing this is in itself; what is decisive is that he knows the relation between the universe and himself. Thereby from out of the midst of the universe something that faces the universe has arisen. And that means that this "from out of the midst" has its own special problematic.

4.

We have seen that the strict anthropological question, which refers to man's specific problematic, becomes insistent in times when as it were the original contract between the universe and man is dissolved and man finds himself a stranger and solitary in the world. The end of an image of the universe, that is, the end of a *security* in the universe, is soon followed by a fresh questioning from man who has become insecure, and homeless, and hence problematic to himself. But it can be shown that a *way* leads from one such crisis to the next, and on to the one after that. The crises have something essential in common, but they are not similar. Aristotle's cosmological image of the universe breaks up from within, through the soul's experience of the problem of evil in its depth, and through its feeling of being surrounded by a divided universe; Aquinas's theological image of the universe breaks up from without, through the universe manifesting itself as unlimited. What causes the crisis is on the one occasion a myth, the dualistic myth of gnosis, on the other occasion it is the cosmos of science itself, no longer clothed with any myth. Pascal's solitude is truly historically *later* than Augustine's; it is more complete and harder to overcome. And in fact something new arises that has not existed before; work is carried out on a new *image* of the universe, but a new *house* in the universe is no longer built. Once the concept of infinity has been taken seriously a human dwelling can no longer be made of the universe. And infinity itself must be included in the image of the universe— which is a paradox, for an image, if it is really an image, is limited, yet now the unlimited itself must enter the image. In other words, when the point is reached where the image ends, the point, say—to use the language of modern astronomy—of the nebulae, which are a hundred million light-years distant from us, then it must be felt with the utmost urgency that the image does not and cannot end. Incidentally it may be noticed, though it is self-evident, that Einstein's concept of finite space would be by no means fit for rebuilding the universe as a house for man, since this "finitude" is essentially different from that which produced the feeling of the universe as a house. And more, it is certainly possible that this concept of the universe, which has been disclosed by the mathematician's genius, freed from sensuality, can one day become accessible to natural human understanding; but it will no longer be in a position to produce a new *image* of the universe, not even a paradoxical image as the Copernican concept could. For the Copernican concept only fulfilled what the human soul had vaguely felt in the hours when the house of universal space, the Aristotelian or the Thomist, seemed too cramped, and it dared to beat on its walls to see if a window could not be thrown out into a world beyond—it fulfilled it, it is true, in a way which deeply perturbed this same human soul, which cannot help being as it is, once and for all. But Einstein's concept of the universe signifies no fulfilment of the spirit's inkling, but the contradiction of all its inklings and imaginings: this universe can still be thought, but it can no longer be imaged, the man who thinks it no longer really lives in it. The generation which works modern cosmology into its natural thought will be the first, after several millennia of changing images of the universe, which will have to forego the possession of an image of its universe; this very fact, that it lives in a universe which cannot be imaged, will probably be its feeling of the universe, so to speak its image of the universe: *imago mundi nova—imago nulla.*

5.

I have far anticipated the course of our investigation. Let us return to our second example and ask how from there we reach our age in its special human homelessness and solitude, and its new setting of the anthropological question.

The greatest attempt to master the situation of post-copernican man, as mediated to us by Pascal, was undertaken shortly after Pascal's death by a man who was destined to die almost as young. Spinoza's attempt, from the point of view of our problem, means that astronomical infinity is both unconditionally accepted and stripped of its uncanniness: extension, of which this infinity is stated and demonstrated, is only one of the infinitely many attributes of infinite substance, and it is one of the two which alone we know—the other is thought. Infinite substance, also called God by Spinoza, in relation to which this infinity of space can be only one of infinitely many attributes, *loves,* it loves itself, and it loves itself also, and especially, in man, for the love of the human spirit for God is only *pars infiniti amoris, quo Deus se ipsum amat.* Here one may say that Pascal's question, what is a man in the infinite, is answered: he is a being in whom God loves himself. Cosmology and anthropology appear here imposingly reconciled, but the cosmos has not again become what it was with Aristotle and Aquinas—a manifold universe, ordered as an image, in which every thing and every being has its place and the being "man" feels himself at home in union with them all. A new security of being in the world is not given; yet for Spinoza this is not necessary: his devotion to the infinite *natura natu-*

rans lifts him above the mere outline character of his *natura naturata,* which is drawn into the system only conceptually, as the aggregate of the divine modes, and in which the kinds and orders of being are not really grasped and united. There is no new house of the universe, no ground-plan of a house and no material for it: a man accepts his homelessness, his lack of a universe, because it enables him to have *adaequata cognitio aeternae et infinitae essentiae Dei,* that is, enables him to know how God loves himself in *him.* A man, however, who knows this can no longer be problematic to himself.

In Spinoza's intellectual separatedness reconciliation was effected. But in actual man's concrete life with the actual world, in the unseparated and inseparable life out of which Pascal spoke and expressed at once man's frailty and the world's terror, it became increasingly difficult to effect it. The age of rationalism, which weakened and adapted Spinoza's objectification of being in which world and man are united, breaks off the point of the anthropological question; but it remains embedded in the flesh and secretly festers.

Certainly, one can point to a man who was a true heir of Spinoza in the post-rationalist age and was made happy by Spinoza's "atmosphere of peace", who was "a child of peace" and minded to keep peace "for ever and ever with the whole world", who grasped and penetrated this world in its living fulness, as a whole which gives us in its synthesis with spirit "the most blissful assurance of the harmony of existence". Goethe, who in his place in history appears to us in many respects like a glorious lethal euphoria before the end of an age was undoubtedly still able to live really in the cosmos; but he, who had plumbed the depths of solitude ("I can speak only with God about many things"), was exposed in his inmost being to the anthropological question. Certainly, man to him was "the first conversation which nature holds with God", yet, like Werther, he heard "the voice of the creature completely driven into itself, lacking itself, and falling irresistibly downwards".

6.

Kant was the first to understand the anthropological question critically, in such a way that an answer was given to Pascal's real concern. This answer—though it was not directed metaphysically to the being of man but epistemologically to his attitude to the world—grasped the fundamental problems. What sort of a world is it, which man knows? How can man, as he is, in his altered reality, know at all? How does man stand in the world he knows in this way—what is it to him and what is he to it?

In order to understand the extent to which the *Critique of Pure Reason* may be taken as an answer to Pascal's question we must consider the question once more. To Pascal infinite space is an uncanny thing which makes him conscious of the questionable nature of man, exposed as he is to this world. But what stirs and terrifies him is not the newly discovered infinity of space in contrast to the finitude previously believed of it. Rather it is the fact that, by the impression of infinity, any concept of space, a finite no less than an infinite, becomes uncanny to him, for really to try and imagine finite space is as hazardous a venture as really to try and imagine infinite space, and makes man just as emphatically conscious that he is not a match for the world. When I was about fourteen years of age I myself experienced this in a way which has deeply influenced my whole life. A necessity I could not understand swept over me: I had to try again and again to imagine the edge of space, or its edgelessness, time with a beginning and an end or a time without beginning or end, and both were equally impossible, equally hopeless—yet there seemed to be only the choice between the one or the other absurdity. Under an irresistible compulsion I reeled from one to the other, at times so closely threatened with the danger of madness that I seriously thought of avoiding it by suicide. Salvation came to the fifteen year old boy in a book, Kant's *Prolegomena to all Future Metaphysics,* which I dared to read although its first sentence told me that it was not intended for the use of pupils but for future teachers. This book showed me that space and time are only the forms in which my human view of what is, necessarily works itself out; that is, they were not attached to the inner nature of the world, but to the nature of my senses. It further taught that it is just as impossible to all my concepts to say that the world is infinite in space and time as to say that it is finite. "For neither can be inherent in experience", and neither can be situated in the world itself, since the world is given to us only as an appearance "whose existence and connexions take place only in experience". Both can be asserted and both can be proved; between the thesis and the antithesis there exists an irresoluble contradiction, an antinomy of cosmological ideas; being itself is not touched by either. Now I was no longer compelled to torture myself by trying to imagine first the one unimaginable and then the opposite equally unimaginable thing: I could gain an inkling that being itself was beyond the reach alike of the finitude and the infinity of space and time, since it only appeared in space and time but did not itself enter into this appearance. At that time I began to gain an inkling of the existence of eternity as something quite different from the infinite, just as it is something quite different from the finite, and of the possibility of a connexion between me, a man, and the eternal.

Kant's answer to Pascal may be formulated after this fashion: what approaches you out of the world, hostile and terrifying, the mystery of its space and time, is the mystery of your own comprehension of the world and the mystery of your own being. Your question *What is man?* is thus a genuine question to which you must seek the answer.

Here Kant's anthropological question is shown in all clarity as a legacy to our age. No new house in the universe is being planned for man, but he, as the builder of houses, is being required to know himself. Kant sees the age after him in all its uncertainty as an age of self-restraint and self-reflection, as the anthropological age. First—as is clear from that well-known letter of 1793—he saw in the treatment of the fourth question a task which he set himself, and whose resolution was to follow that of the first three questions; he did not really set about it, but he set it in such clarity and urgency that it remained a task set to following generations, till at last our own generation is preparing to place itself in its service.

III: *Hegel and Marx*

1.

First, however, there follows such a radical alienation from the anthropological setting of the question as has probably never happened before in the history of human thought. I mean the system of Hegel, that is, the system which has exercised a decisive influence not merely on an age's way of thought but also on its social and political action—an influence which can be characterized as the dispossessing of the concrete human person and the concrete human community in favour of universal reason, its dialectical processes and its objective structures. This influence, as is well-known, has also operated on thinkers who, though deriving from Hegel, have travelled far from him, such as Kierkegaard on the one hand, the critic of modern Christianity, who certainly grasped like no other thinker of our time the significance of the person, but still saw the life of the person entirely in the forms of the Hegelian dialectic as a movement from the aesthetic to the ethical and from there to the religious, and Marx on the other hand, who entered with an unexampled earnestness on the actuality of human society, but considered its development in forms of Hegelian dialectic as a movement from primitive communal economy to private property and from there to socialism.

In his youth Hegel accepted Kant's anthropological setting of the question, which was at that time not published in its final form but whose sense was certainly known to the young man so deeply engaged with Kant. From this point his thought proceeded in a genuinely anthropological fashion, in that he sought to reach, by understanding the organic connexion of the spirit's capacities, what Kant himself knew only as a regulative idea, not as living being, namely, what the young Hegel himself called (about 1798) the "unity of the whole man". What he strove after then has been rightly called an anthropological metaphysic. He took the concrete human person so seriously that it was by him that he demonstrated his conception of man's special position.

To illustrate this I quote a beautiful sentence from the notes *The Spirit of Christianity and its Destiny,* which clearly shows the way in which Hegel, going beyond Kant, seeks to penetrate the anthropological problem: "In every man himself there is light and life, he is the property of light; and he is not illumined by a light like a dark body which has only a reflected brilliance, but his own fuel is being kindled and there is a flame of its own." It is worth noticing that Hegel does not speak of a general concept of man here, but of "every man", that is, of the real person from whom genuine philosophical anthropology must seriously begin.

But this setting of the problem will be sought in vain in the later Hegel, in the one, that is, who has influenced a century's thought. I should go so far as to say that the real man will be sought in vain in the later Hegel. If one, for instance, looks through the section in the *Encyclopaedia of the Philosophical Sciences* which is entitled "Anthropology", one sees that it begins with statements about what spirit is and signifies, then passes to statements about the soul as substance. There follow valuable references to distinctions within mankind and human life, especially to distinctions of age, of sex, between sleeping and waking, and so on—but without our being able to relate all this to a question about the reality and significance of this human life. Also the chapters about feeling, self-feeling, and habit, give no help, and even in the chapter entitled "The real soul" we learn only that the soul is real as the "identity of the inner with the outer". The systematic philosopher Hegel no longer begins, like the young Hegel, with man, but with universal reason; man is now only the principle in which the universal reason reaches perfect self-consciousness and thus completion. All the contradiction in human life and history does not lead to the anthropological questionableness and question, but presents itself as a "ruse" which the idea makes use of in order to reach its own perfection through the very fact that it overcomes contradiction. The claim is made that Kant's fundamental question *What is man?* is finally answered here; in reality it is obscured, even eliminated. Even the first of Kant's three philosophical questions which precede the anthropological question, the question *What can I know?* is silenced. If man is the place and medium in which the universal reason knows itself, then there is simply no limitation to what man can know. In terms of the idea man knows all things, just as in terms of the idea he realizes all things, that is, all that is in the reason. Both the knowing and the realizing take place in history, in which the perfect State appears as the completion of being and the perfect metaphysic appears as the completion of knowledge. By experiencing both we experience simultaneously and adequately the meaning of history and the meaning of man.

Hegel undertakes to give man a new security, to build a new house of the universe for him. No further house can be built in Copernican space; Hegel builds it in *time* alone, which is "the supreme power of all that is" (1805).

Man's new house is to be time in the form of history whose meaning can be perfectly learned and understood. Hegel's system is the third great attempt at security within western thought; following Aristotle's cosmological attempt and Aquinas's theological attempt it is the logological attempt. All insecurity, all unrest about meaning, all terror at decision, all abysmal problematic is eliminated. The universal reason goes its undeflectable way through history, and knowing man knows this way, rather, his knowledge is the real goal and end of the way in which truth as it realizes itself knows itself in its realization. The stages of the way follow one another in an absolute order: the law of dialectic, in which the thesis is relieved by the antithesis and the antithesis by the synthesis, is sovereign over them. As one goes with sure step from storey to storey and from room to room of a well-built house with its solid foundations and walls and roof, so Hegel's all-knowing man goes through the new world-house, history, whose whole meaning he knows. If only he shares thoroughly in the thought of the new metaphysic his glance is saved from dizziness, for he can survey everything. The young man over whom the dread of the infinite swept since the Copernican revolution, when he opened the window of his room at night and stood solitary in the darkness, is to know peace now; if the cosmos, in its infinite greatness and infinite smallness, denies itself to his heart, the reliable order of history, which "is nothing but the realization of the spirit", takes him and makes him at home. Solitude is overcome, and the question about man is obliterated.

But now there appears a remarkable historical phenomenon. In earlier times it took some centuries for criticism to destroy a cosmic security and to reinvigorate the anthropological question. Now the Hegelian image of the universe had, indeed, tremendous effect for a century, penetrating every realm of the spirit; but the rebellion against it was raised immediately, and with it the demand for an anthropological perspective was renewed. The Hegelian house of the universe is admired, explained, and imitated; but it proves uninhabitable. Thought confirms it and the word glorifies it; but the real man does not set foot in it. In the universe of Aristotle real ancient man felt himself at home; similarly with the real Christian in the universe of Aquinas; the universe of Hegel has never become the real universe for real modern man. In the thought of mankind Hegel succeeded in repressing Kant's anthropological question only for a moment; in the life of man he did not overcome even for a moment the great anthropological unrest which in modern times is first expressed in Pascal's question.

I wish to indicate here only one of the reasons for this phenomenon. An intellectual image of the universe which builds on *time* can never give the same feeling of security as one which builds on space. To grasp this fact we must distinguish sharply between cosmological and anthropological time. We can as it were comprehend cosmological time, that is, make use of the concept of it, as if all time were present in a relative way, even though the future is not given to us at all. Anthropological time, on the other hand, that is, time in respect of actual, consciously willing man, cannot be comprehended, because the future cannot be present, since it depends to a certain extent, in my consciousness and will, on my decision. Anthropological time is real only in the part which has become cosmological time, that is, in the part called the past. This distinction is not identical with Bergson's well-known one, whose *durée* means a flowing present, whereas the anthropological time which I mean functions essentially through the memory—of course, in respect of the present, this is always "open" memory: as soon as we experience something *as time,* as soon as we become conscious of the dimension of time as such, the memory is already in play; in other words, the pure present knows no specific consciousness of time. It is true that we do not know cosmological time as a whole either, in spite of our knowledge of the regular movements of the stars, and so on; but our thoughts may be engaged with it as with something real, even in what we do not know of this, and naturally even in what we do not know of future human actions, since in the moment of thought all their causes are present. With the anthropological future, on the other hand, our thoughts cannot be engaged as with something real, since my decision, which will take place in the next moment, has not yet taken place. The same is true of the decisions of other men, since I know, on the basis of the anthropological concept of man as a consciously willing being, that he cannot be understood simply as a part of the world. Within the boundaries of the human world which is given in the problem of human being there is no certainty of the future. The time which Hegel introduced into the groundwork of his image of the universe, cosmological time, is not actual human time but a time in terms of thought. It lies in the power of human thought but not of living human imagination to incorporate perfection in the reality of what is; it is something which can be thought, but not lived. An intellectual image of the universe, which incorporates "the goal of universal history", has no power in this part of it to give assurance, the unbroken line changes as it were into a dotted line, which even the mightiest philosopher cannot transform for us into a continuous line. The only exception is an image of the universe which is grounded on faith: the power of faith alone can experience perfection as something assured, because it is something guaranteed to us by someone we trust—whom we trust as the guarantor also for what has not yet come to be in our world. In the history of religion we know above all two such great images of the universe, that of Persian Messianism, in which the future final and complete victory of light over darkness is guaranteed to the precise hour, and that of Israelite Messianism, which rejects such precision because it understands man himself, frail, contradictory, questionable man himself as an element that can both contribute to salvation and hinder it; but final and complete salvation is guaranteed to this form of Messianism as well, in faith in the saving power of God which carries out in the midst of history its work on resisting man. In the Christian picture of the universe, as we saw it in its finished form in Aquinas, the effect of Messianism persists, though weakened. In Hegel's system Messianism is secularized, that is, it is transferred from the sphere of faith, in which man feels himself to be bound up with the object of his faith, to the sphere of evident conviction, in which man contemplates and considers the object of his conviction. This has been repeatedly remarked. But it has not been sufficiently observed that in such a transference the element of *trust* cannot be taken over at the same time. Faith in creation may be replaced by a conviction about evolution, faith in revelation by a conviction about increasing knowledge, but faith in salvation will not really be replaced by a conviction about the perfecting of the world by the idea, since only trust in the trustworthy is able to establish a relation of unconditional certainty towards the *future*. I say, not *really* replaced, that is, not in and for real life. For in mere thought a conviction about the self-realization of an absolute reason in history does not achieve less, even for man's relation to the future, than a messianic faith in God; in fact, it achieves even more, since it is, so to speak, chemically pure and undisturbed by any kind of adulteration by actuality. But thought does not have the power to build up man's real life, and the strictest philosophical certainty cannot endow the soul with that intimate certitude that the world which is so imperfect will be brought to its perfection. In the last resort the problem of the future does not exist for Hegel, since he saw, in fact, in his own age and in his own philosophy the beginning of fulfilment, so that the dialectical movement of the idea through time has really reached its end already. But what devoted admirer of the philosopher has ever truly shared in this worldly auto-messianism, that is, not merely with thought, but—as has continually happened in the history of religion—with the whole real life?

It is true that there is a significant phenomenon within the sphere of Hegel's influence which seems to contradict what I said about the attitude to the future. I mean Marx's doctrine of history, which is based on the Hegelian dialectic. Here too a certainty with regard to perfection is proclaimed, here too Messianism is secularized; yet real man, in the shape of the modern proletarian masses, has entered into this certainty and made this secularized Messianism his faith. How is this to be understood? What Marx has carried out with Hegel's method can be called a sociological reduction. That is, he does not wish to present any image of the universe; none is necessary any more. (The representation of an image of the universe which Engels later—in 1880—attempted, under the title *Dialectic of Nature,* a quite derivatory rendering of the teaching of Hæckel and other evolutionists, completely contradicts the fundamental restriction made by Marx.) What Marx wants to give the men of his age is not an image of the universe but only an image of society, more precisely, the image of the way by which human society is to reach its perfection. The Hegelian idea or universal reason is replaced by human conditions of production, from whose transformation proceeds the transformation of society. Conditions of production are what are essential and basic for Marx; they are the point from which he starts and to which he retraces everything; there is no other origin and no other principle for him. Certainly, they cannot be considered, like Hegel's universal reason, as the first and the last; sociological reduction means an absolute renunciation of a perspective of being in which there exists a first and a last. In Marx the home in which man can dwell—that is, will be able to dwell when it is ready—is built up on conditions of production alone. Man's world is society. In actual fact a security is established by this reduction which the proletarian masses really did accept and take up into their lives, at least for the duration of an age. When the attempt has been made within Marxism, as by Engels, to eliminate this reduction and to present the proletariat with an image of the universe, the proved vital security has been confused with a completely baseless intellectual security and thus robbed of its genuine force.

Certainly, something else, which is particularly important, is added to the reduction. Hegel perceives the beginning of fulfilment in his own age, in which the absolute spirit reaches its goal. Marx simply cannot see the fulfilment beginning in the heyday of capitalism, which has to be relieved by socialism which brings about the fulfilment. He sees, however, in his age something existing in which fulfilment is manifested and guaranteed—namely, the proletariat. In the existence of the proletariat the elimination of capitalism, the "negation of the negation", is bodily declared. "When the proletariat," says Marx, "proclaims the dissolution of the hitherto existing world-order, then it is only expressing the mystery of its own existence, for it is the actual dissolution of this world-order." By this fundamental thesis Marx is able to provide the proletariat with a security. Nothing else needs to be believed in but its own continuation, till the hour in which its existence becomes its action. The future appears here as bound to the directly experienced present and assured by it. Thought consequently does not have the power to construct man's real life; but life itself has this power, and the spirit has it, if it acknowledges the power of life and joins to it its own power, which is different in nature and effect.

Marx is both right and wrong in this view of the power of social life proper. He is right, since in fact social life, like all life, itself produces the forces which can renew it. But he is wrong, since human life, to which social life belongs, is distinct from all other kinds of life by the power of decision which is distinct from all other kinds of power: this power is different from them all in that it does not appear as quantity, but reveals the measure of its strength only in action itself. It depends on the direction and force of this power how far the renewing powers of life as such are able to take effect, and even whether they are not transformed into powers of destruction. The development depends essentially on something which cannot be explained in terms of the development. In other words, neither in man's personal nor in his social life must anthropological time be confused with cosmological time, not even when the latter is endowed with the form of the dialectical process, as, for example, in Marx's famous statement that capitalist production breeds its negation "with the necessity of a natural process". With all his sociological reduction he does no more than follow in Hegel's tracks and introduce cosmological time—that is, a time which is alien to man's reality—into his consideration of the future. The problem of human decision, as the origin of events and of destiny, including social events and destiny, does not exist here at all. Such a doctrine can persist in power only so long as it does not clash with a moment in history in which the problematic of human decision makes itself felt to a terrifying degree. I mean a moment in which catastrophic events exercise a frightening and paralysing influence over the power of decision, and repeatedly move it to renunciation in favour of a negative élite of men—men who, knowing no inner restraint, do not act as they do from real decision, but only stick to their power. In such situations the man who is striving for the renewal of social life, socialist man, can only share in the decision of his society's destiny if he believes in his own power of decision and knows that it matters, for only then does he actualize, in the effect which his decision has, the highest strength of his power of decision. In such a moment he can only share in the decision of his society's destiny if the view of life which he holds does not contradict his *experience*.

Hegel as it were compulsorily combined the course of the stars and of history into a speculative security. Marx, who confined himself to the human world, ascribed to it alone a security in regard to the future, which is likewise dialectic, but has the effect of an actual security. Today this security has perished in the ordered chaos of a terrible historical revulsion. Gone is the calm, a new anthropological dread has arisen, the question about man's being faces us as never before in all its grandeur and terror—no longer in philosophical attire, but in the nakedness of existence. No dialectical guarantee keeps man from falling; it lies with himself to lift his foot and take the step which leads him away from the abyss. The strength to take this step cannot come from any security in regard to the future, but only from those depths of insecurity in which man, overshadowed by despair, answers with his decision the question about man's being.

IV: *Feuerbach and Nietzsche*

1.

With Marx we are already in the midst of the anthropological rebellion against Hegel. At the same time we can see in perfect clarity in Marx the peculiar character of this rebellion. There is a return to the anthropological limitation of the picture of the universe without a return to the anthropological *problematic* and setting of the question. The philosopher who so rebelled against Hegel, and as whose pupil in this respect Marx has to be regarded, in spite of all differences and even oppositions between them, is Feuerbach. Feuerbach's anthropological reduction precedes Marx's sociological reduction.

In order to understand aright Feuerbach's struggle against Hegel and its significance for anthropology, it is best to begin with the fundamental question, What is the *beginning* of philosophy? Kant, in opposition to rationalism, and based on Hume, had established cognition as the very first thing for philosophizing men, and thus made the decisive philosophical problem what knowing is and how it is possible. This problem then led him, as we saw, to the anthropological question— what kind of a being is man who knows in this way? Hegel, perfectly conscious of what he was doing, passed over this first thing. In his view, as he expressed it with complete clarity in the first edition of his *Encyclopædia of the Philosophical Sciences* (1817), there must not be *any* immediate object at the beginning of philosophy, since immediacy is by nature opposed to philosophical thought; in other words, philosophy is not permitted, as with Kant and Descartes before him, to start from the situation of the philosophizing man, but it must "anticipate". He carries out this anticipating in the sentence: "Pure being is the beginning," which is straightway explained as follows: "Now, pure being is pure abstraction." On this basis Hegel is able to make the development of the universal reason, instead of that of human cognition, into the object of philosophy. This is the point where Feuerbach puts in his attack. The universal reason is only a new concept for God; and as theology, when it said "God", only transferred the human essence itself from earth to heaven, so metaphysics, when it says "universal reason", only transfers the human essence from concrete existence to abstract existence. The new philosophy—so Feuerbach formulates it in his manifesto, *Principles of the Philosophy of the Future* (1843)—has as its principle "not the absolute, that is, the abstract, spirit—in short, not reason *in abstracto,* but man's real, whole being". Unlike Kant, Feuerbach wishes to make the whole being, not human cognition, the beginning of philosophizing. In his view nature too is to be understood only as the "basis of man". "The new philosophy", he says, "makes man . . . the exclusive, universal . . . object of philosophy, and thus

makes anthropology . . . the universal science." Thus the anthropological reduction, the reduction of being to human existence, is carried out. One could say that Hegel, in the position he assigns to man,
follows the first creation story, that of the first chapter of *Genesis,* of the
creation of *nature,* where man is created last and given his place in the
cosmos, yet in such a way that creation is not only ended but also completed in its significance now that the "image of God" has appeared;
while Feuerbach follows the second creation story, that of the second
chapter of *Genesis,* of the creation of *history,* where there is no world
but that of man, man in its centre, giving all living things their true
name. Never before has a philosophical anthropology been so emphatically demanded. But Feuerbach's postulate does not lead beyond
the threshold to which Kant's fourth question led us. More, in one decisive respect we feel that we are not merely no further advanced
than with Kant, but actually less advanced. For in Feuerbach's demand
the question *What is man?* is not included at all. Indeed, his demand
means a renunciation of this question. His anthropological reduction of
being is a reduction to *unproblematic* man. But the real man, man who
faces a being that is not human, and is time and again overpowered by
it as by an inhuman fate, yet dares to know this being and this fate, is
not unproblematic; rather, he is the beginning of all problematic. A
philosophical anthropology is not possible unless it begins from the
anthropological *question.* It can be attained only by a formulation and
expression of this question which is more profound, sharp, strict, and
cruel than it has ever been before. Nietzsche's real significance lies, as
we shall see, in his undertaking of such a deepening and sharpening
of the question.

But we must first continue to deal with Feuerbach, for the sake of a
matter which is extraordinarily important for the thought of our age
about man. By man, whom he considers as the highest subject of
philosophy, Feuerbach does not mean man as an individual, but man
with man—the connexion of I and *Thou.* "The individual man for himself," runs his manifesto, "does not have man's being in himself, either
as a moral being or a thinking being. Man's being is contained only in
community, in the unity of man with man—a unity which rests, however, only on the reality of the difference between I and Thou."
Feuerbach did not elaborate these words in his later writings. Marx did
not take up into his concept of society the element of the real relation
between the really different *I* and *Thou,* and for that very reason opposed an unreal individualism with a collectivism which was just as
unreal. But in those words Feuerbach passing beyond Marx, introduced
the discovery of the *Thou,* which has been called "the Copernican revolution" of modern thought, and "an elemental happening which is just
as rich in consequences as the idealist discovery of the I" and "is bound
to lead to a new beginning of European thought, pointing beyond the

Cartesian contribution to modern philosophy".[2] I myself in my youth was given a decisive impetus by Feuerbach.

2.

Nietzsche depends much more solidly on Feuerbach's anthropological reduction than is usually admitted. He falls short of Feuerbach in that he loses sight of the autonomous sphere of the relation between *I* and *Thou* and is content, in respect of inter-human relations, to continue on the line of the French moral philosophers of the seventeenth and eighteenth centuries and complete it by depicting the origin and development of morality. But he far surpasses Feuerbach in that, like no other previous thinker, he brings man into the centre of his thought about the universe, and not, as with Feuerbach, man as a clear and unambiguous being, but rather man as a problematic being; and thereby he endows the anthropological question with an unprecedented force and passion.

The questionableness of man is Nietzsche's real great theme, which engages him from his first philosophical efforts till the end. As early as 1874, in his study of Schopenhauer as an educator, he puts a question which is like a marginal note to Kant's fourth question, and in which our age is mirrored as Kant's age is mirrored in his question: "How can man know himself?" And he adds by way of explanation: "He is something dark and veiled." Ten years later comes an explanation of this explanation: man is "the animal that is not yet established". That is, he is not a determined, unambiguous, final species like the others, he is not a finished form, but something that is only becoming. If we regard him as a finished form then he must appear "as the supreme aberration of nature and a self-contradiction", for he is the being which, "in consequence of a violent separation from the animal past", suffers from himself and from the problem of what his life means. But that is only a transition. In truth, man—as Nietzsche finally expresses it in the notes which were brought together posthumously under the title *The Will to Power*—is "as it were an embryo of the man of the future", of the real man, of the real species man. The paradox of the situation consists in the fact that the coming of this real future man is not at all assured; present man, the man of the transition, must first create him out of the material which he himself is. "Man is something fleeting and plastic—one can make of him what one will." Man, *animal* man, "has

---

[2] Karl Heim, *Ontologie und Theologie,* Zeitschrift für Theologie und Kirche, neue Folge XI (1930), 333; Karl Heim, *Glaube und Denken* 1.Auflage (1931), 405 ff (in the revised edition of 1934 Heim excised this passage). The English translation, *God Transcendent,* has been made from this third, revised and shortened, and altogether more orthodox edition. For a similar point of view see especially Emil Brunner.

hitherto had no meaning. His existence on earth has had no goal. 'To what end man?' was a question without an answer". He suffered, "but it was not the suffering itself which was his problem, but that there was no answer to the cry 'To what end this suffering?' " The ascetic ideal of Christianity wishes to free man from the meaninglessness of suffering; it does this by separating him from the foundations of life and leading him towards nothing. It is from life that man must take the meaning which he has to give to himself. But life is "the will to power"; all great humanity and great culture has developed from the will to power and from a good conscience to it. The ascetic ideals, which gave man a "bad conscience", have suppressed this will. The real man will be he who has a good conscience towards his will to power. That is the man we should "create" and "breed", for whose sake we should "overcome" what is called man. Present man is "no goal, but only a way, an episode, a bridge, a great promise". That is what, in Nietzsche's view, distinguished man from all animals: he is "an animal that may promise"; that is, he treats a bit of the future as something dependent on him for which he answers. No animal can do that. This human quality has arisen out of the contractual relation between creditor and debtor, out of the debtor's obligation. The "leading ethical concept of 'guilt' (*Schuld*) took its origin from the very material concept of 'debts' (*Schulden*)". And human society has elevated by every possible means the quality which has arisen in this way, in order to keep the individual fulfilling his ethical and social duties. As the supreme means it made use of the ascetic ideals. Man must be free of it all, of his bad conscience and of the bad salvation from this conscience, in order to become in truth the way. Now he no longer promises others the fulfilment of his duties, but he promises himself the fulfilment of man.

Whatever of these ideas is meant as an *answer* is wrong. First, the sociological and ethnological presupposition about the history of man's origins is wrong. The concept of guilt is found most powerfully developed even in the most primitive communal forms which we know, where the relation between creditor and debtor is almost non-existent: the man is guilty who violates one of the original laws which dominate the society and which are mostly derived from a divine founder; the boy who is accepted into the tribal community and learns its laws, which bind him thenceforth, learns to promise; this promise is often given under the sign of death, which is symbolically carried out on the boy, with a symbolical re-birth. Just because the man has learned to promise in this way it is possible for the contract-relation in private economy to develop between the debtor who promises and the creditor who is promised.

Secondly, the psychological and historical view of the will to power is wrong. Nietzsche's concept of a will to power is not so unambiguous as Schopenhauer's concept of the will to life, on which it was modelled. Sometimes he understands by it the will to acquire ever more

and more power; "all purposive happenings", he says, "can be reduced to the purpose of increasing power"; all that lives strives, in his
view, "for power, for increase in power", "for a maximal feeling of
power". But another time he defines the will to power as the "insatiable
desire to display power, or to employ, to practise power". These are
two different things. We may, nevertheless, look on them as the two
sides, or the two moments, of the same event. At any rate we know that
real greatness in history, in the history of the spirit and of culture, as
well as in the history of peoples and of states, cannot be characterized
by either of these. Greatness by nature includes a power, but not a
will to power. Greatness has an inner powerfulness, which sometimes
grows suddenly and irresistibly to power over men, sometimes exerts its
effect quietly and slowly on a company that is quietly and slowly increasing, sometimes, too, seems to have no effect at all, but rests in
itself, and sends out beams which will perhaps catch the glance only
of some far time. But greatness strives neither to "increase" nor to "display" power. The great man, whether we comprehend him in the most
intense activity of his work or in the restful equipoise of his forces, is
powerful, involuntarily and composedly powerful, but he is not avid
for power. What he is avid for is the realization of what he has in mind,
the incarnation of the spirit. Of course he needs power for this realization; for power—when we strip the concept of the dithyrambic splen-
dour with which Nietzsche equipped it—means simply the capacity to
realize what one wants to realize; but the great man is not avid for this
capacity—which is, after all, only a self-evident and indispensable
means—but for *what* he wishes to be capable of. This is the point from
where we can understand the *responsibility* in which the powerful man
is placed, namely whether, and how far, he is really serving his goal;
and also the point from where we can understand the seduction by
power, leading him to be unfaithful to the goal and yield to power
alone. When we see a great man desiring power instead of his real goal
we soon recognize that he is sick, or more precisely that his attitude to
his work is sick. He overreaches himself, the work denies itself to him,
the incarnation of the spirit no longer takes place, and to avoid the
threat of senselessness he snatches after empty power. This sickness
casts the genius on to the same level as those hysterical figures who,
being by nature without power, slave for power, for an ever fresh display of power and an ever fresh increase of power, in order that they
may enjoy the illusion that they are inwardly powerful, and who in this
striving for power cannot let a pause intervene, since a pause would
bring with it the possibility of self-reflection and self-reflection would
bring collapse. From this point, too, the connexion between power and
culture is to be judged. It is an essential element of the history of almost
all peoples that the political leadership which is historically important
strives to win and to increase the power of the nation; that is, precisely
what, as we saw, has a pathological character in personal life is normal

in the relation between the historical representatives of the nation and the nation itself. Now again the characters separate in decisive fashion. It is decisively important whether the man who leads longs in his inmost heart, in his deepest desire and dream, to acquire power for his nation for power's sake, or in order that the nation may attain the capacity to realize what in his view appears as their nature and destiny—what he has discovered in his own soul as the sign of a future which is waiting for this nation, to be realized by it. If a man longs in *this* way for power for his nation then what he does in the service of his will or his vocation furthers, enriches and renews the national culture; if he longs for national power in itself then he may achieve the greatest successes—what he does will only weaken and paralyse the national culture he wishes to glorify. The heyday of a community's culture is only rarely identical with the heyday of its power: great, genuine, spontaneous cultural productivity mostly precedes the time of intense striving and struggling for power, and the cultural activity which follows that time is mostly only a gathering and completing and imitating— unless a conquered people brings a new elemental cultural force to the powerful conqueror and enters into an association with it in which the people which has becoming politically powerless represents culturally the powerful, male, generative principle. No one knew more clearly than the historian Jakob Burckhardt that political predominance and the capacity to realize the hidden form, the "idea", thus producing culture, are only seldom compatible. Burckhardt was the man whom Nietzsche admired as he did scarcely any other of his contemporaries, though Burckhardt more and more set him quietly aside. It is noteworthy that the spark which kindled Nietzsche's enthusiasm for the will to power probably came from a lecture by Burckhardt which he heard in 1870. We possess these lectures now in Burckhardt's posthumous book, published with the title *Reflections on World History,* one of the few important books about the powers which determine what we call history. We read there that the real inner incentive for the great historical individual is not love of glory, not ambition, but "the sense of power, which as an irresistible impulse drives the great individual into the light of day". But Burckhardt understands by that something quite different from the will to power in itself. He sees "the characteristic of greatness" in "its carrying out a will which goes beyond the individual". It is possible that the community and the age are unconscious of this will; "the individual knows what the nation's will should really be, and carries it out", because "the force and capacity of infinitely many are concentrated" in him. There appears here, as Burckhardt says, "a secret coincidence of the egoism of the individual" with the greatness of the whole. But the coincidence can be broken up if the means of power which are adopted "react on the individual and in the long run deprive him of the taste for great aims". On the basis of this insight Burckhardt uttered, in another lecture at that time—taking up the words of an earlier historian, Schlosser—the memorable, much-repeated and much-misunderstood words: "Now power in itself is evil, no matter who exercises it. It has no persistence, but is greed and *eo ipso* cannot be fulfilled, hence it is unhappy in itself and is bound to be the cause of unhappiness in others." These words can only be understood in the context of Burckhardt's thoughts, when one notes that he is speaking here of power *in itself*. So long as a man's power, that is, his capacity to realize what he has in mind, is bound to the goal, to the work, to the calling, it is, considered in itself, neither good nor evil, it is only a suitable or an unsuitable instrument. But as soon as this bond with the goal is broken off or loosened, and the man ceases to think of power as the capacity to do something, but thinks of it as a possession, that is, thinks of power in itself, then his power, being cut off and self-satisfied, is evil; it is power withdrawn from responsibility, power which betrays the spirit, power in itself. It corrupts the history of the world. Genuine knowledge of historical reality must rectify in this way Nietzsche's wrong answer to the anthropological question, when he says that man is to be understood, and released from his problematic nature, from the standpoint of the will to power.

As we see, Nietzsche did not give a positive foundation for a philosophical anthropology. But in elevating, as no previous thinker has done, the questionableness of human life to be the real subject of philosophizing he gave the anthropological question a new and unheard-of impulse. Yet it is specially noteworthy that from beginning to end of his thought he endeavoured to overcome the special problem of man in its strict sense. With Augustine, with Pascal, and even with Kant, the pathos of the anthropological question lies in our perceiving something in ourselves that we cannot explain to ourselves from nature and its development alone. For philosophy till Nietzsche, so far as it has an anthropological concern, "man" is not merely a species, but a category. But Nietzsche, who is very strongly determined by the eighteenth century, and whom one would sometimes like to call a mystic of the Enlightenment, does not acknowledge such a category or basic problem. He attempts to follow out a thought indicated by Empedocles, but since then never discussed in a genuinely philosophical fashion: he wants to understand man purely *genetically,* as an animal that has grown out and stepped forth from the animal world. He writes: "We no longer derive man from the 'spirit', we have put him back among the animals." These could be the words of one of the French encyclopædists. But all the same Nietzsche remains deeply conscious of the specifically human questionableness. It is this very questionableness which he wants to explain by the fact of man's breakaway from the animal world and his aberration from his instincts; man is problematic because he is an "overwrought kind of animal" and thus a "sickness" of the earth. For Kant the problem of man is a *frontier* problem, that is, the problem of a being which belongs, certainly, to nature, but not to nature alone, of a being that is established on the frontier between nature and another realm. For Nietzsche the problem of man is a problem of the *edge,* the problem of a being that has moved from within nature to its utmost edge, to the perilous end of natural being, where there begins, not as for Kant the ether of the spirit but the dizzying abyss of nothing. Nietzsche no longer sees in man a being in himself, a "new thing", which has come out of nature but in such a way that the fact and the way of this coming cannot be grasped by concepts of nature; he sees only a *becoming,* "an attempt, a groping, a missing the mark", not precisely a being but at best the pre-form of a being, "the animal that is not yet established", thus an extreme piece of nature, where something new has only begun to grow, which till now has certainly seemed very interesting but, considered in respect of its totality, not really a success. Yet two definite things, he thinks, can arise from this indefinite thing. Either man, in virtue of his "growing morality", which suppresses his instincts, will develop in himself "merely the herd animal" and thus "establish" the animal Man as the species in which the animal world goes into decline, as the decadent animal. Or man will overcome what is "fundamentally amiss" with him, give new life to his instincts, bring to light his unexhausted possibilities, build up his life on the affirmation of the will to power, and breed the superman who will be the real man, the successful new being. For this goal Nietzsche apparently does not think how it could come to pass that such an "ill-bred" animal could pull itself out of the bog of its own ambiguity. He demands conscious breeding on a widespread scale, and does not think of what he himself wrote: "We deny that anything that is being consciously made can be made perfect." We are, however, not concerned here with these inner contradictions in Nietzsche's thought, but with something else. Nietzsche, as we have seen, undertook with passionate earnestness to explain man in terms of the animal world; the specific problem of man does not thereby fade out, but has become more visible than ever. Only, from this point of view, the question ceases to be, *How is it to be understood that there is such a being as man?* but is *How is it to be understood that such a being as man has emerged and stepped forth from the animal world?* But in spite of all the arguments he brought to bear throughout his thought Nietzsche has not made this clear. He has scarcely troubled about what is for us the fundamental anthropological fact and the most amazing of all earthly facts—that there is in the world a being who knows the universe as a universe, its space as space, its time as time, and knows himself in it as knowing it. But that does not mean, as has been asserted, that the world exists "over again" in man's consciousness, but that a *world* in our sense, a unified, spatio-temporal world of the senses, only exists in virtue of man, because only the human person is able to combine into a cosmic unity the data of his own senses and the traditional data of the whole race. Certainly, if Nietzsche had troubled about this fundamental fact it would have led him to the sociology he despised, namely, to the sociology of knowledge and the sociology of tradition, to that of language, and that of the generations—in brief, to the sociology of human thinking together, which Feuerbach had in principle already pointed out. The man who knows a world is man *with* man. The problem which Nietzsche neglected, that such a being exists, is only shifted in his view from the realm of the being of a species to the realm of its becoming. If a being has emerged from the animal world who knows about life and about his own life, then the fact and the manner of this emergence cannot be explained by his place in the animal world or comprehended by concepts of nature. For post-nietzschian philosophy man is more than ever not merely a species, but a category. Kant's question *What is man?* is put to us with new urgency by Nietzsche's passionate anthropological concern. We know that to answer it we must invoke not merely the spirit but also nature to tell us what it has to tell; but we know that we have also to approach another power for information, namely, community.

I say "we know". But it is true that modern philosophical anthropology, even in its most significant representatives, has not yet realized this knowledge. Whether it has turned more to the spirit or more to nature, the power of community has not been invoked. If this power is not invoked the others lead not only to fragmentary knowledge but of necessity also to knowledge which is inadequate in itself.

ABOUT THE EDITORS

HENRY AIKEN was born in Portland, Oregon, and after attending Reed College in Oregon, received his M.A. degree from Stanford and his Ph.D. from Harvard. At present a Professor of Philosophy at Harvard, he has edited a number of books including *Humes' Moral and Political Philosophy*, *Humes' Dialogues Concerning Natural Religion,* and *The Age of Ideology,* for which he wrote the long introduction.

WILLIAM C. BARRETT was born in New York City, attended C.C.N.Y., and received both his M.A. and Ph.D. from Columbia. At present a Professor of Philosophy at New York University, he has taught at the University of Illinois, Brown University, the University of California, and served as an Instructor for the Naval Air Forces. Professor Barrett is the author of *What Is Existentialism?, Irrational Man,* and the co-editor (with D. T. Suzuki) of *Zen Buddhism.*